AREA STUDIES

Europe

David Waugh

Head of the Geography Department
Trinity School, Carlisle

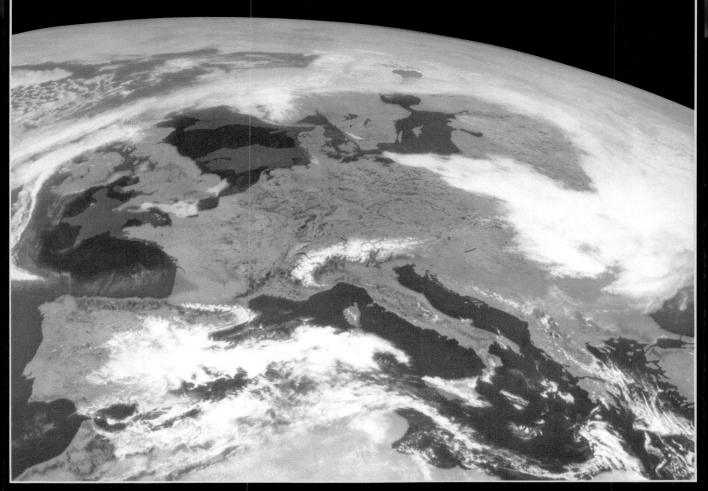

Nelson

Thomas Nelson and Sons Ltd
Nelson House Mayfield Road
Walton-on-Thames Surrey
KT12 5PL UK

51 York Place
Edinburgh
EH1 3JD UK

Thomas Nelson (Hong Kong) Ltd
Toppan Building 10/F
22a Westlands Road
Quarry Bay Hong Kong

Thomas Nelson Australia
102 Dodds Street
South Melbourne Victoria 3205
Australia

Nelson Canada
1120 Birchmount Road
Scarborough Ontario
M1K 5G4 Canada

© David Waugh 1985
First published by Thomas Nelson and Sons Ltd
ISBN 0-17-434209-8
NPN 19 18 17 16 15 14 13 12 11 10

Title page photograph supplied by the Daily Telegraph Colour Library.

The author and publisher are grateful to the following for permission to use their photographs:
A.G.I.P. Fig. no. 11.13, 12.8, 12.9; Aerofilms Fig. no. 1.26, 11.6, 13.9; Aerphoto Schipol Fig. no. 11.17, 11.18; Art Directors Photo Library Fig. no. 2.21, 6.9, 10.17, 15.20; Camerapix Hutchison Fig. no. 4.21, 15.9, 15.27; Camera Press Fig. no. 8.24, 11.4, 11.14, 12.4, 12.22, 14.19; Colorific Fig. no. 10.21, 10.25, 11.9, 11.9, 13.3; Compaignie Nationale du Rhône Fig. no. 8.21; Commission of the European Communities Fig. no. 16.2; James Davis Fig. no. 4.24, 4.26, 8.20, 10.10, 10.32, 15.13; Fjellanger Widere Fig. no. 10.31; French Government Tourist Office Fig. no. 1.32, 2.10, 4.13; French Railways Fig. no. 12.12, 12.14; Geoslides Fig. no. 2.18; Susan Griggs Agency Fig. no. 1.16, 2.16, 8.9, 8.11, 11.8B, 15.5; Robert Harding Fig. no. 1.21 (1), 13.2, 14.11, 14.12, 15.26a, 15.26b, 16.10; Knudsen Fotosenter Fig. no. 10.30, 10.33, 10.34; Kommunalverband Ruhrgebiet Fig. no. 15.11; Krupp Gmbtt Stabsalsteilung Information und Wirtschaftspolitik Fig. no. 9.10; G. C. Morlin Fig. no. 2.8, 7.3; The Photo Source Fig. no. 8.25, 15.3; Picturepoint Fig. no. 1.12 (3), 1.29, 4.23, 7.2, 10.1, 11.8a, 11.9 (2), 12.2, 13.5, 13.7; Popperfoto Fig. no. 1.23, 1.27, 10.9; Schools Abroad Fig. no. 14.10, 14.15; Science Photo Library Fig. no. 15.6; tony Stone Associates Fig. no. 1.30, 2.7, 4.34, 4.8, 5.1, 6.3, 8.26, 11.9 (1), 11.9 (4), 14.23 (3), 14.23 (4), 14.24 (3), 14.3, 15.16; Swiss Tourist Board Fig. no. 10.23; Solar Filma Fig. no. 1.13, 1.14; Thomsons Fig. no. 14.4, 14.5; Tiofoto (Lennart Olson) Fig. no. 9.1, (Tore Johnson) 9.3; John Topham Picture Library Fig. no. 9.9; Travel Photo International Fig. no. 2.12, 4.11, 9.4, 13.1, 13.6, 14.24, (4), 15.28; University of Dundee Electronics Lab Fig. no. 2.9; Vereine Schweizerischer Fig. no. 10.24; Volkswagon (U.K.) Ltd Fig. no. 10.28; David Waugh Fig. no. 2.17, 11.9 (1), 12.19, 14.23 (2); J. S. Waugh Fig. no. 1.28, 2.6, 4.9, 13.4; Yugoslavian National Tourist Office Fig. no. 1.32.

We are indebted to the following for permission to produce diagrams based on copyright materials:
British Geological Survey (Figures 1.7, 1.11) reproduced by permission of the Director, British Geological Survey (NERC): Crown copyright reserved; Chancerel Publishers Limited, Schools Abroad (Figure 2.19 from *The Mountain Environment*); Commission of the European Communities (Figures 8.2, 8.3, 8.4, 8.14, 10.5, 10.6, 16.3, 16.5, 16.7 from various publications); Director of Public Works, Rotterdam (Figure 12.17 produced by the Cartography Department of Public Works, Rotterdam); Financial Times Business Information (Figure 8.27); *The Geographical Magazine* (Figure 10.8); Chas. E. Goad Ltd. (Figure 13.8); Information and Documentation Centre for the Geography of the Netherlands (Figures 11.6, 11.20); *National Geographic Magazine*, November 1972 (Figure 15.8); Oxford University Press (Figures 14.18, 15.25 redrawn from *Problem Regions of Europe: The Lower Rhone and Marseille* by I. B. Thompson © Oxford University Press 1975, and Figure 7.1 redrawn from *The Oxford Regional Economic Atlas of Western Europe* © Oxford University Press 1971); Schools Abroad (Figures 14.13, 14.14); Southern Universities Joint Board from question papers in O.L. Geography (AH) (Figures 14.8, 14.22); Thomson Holidays (for information incorporated in Figures 14.4, 14.5, 14.6); Times Newspapers Limited (Figure 1.21, Mount Etna eruption diagram only, *Sunday Times* 8 May 1983, and Figure 16.4 *Sunday Times* March 1984).

Every effort has been made to trace owners of copyright. It is hoped that any omission will be pardoned.

We are indebted to the following for permission to reproduce copyright material:
Collins Publishers, Hammond Innes, *Blue Ice* (p. 16); Harrap Ltd., Carlo Levi, *Christ Stopped at Eboli* (p. 114); Hodder and Stoughton Educational, G. N. Minshull, *New Europe: Economic Geography of the EEC* (p. 63).

Maps supplied by Marlborough Design, Oxford.

Diagrams supplied by Maltings Partnership, Duffield.

Printed and bound in Hong Kong

Contents

What is Europe?

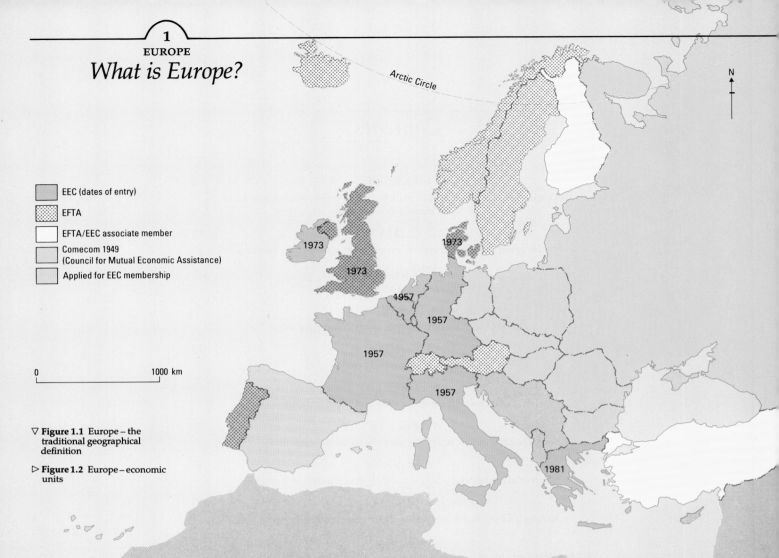

Legend:
- EEC (dates of entry)
- EFTA
- EFTA/EEC associate member
- Comecom 1949 (Council for Mutual Economic Assistance)
- Applied for EEC membership

0 ⎯⎯⎯⎯ 1000 km

▽ **Figure 1.1** Europe – the traditional geographical definition

▷ **Figure 1.2** Europe – economic units

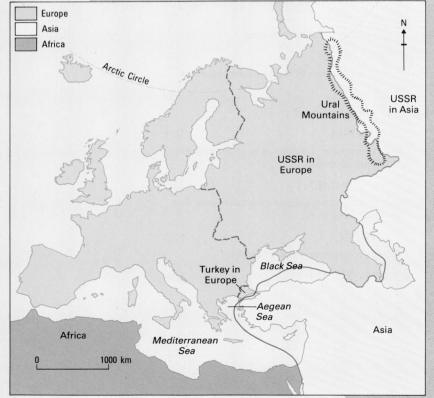

Legend:
- Europe
- Asia
- Africa

There are numerous definitions of Europe including:

- The traditional one – the geographical limits being the Mediterranean to the south, the Aegean and Black Seas to the south-east, and the Ural Mountains to the east (Figure 1.1).

- More recently Europe has become divided into economic units (Figure 1.2).

- And into military areas (Figure 1.3).

- A further definition could be made by accepting those countries which are members of the Council of Europe (Figure 1.4).

- Perhaps you feel your idea of Europe may be confined to those countries which entered the European Football Cup, (Figure 1.5).

Which of these, if any, do you feel to be the most accurate?

For the purposes of this book, Europe has been taken to be those countries in the European Economic Community (EEC) and those belonging to the European Free Trade Association (EFTA). Of the two associate members, Finland has been accepted as 'European', but Turkey as 'Asian'.

One aim of this book is to try to raise problems and to ask questions – yet few have simple answers. The hope is that you can appreciate various suggested solutions, and try to come to your own informed answer.

NATO member

Warsaw Pact member

Non-aligned

— — 'Iron Curtain'

▽ **Figure 1.3** Europe – military areas

▷ **Figure 1.4** Europe – justice

Council of Europe members

Non-members

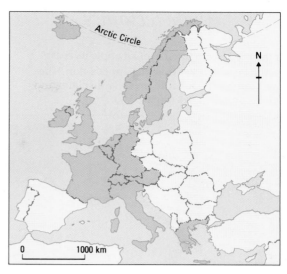

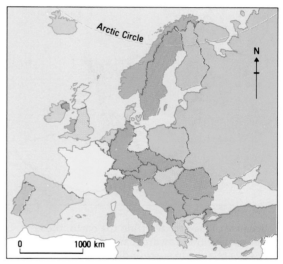

▷ **Figure 1.5** Europe – teams in the European Nations Football Cup qualifying groups, 1984

1	4	7
2	5	host
3	6	

▽ **Figure 1.6** Latitude, longitude and time

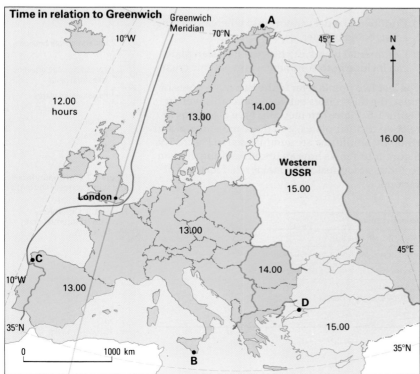

Size of Europe

Figure 1.6 shows the extent of Europe. How many kilometres is it:

1 From the north of Norway to Sicily (A to B on the map)?

2 From the west coast of Spain to Istanbul (C to D on the map)?

Figure 1.6 also shows that the western USSR is three hours ahead of the time experienced in the British Isles. Why is this?

The earth takes 24 hours to rotate through its 360° of longitude, and places in the east receive daylight before places in the west.

$$\frac{24 \text{ hours}}{360°} = \text{1 hour time difference for every 15° of longitude}$$

As a result the world is divided into a series of time zones, each approximately 15° in longitude. Figure 1.6 shows how Europe is divided into time zones.

1 Why is the time in Istanbul (D on the map) two hours different from time in London?

2 Why is Istanbul ahead of London in time?

Plate tectonics

If the earth were the size of an apple its crust would be no thicker than the apple's skin. The crust can be divided into seven large plates and several smaller ones (Figure 1.7).

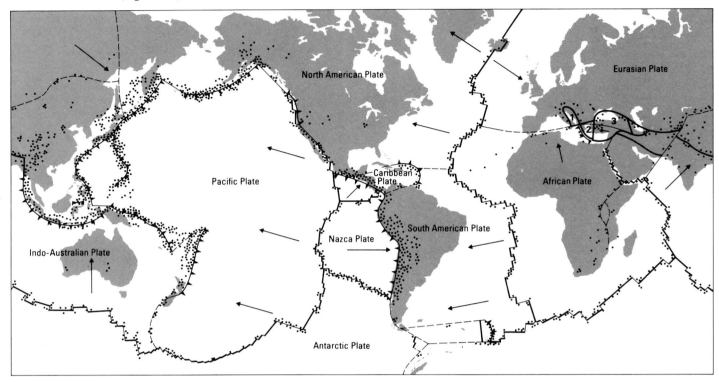

Because of heat from within the earth, these plates move either towards, away from, or sideways relative to surrounding plates. It is at plate boundaries that most of the world's major landforms occur, and where earthquake, volcanic and mountain building zones are located. It must be remembered, however, that:

□ Most changes take place at plate boundaries, and very little change occurs in the centre of plates.

□ No gaps can occur on the earth's surface so, if two plates move apart, new oceanic crust must form, originating from underneath the crust (i.e. the mantle).

□ Plates cannot overlap, which means that either they must be pushed up on impact to form mountains, or one must be forced downwards and destroyed.

□ Continental crust cannot sink, whereas oceanic crust, being heavier, can.

□ Continental plates, such as the Eurasian plate, can include both continental and oceanic crust.

The last two points refer to the two main types of crust; the differences between them are given in Figure 1.8. Plates can move in three directions in relation to other plates, and these movements and resultant landforms are summarised in Figure 1.9. Figure 1.10 shows how an understanding of plate tectonics accounts for the major relief features of Europe.

: : : : earthquake foci

subduction zone

collision zones

uncertain plate boundary

spreading ridge offset by transform faults

→ movement of plates

1 Adriatic
2 Aegean
3 Turkish

△ **Figure 1.7** Plate boundaries and active zones of the earth's crust

◁ **Figure 1.8** Differences between continental and oceanic crust

	Continental Crust	Oceanic Crust
thickness	35 to 70 km on average	6 to 10 km on average
age of rocks	very old, mainly over 1500 million years	very young, mainly under 200 million years
weight of rocks	lighter with an average density of 2.6	heavier with an average density of 3.0
nature of rocks	light in colour; numerous types, many contain silica and oxygen, granite is the most common	dark in colour; few types, mainly basalt

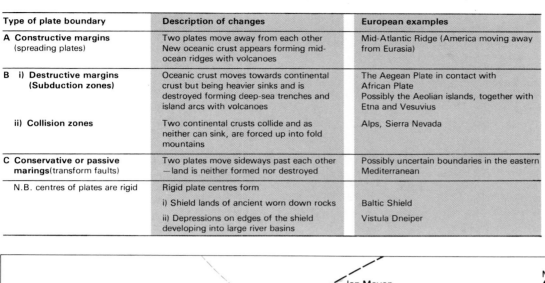

Type of plate boundary	Description of changes	European examples
A Constructive margins (spreading plates)	Two plates move away from each other New oceanic crust appears forming mid-ocean ridges with volcanoes	Mid-Atlantic Ridge (America moving away from Eurasia)
B i) Destructive margins (Subduction zones)	Oceanic crust moves towards continental crust but being heavier sinks and is destroyed forming deep-sea trenches and island arcs with volcanoes	The Aegean Plate in contact with African Plate Possibly the Aeolian islands, together with Etna and Vesuvius
ii) Collision zones	Two continental crusts collide and as neither can sink, are forced up into fold mountains	Alps, Sierra Nevada
C Conservative or passive marings(transform faults)	Two plates move sideways past each other —land is neither formed nor destroyed	Possibly uncertain boundaries in the eastern Mediterranean
N.B. centres of plates are rigid	Rigid plate centres form	
	i) Shield lands of ancient worn down rocks	Baltic Shield
	ii) Depressions on edges of the shield developing into large river basins	Vistula Dneiper

◁ **Figure 1.9** Plate boundaries and resultant landforms

▽ **Figure 1.10** Europe – plates, shield lands, fold mountains and volcanoes

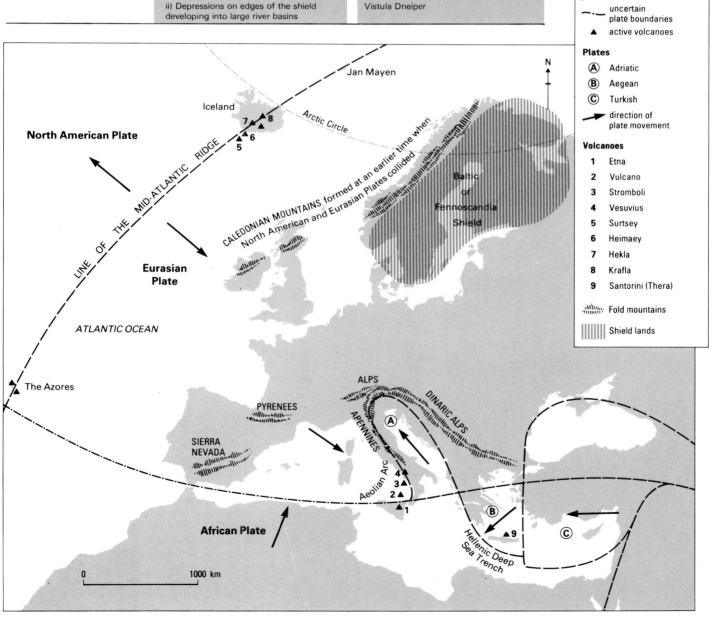

Landforms

Figure 1.9 lists three types of plate boundaries.

Constructive margins

At constructive margins, such as the Mid-Atlantic Ridge (Figure 1.11), two plates move away from each other. Molten rock, or magma, immediately rises to fill any possible 'gap' and so new rocks are formed. The Atlantic Ocean is widening by about 9 centimetres a year as a result of convection currents moving the American plate away from the Eurasian plate. Most of the Mid-Atlantic Ridge is submerged but in a few places volcanic islands rise above the surface (see Figure 1.10).

Iceland is composed almost entirely of lava and other volcanic rocks. The island is estimated to be widening by 5 cm a year. One-third of the lava poured out onto the earth's surface in the last 500 years has been in Iceland, and over 200 volcanoes have erupted in recent geological times.

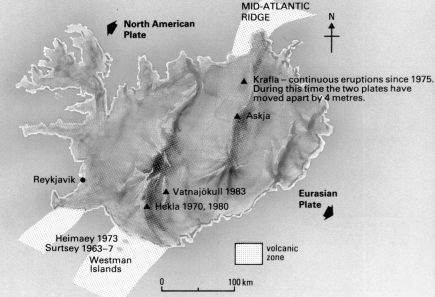

Figure 1.12 Some recent volcanic eruptions in Iceland

▽ **Figure 1.11** Landforms found near constructive plate margins

▽ **Figure 1.13** The fifth day of the Surtsey eruption, 18 November 1963 (bottom)

▷ **Figure 1.14** April 1964, lava overflows the crater rim and flows down to the sea

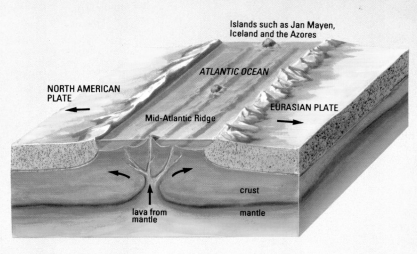

1 Surtsey

On 14 November 1963 an Icelandic fishing boat reported an explosion under the sea south-west of the Westman Islands (Figure 1.12). This was followed by further explosions accompanied by smoke, steam and pumice stone (Figure 1.13) which gave birth to the island of Surtsey. Even so, the submarine eruptions had first to build up an ash cone 130 metres high from the sea bed to the ocean surface. On 4 April 1964 the permanence of the island was guaranteed when lava began to flow from the central vent (Figure 1.14). When eruptions ceased in 1967, the island measured 2.8 km² and rose to 178 metres, and within months plants and insects had begun colonisation.

2 Heimaey

Just before 02.00 hours on 23 January 1973 an earth tremor stopped the clock in the main street of Heimaey, Iceland's major fishing port, in the Westman Islands (Figure 1.12). Soon afterwards, fishermen at sea witnessed the crust of the earth, east of the island's main volcanic cone of Helgafell, break open (Figure 1.15). Lava and ash poured out of a fissure 2 km in length, igniting some houses nearby, and covering others in ash. The town's 5300 inhabitants were evacuated as the new cone of Kirkefell began to form (Figure 1.16).

A month later with the town still threatened, workers started to spray the still advancing lava with 12 000 tons of water per hour to try to cool the lava, enabling it to solidify into a natural defence, and to try to prevent it blocking the harbour entrance. However, two rapid lava surges in March, destroying first 70 and then another 40 houses, meant that over a quarter of Heimaey had been engulfed by lava, and many more buildings had collapsed under the weight of over 5 metres of ash. The eruption started to subside in April, and ended by the beginning of July. Villagers, returning soon after that, found the harbour entrance narrower, but better protected against bad weather.

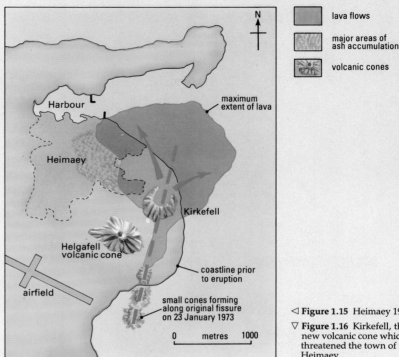

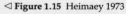

◁ **Figure 1.15** Heimaey 1973

▽ **Figure 1.16** Kirkefell, the new volcanic cone which threatened the town of Heimaey

Destructive margins

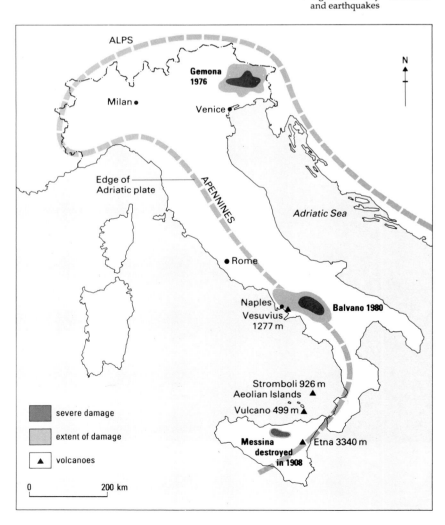

Figure 1.17 Destructive margins

△ **Figure 1.17** Destructive margins

▽ **Figure 1.18** Italy – volcanoes and earthquakes

In about 1470 B.C. a huge explosion occurred on the island of Thera (known as Santorini today) in the Aegean Sea, which gave rise to the legend of the lost 'Continent' of Atlantis. The island, which was originally 16 to 18 km in diameter and rose to a height of 1500 m, was turned into a large lagoon by the explosion. The huge ashfall and tsunamis (tidal waves produced by sub-ocean earthquakes) buried the local city of Akrotiri, and destroyed the ancient Minoan civilisation centred on the island of Crete. Since then, numerous earthquakes and volcanic eruptions have taken place along a line marking the junction of the African and Eurasian plates (Figure 1.10) – an area where, according to the Geological Museum, the movement of plates is very complex.

A small part of the Eurasian plate, the Aegean plate, is moving slowly south-east, while the African plate, is trying to move northwards. As a result, part of the oceanic crust fringing Africa is forced downwards beneath the continental crust to form a destructive margin (remember oceanic crust is heavier than continental) where the deep-sea Hellenic trench off the south coast of Crete descends to 4925 metres below sea level.

Further west (Figure 1.17), under the Tyrrhenian Sea, another part of the African plate is forced downwards as pressure builds up. This causes a jerking movement which produces earthquakes as well as destroying the crust. Friction causes a rise in temperature which may cause lava to rise to the surface to form either offshore volcanic island arcs, or larger volcanoes on the mainland. The location of present day volcanoes, and of three major twentieth century earthquakes in Italy are shown in Figure 1.18.

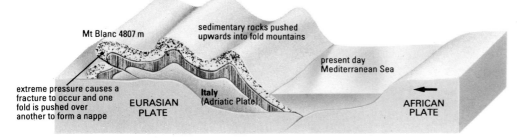

2 Today

3 And if Africa continues to move northwards –

The volcanic eruption of Vesuvius in A.D. 79 led to the town of Pompeii being destroyed by ash, and Herculaneum by mud flows. The 1983 eruption of Mount Etna was its fortieth since 1662.

Present day Italy is believed to have been formed when the small Adriatic plate, part of the continental crust of Africa, moved northwards and collided with the Eurasian plate. As both plates consisted of continental crust, neither could sink, and so parts of what had been an earlier enlarged Mediterranean Sea (the Tethys Sea) were forced upwards to form young fold mountains – the Alps (Figure 1.19). The force of the collision was large enough for deposited sediments, including sea shells, to be lifted high up onto the upper parts of the Matterhorn (4478 metres). The continuing movement of these plates has produced numerous serious earthquakes, including ones at Gemona, Skopje and Bucharest (see Figure 1.21). When the quake itself occurs in inhabited areas, the major causes of death come in the aftermath in the form of:

□ Flooding – if on the coast, or if dams fail.

□ Fires – caused by broken gas mains.

□ Disease – spread after the disruption of water supply and sewerage.

□ Exposure – inhabitants are left without any shelter.

Conservative margins

These occur when two plates slide past each other, forming transform faults (Figure 1.20). They are rare on the mainland of Europe, although the Great Glen of Scotland, which includes Loch Ness, is on such a fault. The most famous, or notorious, transform fault is the San Andreas Fault, which passes underneath San Francisco in North America.

△ **Figure 1.20** A transform fault

Side effects

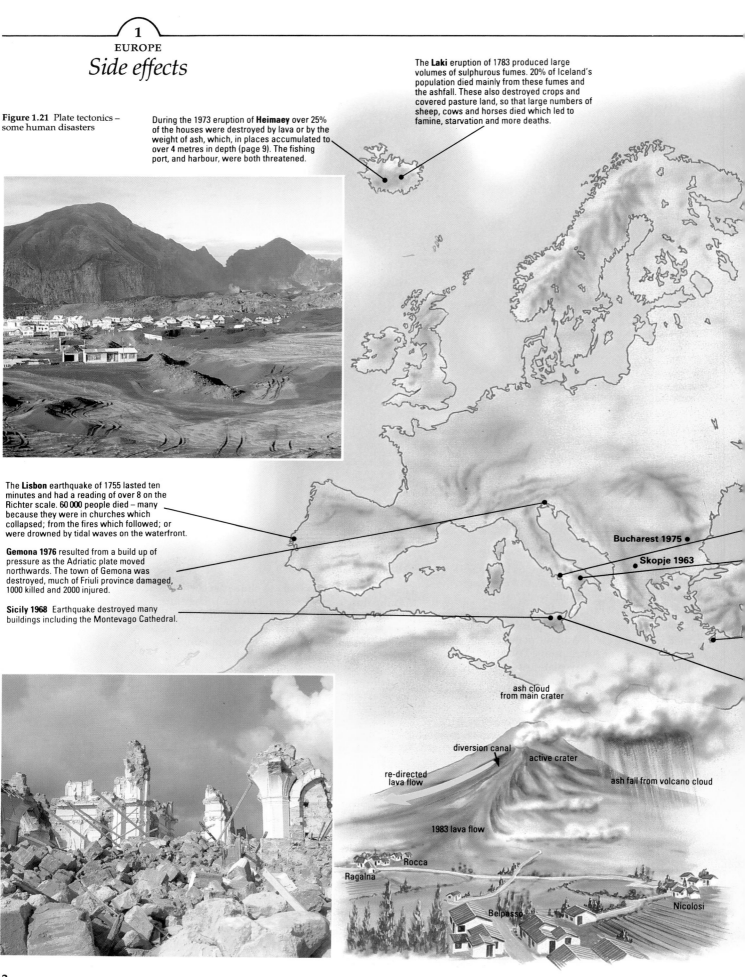

Figure 1.21 Plate tectonics – some human disasters

During the 1973 eruption of **Heimaey** over 25% of the houses were destroyed by lava or by the weight of ash, which, in places accumulated to over 4 metres in depth (page 9). The fishing port, and harbour, were both threatened.

The **Laki** eruption of 1783 produced large volumes of sulphurous fumes. 20% of Iceland's population died mainly from these fumes and the ashfall. These also destroyed crops and covered pasture land, so that large numbers of sheep, cows and horses died which led to famine, starvation and more deaths.

The **Lisbon** earthquake of 1755 lasted ten minutes and had a reading of over 8 on the Richter scale. 60 000 people died – many because they were in churches which collapsed; from the fires which followed; or were drowned by tidal waves on the waterfront.

Gemona 1976 resulted from a build up of pressure as the Adriatic plate moved northwards. The town of Gemona was destroyed, much of Friuli province damaged, 1000 killed and 2000 injured.

Sicily 1968 Earthquake destroyed many buildings including the Montevago Cathedral.

Bucharest 1975 ●

Skopje 1963 ●

ash cloud from main crater

diversion canal

active crater

re-directed lava flow

ash fall from volcano cloud

1983 lava flow

Rocca

Ragalna

Belpasso

Nicolosi

Plate tectonics – benefits

Geothermal heat

Figure 1.22 illustrates how electricity can be obtained from heated rocks if they are near enough to the earth's surface. The oldest geothermal power station in the world is at Lardarello in Tuscany (Italy). In Iceland hot springs provide all the homes in the capital city of Reykjavik with central heating, as well as providing heating for swimming pools and greenhouses.

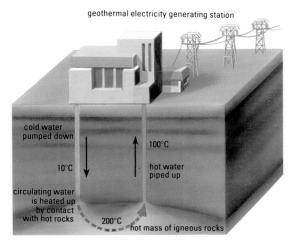

geothermal electricity generating station

cold water pumped down

100°C

10°C

hot water piped up

circulating water is heated up by contact with hot rocks

200°C

hot mass of igneous rocks

△ **Figure 1.22** Geothermal heat

Fertile soils

Although the first falls of ash from an erupting volcano will kill off all crops, the ash, which is composed of fine glassy particles, is easily weathered into a rich soil full of elements such as potassium. Lava flows also break down, though less quickly, into fertile soils. The result is a high crop yield which encourages a high density of population (e.g. Mount Etna).

Building materials

Some eruptions produce ignimbrites which can be used as a building material (e.g., in Naples and its nearby villages).

Tourism

The spectacular fold mountains, volcanoes and geysers (hot springs which eject hot water and steam into the air at intervals) attract both those who wish to look at such attractions and those more active who enjoy climbing and walking.

Mineral wealth

Europe is less fortunate than the Americas where considerable mineral wealth is found in the volcanic rocks of the young fold mountains, and especially where oceanic crust has been destroyed under continental crust. In Europe:

- Sulphur is mined in Sicily.
- Spain and Yugoslavia are the world's 10th and 12th largest producers of silver.
- Both the Spanish Sierra Nevada, and the Yugoslav Dinaric Alps have deposits of copper, lead and zinc. (Cornwall used to be a major source of copper and tin).

Vesuvius was thought to have been extinct until the violent eruption of A.D. 79 which led to the destruction of Pompeii, by ash, and Herculaneum by mudflow. Many thousands were killed. Other major eruptions occurred in 1794, 1822, 1906 and 1944.

Balvano 1980 At 19.35 local time on Sunday 23 November, southern Italy was struck by an earthquake of magnitude 6.8 on the Richter scale. The main tremor lasted 1 minute 20 seconds and was followed by several secondary shocks and led to 3000 deaths, and made 180 000 homeless.

An earthquake in 226 B.C. destroyed the town of **Rhodes** and also the high statue of the Colossus which was one of the seven wonders of the ancient world.

Mount Etna During the 1971 eruption most of the ski slopes and cable car stations, together with the vulcanological observatory, were destroyed. In 1983 an eruption began in late March. Millions of tons of lava gushed out of a small crater on the mountain side, and by the end of April a hotel, 3 restaurants, 25 houses and numerous orange groves and vineyards had been engulfed. The lava flowed at an average speed of 15 km per hour along a channel confined by ridges of solidified lava. On 15 May attempts were made to divert the flow of lava from this channel into a diversion canal cut parallel to it. However, following a series of explosions only 30% of the lava was actually diverted.

Colossus of Rhodes

Rivers

Although rivers can be used for considerable human and economic advantage, extremes of climate can cause an inconvenience to human and animal life, damage to property, and even, under extreme conditions, loss of life.

The upper sections of rivers can provide hydro-electricity, and lakes in which to store water and fish. The lower parts can be used to provide water for transport, recreation, irrigation, cooling in industry and waste disposal; while the wider, flat valley floor provides land for domestic and industrial building, road and rail links and farming.

However, seasonal drought can lower river levels to interrupt economic activity, whilst periods of heavy rainfall and snow-melt can cause flooding. Two natural disasters, resulting from flooding, are described here.

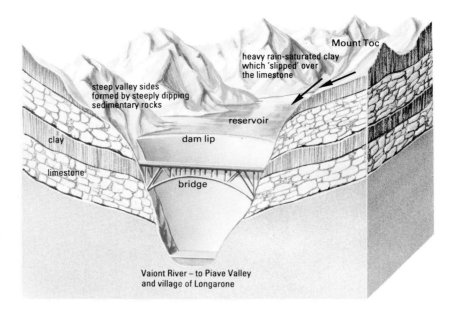

△ **Figure 1.24** The Vaiont Dam

Two Italian disasters

1 Florence flood 1966

Severe gales and frequent cloud bursts struck most of western Europe in the late autumn of 1966. In Italy these storms reached a peak in early November when 6 months equivalent of rain fell in only 48 hours. The Apennines behind Florence are steep-sided, and flood water from many tributaries soon collected into the River Arno. The river rose 6 metres overnight on 3 November, and the following morning burst its banks, and flooded many streets and buildings in Florence to a depth of 5 metres. Cars and lorries were swept away, and all roads out of the city were blocked. When the waters receded, a thick layer of yellow mud was left; 17 people had drowned; one-tenth of the inhabitants (45 000) were homeless; 40 000 cars had been wrecked; shops on the famous Ponte Vecchio belonging to goldsmiths and leather workers (Figure 1.23) had been destroyed, and many of Italy's most famous paintings and books needed urgent treatment after being submerged in museums, galleries and libraries for several hours.

2 Vaiont Dam 1963

This dam was built in the Italian Alps and, when opened in 1960, was the third highest concrete dam in the world. It was built in a steep sided valley, and on alternate bands of clay and limestone (Figure 1.24). Down valley was the village of Longarone and several hamlets. Heavy rain in October 1963 saturated the clay, and at 23.00 hours on 9 October an avalanche of rocks, mud, earth and trees slipped over the harder beds of limestone and into the reservoir. The dam itself stood, but a wave of water spilled over the lip creating a towering wall of water which swept down the valley and destroyed settlements. Longarone was virtually totally destroyed, and the final death toll was put at 1189, although several bodies were never found. The landslide filled in two-thirds of the lake. A court of inquiry discovered that the site was geologically unsuitable, and that even during construction many landslides had occurred. The outcome was that the dam was closed.

◁ **Figure 1.23** Florence 1966 – the famous Ponte Vecchio remains intact across the swollen River Arno. Jewellery shops lining the bridge were almost completely destroyed by the rampaging flood waters.

The sea

Coastlines are continually changing, and throughout Europe it is possible to see areas where land is being lost to the sea through erosion, and others where the eroded materials are being deposited. The major types of coastline reflect both the structure of an area, and the changes in sea level both during, and since, the last ice age. During the ice age, sea level fell as water was stored on the land as ice. After the ice age, this water was released and returned to the sea flooding many low-lying areas and forming fjords and rias (Figure 1.25). If all the ice caps in the world melted, the estimated further rise of 60 m would flood most of industrial western Europe (Figure 1.25).

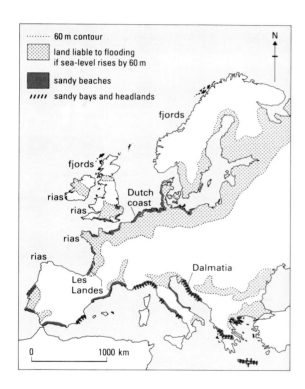

The balance between protection and flooding

Sand dunes along the coast of the Netherlands have been used to try to prevent the interior, which is below sea level, from being flooded by the sea. Sand, deposited on beaches, dries as the tide ebbs, and is then blown inland by the prevailing westerly winds to form dunes of up to 30 metres in height (Figure 1.26). These dunes were breached in the Middle Ages leading to the formation of the Zuider Zee. Further south, in the Delta area of the Scheldt and Rhine, the sand dunes are less high, or absent. During the night of 31 January–1 February 1953, a severe northerly gale, coinciding with high tides, caused a surge of water to move southwards down the North Sea, which breached the natural dunes and artificial dykes which were

protecting land, much of which lies over one metre below sea level. The tide was 3 m higher than ever experienced before. The sea covered one-sixth of the country, flooded 90 villages, claimed the lives of over 1800 victims and made 300 000 people homeless. For ten months tides swept unchecked through gaps in the defences and battered homes and windmills (Figure 1.27). The last dyke was repaired on 6 November, but the battle between the Dutch people and the sea continues. (See pages 110–11).

△ **Figure 1.25** Types of coastline in Europe (above left)

△ **Figure 1.26** Sand dunes along the Dutch coast near Zoutelande protect the interior from flooding (top)

△ **Figure 1.27** Flooding on the island of Tholen in the Netherlands, 1953, caused damage to property, land and livestock

Ice

Permanent snowcover and glaciers can still be found in parts of Alpine Europe, and in places near the Arctic Circle.

FROST SHATTERED PEAKS

HORN

ARÊTE

CORRIE GLACIER

TRUNCATED SPURS

HANGING VALLEY

GLACIAL TROUGH

LATERAL MORAINE

LATERAL MORAINE

MEDIAL MORAINE

△ **Figure 1.28** Mer de Glace above Chamonix, French Alps

◁ **Figure 1.29** Upland glacial features, the Aletsch Glacier, Swiss Alps

▽ **Figure 1.30** Geiranger Fjord, Norway

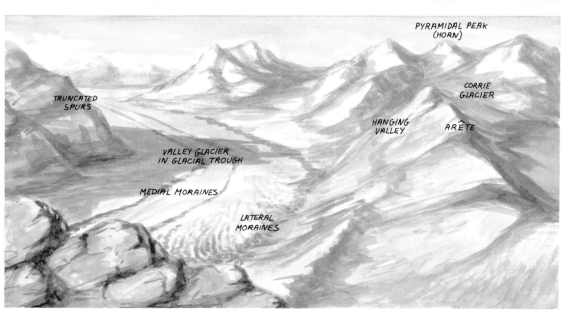

PYRAMIDAL PEAK (HORN)

TRUNCATED SPURS

CORRIE GLACIER

HANGING VALLEY

ARÊTE

VALLEY GLACIER IN GLACIAL TROUGH

MEDIAL MORAINES

LATERAL MORAINES

1 Using Figures 1.28 and 1.29 describe how the various glacial features have formed.

2 Using these figures and your own knowledge:

   (a) list the obstacles to human development in such parts of Europe.

   (b) list the ways in which such areas may be developed.

Fjords

The rise in sea level at the end of the ice age drowned valleys which had been over-deepened by glaciers (Figure 1.30). A description of one such fjord reads: *'As we sailed up the fjord, the wind died away leaving the water as flat as glass. The view was breathtakingly beautiful. Mountains rose to snow-covered, jagged peaks. The dark green of the pines covered the lower slopes, but higher up the vegetation vanished leaving sheer cliffs of bare rock which seemed to rise to the blue sky. In the distance, on a piece of flat land was Balestrand, with a steamer moving to the quay. Beyond was the hotel on a delta of green and fertile land.*

"Isn't it lovely?" Dahler said, "It is the sunniest place in all the Sogne Fjord. The big hotel you see is built completely of wood. Here the fjord is friendly, but when you reach Fjaerlandsfjord you will find the water like ice, the mountains dark and terrible, rising to 1300 metres in precipitous cliffs. High above you will see the Boya and Suphelle glaciers, and from these rivers from the melting snow plunge as giant waterfalls into the calm, cold, green coloured fjord"'.
(Hammond Innes, *Blue Ice*)

Limestone

Limestone is composed of calcium carbonate and forms its own distinctive 'karst' scenery. This is because:

☐ It is a sedimentary rock, having been laid down in layers. The horizontal junctions between layers are called bedding planes, and the vertical lines of weakness are known as joints. The rock is exposed in many parts of Mediterranean Europe, and together with its thin soils, can give an appearance like that shown in Figure 1.31.

☐ Calcium carbonate is soluble in rainwater. As the water dissolves the limestone, any surface moisture soon disappears leaving the ground dry, and forming underground passageways and caverns (Figures 1.32 and 1.33).

▽ **Figure 1.31** Karst scenery in the Gorges du Tarn, Aveyron, France

△ **Figure 1.32** Caves in limestone areas were used in prehistoric times. These paintings are in the caves at Lascaux in the French Dordogne.

◁ **Figure 1.33** Where limestone has been redeposited in caves as stalactites or stalagmites, the caves form tourist attractions. These caves are at Postojna, Yugoslavia.

Climates of Europe

Figure 2.1 This diagram shows the broad types of climate found in Europe, although the division lines between climates are often broad transition zones. The central European climate is really no more than a transition between the: (*a*) Maritime (to the west) and continental (to the east) and, (*b*) cold (to the north) and Mediterranean (to the south).

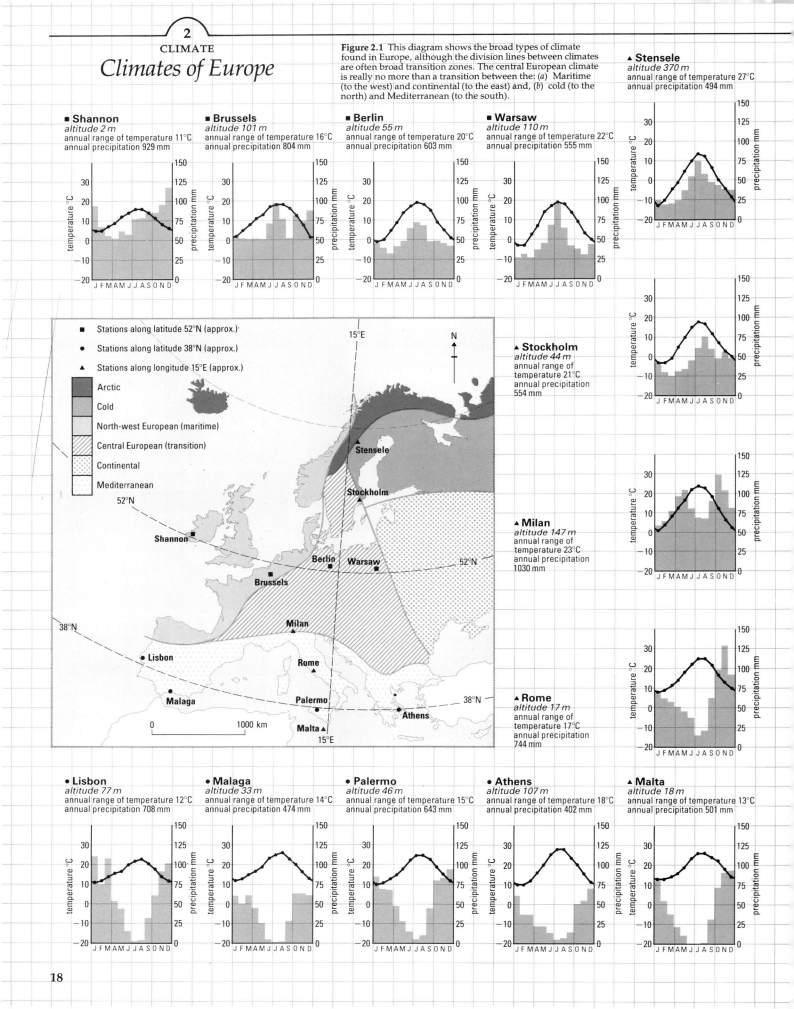

■ **Shannon**
altitude 2 m
annual range of temperature 11°C
annual precipitation 929 mm

■ **Brussels**
altitude 101 m
annual range of temperature 16°C
annual precipitation 804 mm

■ **Berlin**
altitude 55 m
annual range of temperature 20°C
annual precipitation 603 mm

■ **Warsaw**
altitude 110 m
annual range of temperature 22°C
annual precipitation 555 mm

▲ **Stensele**
altitude 370 m
annual range of temperature 27°C
annual precipitation 494 mm

■ Stations along latitude 52°N (approx.)
● Stations along latitude 38°N (approx.)
▲ Stations along longitude 15°E (approx.)

Arctic
Cold
North-west European (maritime)
Central European (transition)
Continental
Mediterranean

▲ **Stockholm**
altitude 44 m
annual range of temperature 21°C
annual precipitation 554 mm

▲ **Milan**
altitude 147 m
annual range of temperature 23°C
annual precipitation 1030 mm

▲ **Rome**
altitude 17 m
annual range of temperature 17°C
annual precipitation 744 mm

● **Lisbon**
altitude 77 m
annual range of temperature 12°C
annual precipitation 708 mm

● **Malaga**
altitude 33 m
annual range of temperature 14°C
annual precipitation 474 mm

● **Palermo**
altitude 46 m
annual range of temperature 15°C
annual precipitation 643 mm

● **Athens**
altitude 107 m
annual range of temperature 18°C
annual precipitation 402 mm

▲ **Malta**
altitude 18 m
annual range of temperature 13°C
annual precipitation 501 mm

The four climate graphs above Figure 2.1. refer to four stations from west to east approximately along latitude 52°N, and the four graphs below Figure 2.1 to the four stations, also from west to east, approximately along latitude 38°N.

1 Describe the changes which take place along these two lines of latitude, going from west to east, in terms of:
(a) maximum temperatures
(b) minimum temperatures
(c) annual range of temperature
(d) total rainfall
(e) seasonal distribution of rainfall

2 The five graphs to the side of Figure 2.1 refer to five stations from north to south along approximately longitude 15°E. Describe the changes which take place along this line of longitude going from north to south under the same five headings given in question one.

Factors affecting the climate in Europe

Latitude Europe extends from 35°N in Crete to 71°N at North Cape in Norway. Temperatures decrease polewards.

Altitude For every 150 metres above sea level the temperature drops approximately 1°C. If it is 20°C at sea level what will the temperature be on top of Mont Blanc at 4807 metres?

Influence of the sea Water takes longer to heat up than land, but then retains its heat longer. This means that places nearer to the sea will not be as warm as places away from the sea in summer, but will remain much milder in winter.

Ocean currents Much of western Europe is kept remarkably warm for its latitude in winter by the influence of the North Atlantic Drift. This is a current of warm water originating in the Caribbean Sea and which flows northwards up the east coast of the USA (where it is known as the Gulf Stream) before turning north-west to Europe.

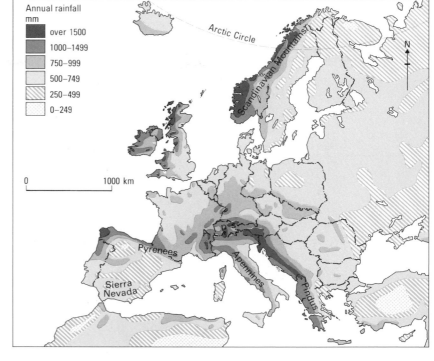

△ **Figure 2.2** Annual rainfall in Europe

▽ **Figure 2.3** Natural vegetation

Tundra

Mountain vegetation

coniferous forest, i.e., the Taiga

mixed forest

deciduous forest

Mediterranean evergreen forest and shrubs

Steppe vegetation

Prevailing winds over most of Europe come from the south-west (only in winter in the Mediterranean). Apart from affecting temperatures, these winds pick up moisture as they cross the Atlantic Ocean, and deposit it when crossing the land, especially in mountainous areas.

3 Account for the changes in climate which you described in questions 1 and 2.

Precipitation

Figure 2.2 shows the annual rainfall totals for Europe. These figures are important for:

☐ **Farming**, where the wetter, cloudier areas tend to favour cattle on lowlands, and sheep and goats at higher levels, and the drier, sunnier areas which are used for crops.

☐ **Water supply**, where there tends to be a water surplus in the north and west, and a water deficit to the south and east (Chapter 7).

Reliability of precipitation

It is not usually how much rain falls that is important, but when it falls, the intensity of the fall and the form it takes which is more significant.

Drought affects Mediterranean areas each summer.

Floods result from prolonged rain and can be serious if this coincides with a time of snow-melt when the ground is frozen. However the worst floods tend to follow summer thunderstorms when the hard ground cannot absorb the water and the resultant rapid run-off can disrupt transport, ruin crops and damage homes.

Snow is common in winter in many mountainous and northern areas. Though giving rise to tourism it can disrupt normal life.

Hail and frost can also damage crops.

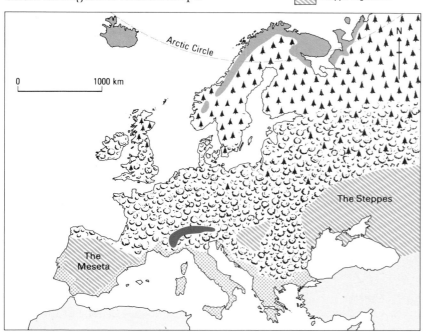

Temperatures

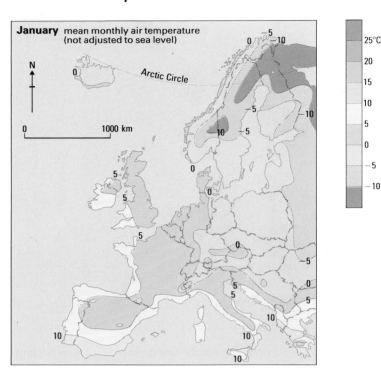

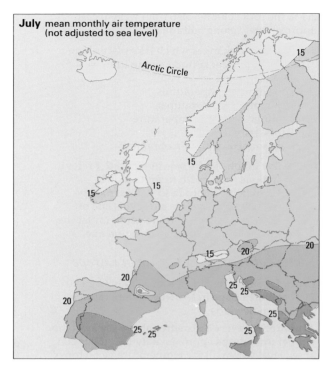

△ **Figure 2.4** Temperatures in Europe

Summer temperatures (Figure 2.4) Although these are too low in northern Scandinavia for cereals and fruit to ripen, they are high enough for olives, vines and sub-tropical fruit to grow around the Mediterranean Sea. The high temperatures of these southern areas attract large numbers of tourists (Chapter 14), but the high rates of evaporation and low rainfall cause water shortages.

Winter temperatures (Figure 2.4) Although still warm enough in southern Spain, France, Italy and Greece to attract tourists and retired people, many areas such as the Alps and Scandinavia are cold enough to have several months of snow. Although this discourages farming, it does attract winter sports.

The length of the growing season increases southwards. This is important to farmers, and the Mediterranean is warm enough for plants to grow all year. This means fruit and vegetables can be sold 'early' to the northern parts of the continent.

▽ **Figure 2.5** Winds of the Mediterranean

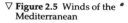

Winds

Northern and central Europe The south-westerlies are the prevailing winds here, with, in winter, colder winds from the Arctic or central Asia.

Mediterranean Europe This only receives the south-westerly winds in winter – the rainy season. However, the area is characterised by several local winds, including (Figure 2.5):

☐ Sirocco and Khamsin which are very hot and dry winds which blow from the Sahara Desert. Temperatures can rise to 40°C, and even vines and olives can be destroyed. The Sirocco can produce 'Blood Rain', the name derived from the red dust carried from the Sahara.

☐ The Mistral is a cold, winter wind which originates over the Alps and is funnelled down the Rhône Valley where it can reach speeds of 130 km per hour. Many farmhouses have no north-facing windows and rows of poplar trees have been planted to try and protect both homes and crops. *'Then came the mistral.*

  It trumpeted down the overflow pipe, strained at the windows, whistled under the doors and moaned and shrieked in the chimney. The house shuddered. The countryside was ravaged by its violence. The sheep and lambs huddled closely together. The sky was piercingly blue, the wind as piercingly sharp.

  "It's very dangerous. A man was blown off his bicycle yesterday and killed, and this morning a car was swept off the middle of the road, crashing into another one. But of course it can blow harder than this".' (*The Times*)

☐ The Bora is similar to the Mistral, but affects the Adriatic Sea.

Mediterranean areas

This climate is usually found on west coasts of continents between latitudes 30° and 40° north and south of the Equator (Figure 2.1). The climate, as shown by the graph for Malta (Figure 2.1) is characterised by:

☐ Hot, dry summers

☐ Warm, wet winters

Indeed, it forms a transition between the hot deserts towards the Equator (and like them it receives dry offshore trade winds in summer) and the cool temperate western margins towards the pole (with their winters being both mild and moist because the prevailing winds at the time blow from the sea).

Vegetation

The vegetation has to adapt to the seasonal drought. It is mainly broad leaved evergreen forest with:

☐ Small, waxy, glossy leaves to reduce transpiration.

☐ Long tap roots to reach underground water supplies.

☐ Grass and aromatic herbs which complete their life-cycles before the onset of the drought (Figure 2.7).

☐ A slow annual growth, checked by drought in summer but permitted in winter by the mild temperatures.

At one time the Mediterranean hillsides were extensively wooded. Where this is still so, they are frequently dominated by evergreen oaks (e.g. the cork oak), and conifers (e.g. the Corsican pine). Much, however, has been deforested, and a secondary scrub-type vegetation has developed. The two major types of scrub, differing due to soil and climatic conditions, are:

(a) *Maquis* – the French word for dense, tangled undergrowth more typical of granite areas (Figure 2.8).

(b) *Garigue* – a much sparser, lower-lying scrub with many aromatic plants such as rosemary and lavender (Figure 2.7), which develops on dry, limestone areas.

Problems of development

☐ The summer drought affects agriculture by retarding the growth rate of plants. The highest temperatures (and therefore evaporation rates), coincide with the time of minimum rainfall, but otherwise the high incidence of sunlight is ideal for crops and fruit.

☐ Heat and drought in summer can produce serious forest and bush fires. These are especially common in the Provence region of the south of France (Figure 6.10).

☐ There are relatively large amounts of mountainous land with thin soils.

▽ **Figure 2.6** The photograph shows part of the island of Rhodes. It was taken in mid-October, a day after the first rain of 'winter'. The rain had caused the evergreen trees to immediately put out new needle-like leaves. The background shows the scorched vegetation, and lack of grass and greenery, following the summer drought.

◁ **Figure 2.7** *Garigue* vegetation, lavender in Provence, France

▽ **Figure 2.8** *Maquis* vegetation growing in Sicily

Temperate western margins (Maritime climate)

Climate

These are found to the poleward side of 40° north and south of the Equator (Figure 2.1) which, in the case of Europe includes the north coast of Spain, western and northern France, the Benelux countries, Norway and the British Isles. The climate (see Shannon Figure 2.1) has mild winters, due to the presence of the warm North Atlantic Drift and prevailing south-westerly winds, but cool summers. The annual temperature range is small due to the moderating influence of the sea. Frosts and snow are relatively uncommon at sea level. Only the higher parts of Norway experience heavy snowfalls.

However, several areas have high coastal mountains. These mountains force the warm, moist air brought in by the westerly winds from the Atlantic, in the form of depressions with their associated fronts, to rise rapidly to give heavy amounts of precipitation (over 1500 mm a year in Norway). These depressions tend to be more frequent in winter which explains the precipitation maxima for that season of the year. Figure 2.9 shows some characteristic conditions associated with a depression over north-west Europe.

△ **Figure 2.9** The satellite photograph shows the cloud associated with the warm front of the depression covering Denmark, Norway, Sweden and Germany, whilst the skies over the Mediterranean remain relatively clear

▽ **Figure 2.10** Deciduous woodland in the Doubs valley, France

Vegetation

At sea level the natural vegetation is deciduous forest as winters are sufficiently cool to limit growth and so the trees shed their leaves. Summer temperatures and moisture encourage rapid leaf growth. Deciduous trees need a minimum growing season of five months over 10°C, and have large, thin leaves to allow transpiration to take place during warm spells. (Figure 2.10). These forests include several species of trees, with oak, ash and elm predominant in the west, and beech in the east. There are often four layers – the tree, shrub, herbaceous and ground layers – the latter often quite thick as sunlight can penetrate the forest canopy. Where trees are more spaced out (or, more likely in western Europe cleared for economic gain) lush, green meadow grass grows.

As height above sea level increases, and the growing season decreases, coniferous trees form the climax vegetation.

Temperate continental

This continental climate is really only found in the extreme east of the continent where distance from the sea is greatest (Figure 2.1). However, characteristics of this climate can be found in eastern Europe (Warsaw, Figure 2.1.) and on parts of the Spanish Meseta.

Eastern Europe

Temperatures Because there is no moderating influence of the sea, the annual range is high (Warsaw 22°C, Moscow 31°C). Central areas of continents absorb incoming radiation from the sun and heat up faster than areas near to the sea to give warm summers (Warsaw 19°C, Moscow 18°C maximums). But they also lose heat rapidly in winter when skies are clear and the sun is at a low angle in the sky, to give extremely low temperatures (Warsaw −3°C, Moscow −13°C in January), and several months of frost. The clear skies also give large daily temperature ranges.

Precipitation Amounts are light (about 500 mm a year) and decrease eastwards due to increasing distance from the sea. Amounts tend to be unreliable, and droughts can occur. Although there is a summer maximum of rain, this often comes as destructive convectional and hail storms. Winters give powdery snowfalls.

Blizzards result from high winds and cold temperatures.

Vegetation

Due to the deficiency of rainfall, trees can only grow along water-courses (e.g. willow), otherwise the natural vegetation is (if indeed any remains in Europe) tall, coarse grasses (Figure 2.11). These lie dormant in winter, which experiences several months below 6°C (the minimum temperature for grass growth) but grow rapidly as the temperatures rise and the snow melts in spring. As the climate becomes drier in the east, the grass becomes shorter, more tussocky and provides a less even cover. Individual blades turn inwards to reduce moisture loss. In flatter areas, marshland can occur (Pripet marshes).

The Spanish Meseta

This area also shows continental characteristics, since upland areas surrounding it block out rain-bearing winds from the sea (Figure 2.12).

▽ **Figure 2.11** Grasses of Hortobágy, Eastern Hungary

▽ **Figure 2.12** Spain – the vegetation found here reflects the lack of rainfall (bottom)

Cold climates

As Figure 2.1 shows, this climate extends eastwards from north Sweden through Finland and into the USSR, as well as being found in the higher parts of such fold mountains as the Alps.

☐	snow covered more than 6 months of the year
▨	snow covered 3 to 6 months
▨	sea frozen each winter
▨	sea occasionally freezes

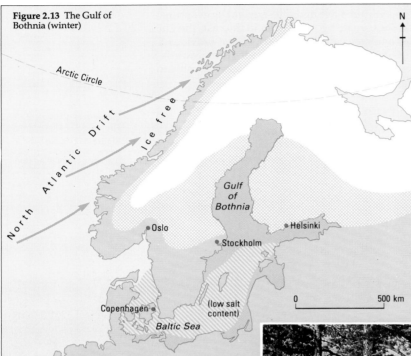

Figure 2.13 The Gulf of Bothnia (winter)

Arctic Circle

North Atlantic Drift

Ice free

Gulf of Bothnia

• Oslo
• Stockholm
• Helsinki

Copenhagen •

(low salt content)

Baltic Sea

0   500 km

N

Climate (See Stensele, Figure 2.1)

Winters are both very long and cold, with hours of daylight very limited nearer the Arctic Circle. The Gulf of Bothnia freezes each winter (Figure 2.13). Summers are cool (the sun is still low in the sky) and the growing season is short although there are long hours of daylight.

Precipitation is light, partly due to being in the rain shadow of the Norwegian mountains, and is mainly snow in winter and convectional rain in summer. However, amounts are not so critical to vegetation growth as the temperatures are.

Vegetation

Vegetation consists of vast stands of coniferous trees (Figure 2.14). The most common trees are the Norwegian spruce, scots pine, fir and larch (the latter is not an evergreen). These are adapted to the severe climatic conditions. These adaptations are shown in Figure 2.15. These trees are softwoods valuable not just for timber, but also for the manufacture of pulp and paper. To the north the vegetation thins out into the tundra, with the trees getting increasingly more stunted in growth and more widely spaced out.

▽ **Figure 2.15** Coniferous trees in Finland. The trees are adapted to the climatic conditions: they are evergreen (no need to renew leaves for the short growing season); they have needles instead of leaves which reduce moisture loss; the thick bark acts as a protection against cold winds, whilst the thin girth is a result of rapid upward growth; cones protect the seeds during very cold winters.

△ **Figure 2.14** Coniferous forest in Sweden

Arctic climates

These occur in the northern parts of Scandinavia, and in Iceland.

Climate

☐ Winters are extremely long and cold, and air temperatures can fall to −30°C. For several weeks the sun never rises.

☐ The wind-chill factor is high. This is the result of strong winds which evaporate moisture, freeze the skin and cause frost-bite.

☐ Blizzards result from strong winds blowing the dry, powdery snow.

☐ The long, continuous frosts of the northern area can cause some areas to be permanently frozen – the so-called permafrost. This is not nearly so intensive in Europe as in Siberia and northern Canada.

☐ The more southern areas have up to four months above freezing point, and with the sun low in the sky often for several weeks, the surface melts, forming the active layer. Because of the frozen subsoil, the low rates of evaporation and the gentle relief, much of the surface becomes waterlogged (Figure 2.16).

Vegetation

This area is known as the tundra ('tree-less plain'). Figure 2.17 was taken in the north of Iceland. In winter the land is snow-covered. The growth of tundra vegetation is seriously affected by the permafrost, for even where the snow does melt, roots cannot penetrate into the frozen ground. Plants must adapt to a short life cycle, to the thin active layer (for which they need short roots) and to find shelter against the biting winds (for which they must be low-growing). On south facing, sheltered, drier slopes carpets of brightly coloured flowers called 'bloom-mats' grow (Figure 2.18) together with such berry-bearing plants as the bilberry. In the more poorly drained areas mosses predominate, and the numerous exposed rocks are covered in lichens. Nearer to rivers, stunted willow, alder and birch struggle for survival.

▷ **Figure 2.16** Tundra vegetation – found in areas with Arctic climates

▽ **Figure 2.17** The tundra in Iceland

▽ **Figure 2.18** Brightly coloured 'bloom-mats' grow in the short summer (inset)

Mountain climates

Although the mountains in Europe are less high than in other continents (the Alps reach 4807 m and the Pyrenees 3404 m) the differences in altitude cause rapid modification and local variation in climate.

Temperatures As the air is thin and clear it has little ability to absorb heat from the sun. Temperatures decrease, on average, by 1°C for every 150 m of height. This means that while summer afternoon temperatures could rise to 30°C on the south coast of France, the temperature on top of Mount Blanc would be −2°C, hence its permanent snow cover. In winter, days may be sunny but the incoming energy is reflected by the snow. The snow-line is the lowest level of permanent snow cover (Figure 2.19). Also in the mountains fewer ultra-violet rays are filtered out. These rays cause sunburn and this explains why skiers and mountaineers have tanned faces.

Precipitation Where moist, warm air is forced to rise by mountains, it is cooled until the vapour is condensed into clouds and rain or, where temperatures are low enough, into snow. The windward sides may receive high amounts of precipitation while the sheltered leeward slopes are in a rain shadow. Heavy rains also wash away any accumulations of soil.

Winds These are frequent and often strong. At least three types can be recognised.

(a) Prevailing winds which means that windward slopes suffer from exposure which results in less vegetation cover than on sheltered leeward slopes.

(b) Mountain and valley winds caused by air in valleys being warmed during the day and rising up the hillsides, whereas at night as temperatures drop, cold air descends and so winds blow down hillsides.

(c) The Föhn (Figure 2.20) which can aid human development by melting the snow and increasing the length of the growing season yet can cause avalanches (Figure 2.21).

Pressure The decrease in pressure and oxygen can cause mountain sickness on the highest peaks.

Vegetation

Vegetation is also modified by height. Figure 2.19 shows the altitudinal changes in the Alps. Why is the level of the tree-line and the snow-line lower on north facing slopes than it is on south facing ones?

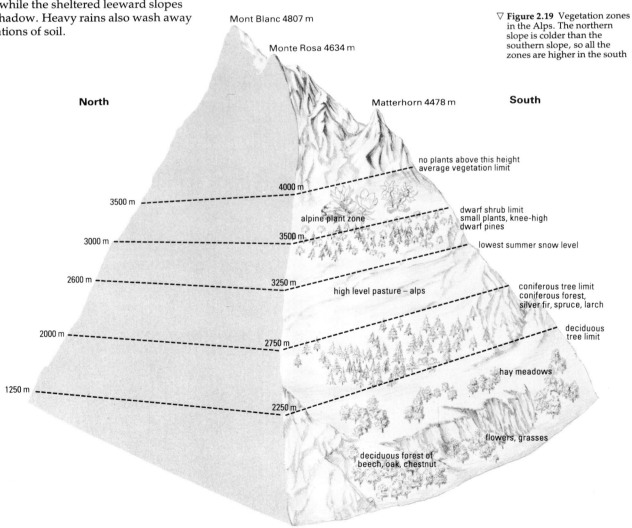

▽ **Figure 2.19** Vegetation zones in the Alps. The northern slope is colder than the southern slope, so all the zones are higher in the south

Mont Blanc 4807 m

Monte Rosa 4634 m

Matterhorn 4478 m

North   **South**

no plants above this height
average vegetation limit

4000 m

3500 m

alpine plant zone

dwarf shrub limit
small plants, knee-high
dwarf pines

3500 m

3000 m

3500 m

lowest summer snow level

2600 m

3250 m

high level pasture – alps

coniferous tree limit
coniferous forest,
silver fir, spruce, larch

2000 m

2750 m

deciduous
tree limit

hay meadows

1250 m

2250 m

flowers, grasses

deciduous forest of
beech, oak, chestnut

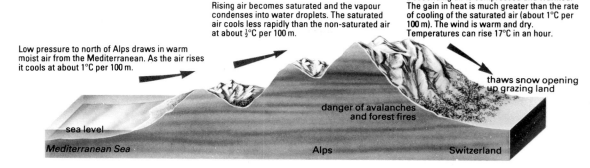

Low pressure to north of Alps draws in warm moist air from the Mediterranean. As the air rises it cools at about 1°C per 100 m.

Rising air becomes saturated and the vapour condenses into water droplets. The saturated air cools less rapidly than the non-saturated air at about ½°C per 100 m.

Descending air is compressed and warmed. The gain in heat is much greater than the rate of cooling of the saturated air (about 1°C per 100 m). The wind is warm and dry. Temperatures can rise 17°C in an hour.

thaws snow opening up grazing land

danger of avalanches and forest fires

sea level

Mediterranean Sea

Alps

Switzerland

◁ **Figure 2.20** The Föhn

▽ **Figure 2.21** Airolo, February 1951. Soliders and civilians dig for four people missing in the avalanche which enveloped the whole of the eastern part of the village. The avalanche carried a complete forest away as it thundered down from the mountains.

Avalanches

Winter snows reduce heat loss from the ground keeping the soil frost-free and ready for planting, and on melting, the moisture encourages the growth of new grass on Alpine pastures. However, the heavy snow falls, up to eight metres a year in some Alpine valleys, can block roads and isolate communities. More dangerous, in areas of steep slopes, is the threat of avalanches. These can result from:

(a) the weight of heavy snowfalls

(b) instability resulting from spring snow melt (especially when the Föhn is blowing).

Both cause snow, under gravity, to detach itself from steep slopes and to rush downhill at speeds of over 300 km per hour. Figure 2.21 shows the after effects of an avalanche in the Alps in February 1951. Snow rushed downhill, fanned out without losing momentum, swept over the big avalanche wall shielding the village of Airolo, and covered the first few lines of houses. A worse disaster occurred in France in 1970 when 50 French school children were killed when the hospital in which they were convalescing was hit by an avalanche.

Snow fences are built to try to protect villages and transport routes, and in mountain areas there is an avalanche warning watch service.

Land use

The way in which an area can be utilised can depend partly upon the physical environment (Chapter 1 – relief, soils) and partly upon its climate (Chapter 2 – temperatures, rainfall). Figure 2.22 shows the types and amount of land use in western Europe. Using this data, and your own knowledge:

1 Why does Iceland have no forest land?

2 Which is Europe's major timber producer?

3 Why do Norway and Sweden have such a high percentage of tundra, bare rock, urban and non-agricultural land?

4 The Netherlands has the highest population density in Europe. How is this reflected in the figures?

5 Why does Switzerland have so much pasture and heathland, yet little arable land?

6 Which two countries are most famous for their dairy produce?

7 What evidence is there that Spain and Italy are important producers of cereals and fruit?

▽ **Figure 2.22** Land use (%) of selected countries

	tundra, bare rock, urban and non-agricultural land	pasture and heath	arable land	forests
Iceland	78.2	21.0	0.8	0
Norway	73.5	1.0	3.0	22.5
Sweden	40.0	2.0	8.0	50.0
Denmark	17.5	7.5	65.0	10.0
West Germany	16.9	21.7	32.6	28.8
Netherlands	23.9	38.4	29.1	8.6
Belgium	25.5	24.0	30.8	19.7
France	14.2	25.3	34.2	26.3
Switzerland	23.0	43.0	10.0	24.0
Italy	3.7	18.7	55.3	22.3
Spain	5.1	30.4	41.6	22.9

Distribution and density

Reasons for high population densities	European examples		Reasons for low population densities	European examples	
	1	2		1	2
lowlands	Netherlands		mountains	Alps	
moderate climates			extreme climates		
i) warm climates	Costa Brava		i) too cold	Northern Finland	
ii) Adequate, evenly distributed rainfall	Northern France		ii) too dry	Spanish Meseta	
deep, rich soils	Po Valley		thin, rocky soils	Norway	
broad, flat river valleys	Po Valley		narrow river valleys	Massif Central	
rich 'natural' vegetation	Paris Basin		lack of any 'natural' vegetation	Lappland	
ports	Antwerp		inland areas with limited communications	Finland	
holiday resorts	French Riviera		areas with limited tourist appeal	Lappland	
economic resources	Ruhr coalfield		lack of economic resources	Eire	
capital cities – administrative, educational, ecclesiastical and commercial centres	Paris		areas furthest from capital cities	Western Eire	

△ **Figure 3.1** Population density and distribution

▷ **Figure 3.2** Density of population in Europe

People have always been unevenly distributed over the earth's surface. Chapters 1 and 2 should have given you some idea as to how relief and climate can affect this distribution, and later chapters will stress the importance of economic factors. Complete the table in Figure 3.1 using your general knowledge and Figure 3.2.

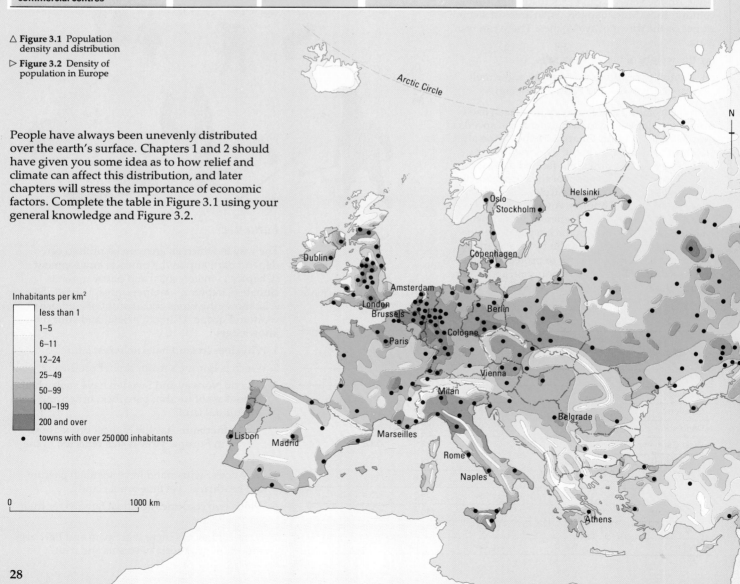

Inhabitants per km²

less than 1
1–5
6–11
12–24
25–49
50–99
100–199
200 and over

• towns with over 250 000 inhabitants

0 ——— 1000 km

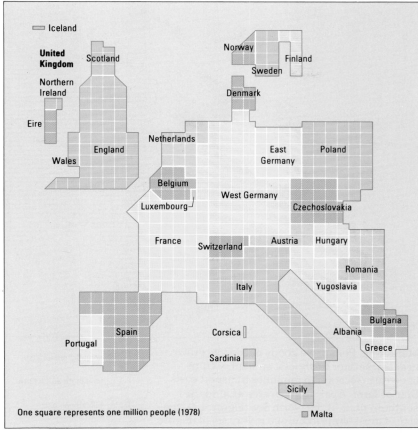

One square represents one million people (1978)

△ **Figure 3.3** Demographic map of Europe

Figure 3.3 is a demographic map. It shows areas in proportion to population and not, as is usual, to the amount of land. One square on the map represents one million people. Some countries appear much smaller than usual indicating that they have a low population density. Other countries appear larger than usual indicating that they have a high population density. Using this map:

1 How many people (in millions) live in the Netherlands, Norway, and West Germany?

2 Which countries have a low population density?

3 Which countries have a high population density?

4 What do you consider to be the advantages and disadvantages of showing population densities on this type of map?

Growth of population

This is much smaller in Europe than in any other continent. At present Latin America's population is increasing by, on average, 2.8% a year, with North America's by 0.8% and Europe's by only 0.3%. In Europe, only Eire and Spain exceed a 1% growth rate a year (the world's average is 2%). The UK will have a declining population before the end of the decade, and indeed, estimates suggest that Europe will have a zero growth rate by A.D. 2030. This is partly due to a low birthrate, to family planning, to improved education and a desire for material possessions rather than a large family.

Population structure

An age-sex pyramid (Figure 3.4) divides the population into age groups with the percentage of females on the right and males on the left of the central axis. This method of representing population also allows easy comparison between countries. West Germany, like most western European countries has a 'narrow' pyramid where the numbers in each age group are approximately equal. (Unlike developing countries which, with their high birth rates have a very wide base and a rapidly tapering pyramid). The 'dependency age' groups are large in relation to those in the economically active and reproductive sections. This represents a country with no significant population growth and an ageing population, as well as a low infant mortality rate and a high standard of medical care. In West Germany's case how do you account for fewer people in both the 25–29 and 55–59 age groups, and fewer males than females in the age groups over 60 years old?

The Dependency Ratio is

$$\frac{\text{the non-economically active}}{\text{economically active}}$$

i.e. $\dfrac{\text{children} + \text{elderly}}{\text{those of working age}}$

How does this ratio affect:

(a) the working population

(b) the gross national product of a country

(c) the planning and cost of social services such as hospitals, old people's homes, schools and nurseries?

Figure 3.4 Population pyramid for West Germany 1980 (Source of data: *Facts about Germany*)

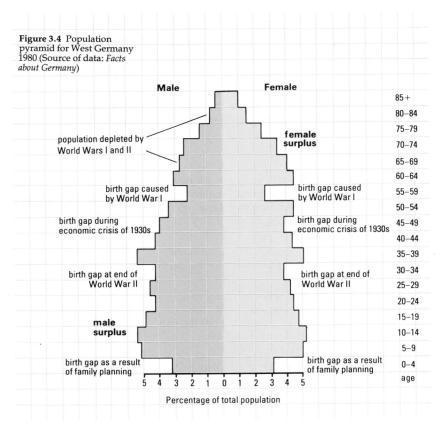

29

Farming systems

Farming is an industry, and like any other industry it has its **inputs** into the farm, **processes** which take place on the farm, and **outputs**.

Inputs include the physical environment (natural inputs) together with human (artificial) inputs.

Processes are the types of farming, such as growing crops or rearing animals.

Outputs are the farm products available for sale. These must be greater, in monetary terms, than the inputs if the farmer is to make a profit.

Factors affecting farming in Europe

Farmers decisions on what crops to grow or animals to rear, and what methods to use to produce the outputs depends upon an understanding of the most favourable physical and economic conditions of their location. A simplified map to show the major areas of specialisation is shown in Figure 4.1.

Physical inputs

Relief Usually the flatter the land the larger and more efficient is the farm. Output tends to decline as land gets steeper and higher (Figures 4.1 and 4.2).

Soils The deeper and richer the soil the more intensive the farming and higher the output e.g. limon of the Paris Basin, alluvium of the Po Valley and the estuarine deposits in the Netherlands. Soils ideally should be reasonably well drained.

Rainfall Those areas in more northern and western Europe with adequate moisture spread evenly throughout the year, and which is reliable, tend to produce good grass and concentrate on animal rearing. The drier areas with less reliable rainfall in the south and east concentrate more on arable farming.

Temperatures In the north the length of the growing season is limited, whereas in the warmer, sunnier south cereals and fruit ripen more readily. Aspect is an important local factor.

Human inputs

Government aid Farmers rely on grants for new stock and machinery, and subsidies to guarantee a fixed price. Many of western Europe's farm prices are fixed by the Common Agricultural Policy (CAP) of the EEC.

Fertilisers These have increased in amounts and effectiveness raising outputs in especially the more affluent farming regions.

Mechanisation The introduction of many new labour-saving machines, even since 1950, has increased outputs even if (Figure 4.2) it has led to a sharp decline in the numbers employed in agriculture.

Improvement in varieties Output has also increased due to better strains of seed, better quality animals, and new pesticides.

Marketing Perishable goods need to be grown near markets for freshness, and bulky crops likewise in location to minimise transport costs.

Size of farm Apart from an area around the southern parts of the North Sea (Figure 4.4), the size of most farms in Europe is very small (Figure 4.2). Attempts are being made to amalgamate farms but while this may increase their efficiency it also increases rural depopulation. Notice how farm sizes decrease to the peripheral areas such as Portugal, Greece and Finland.

Competition for land Traditional farming areas are under threat from new industry, housing, roads and recreational demands.

Variable inputs

The farmer is vulnerable to changes in market prices and demands, to government policies, and especially to changes in the weather (flood, drought, frosts).

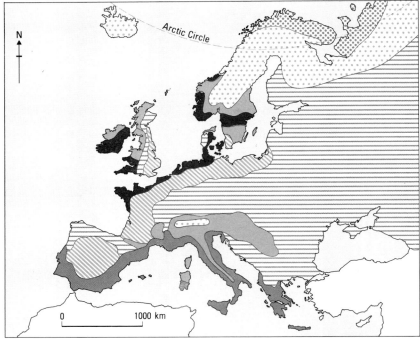

nomadic pastoralism

little or no agriculture

hill farming and marginal land

crop and livestock

commercial grain

commercial dairying

Mediterranean

△ **Figure 4.1** Generalised map showing specialised farming types

▽ **Figure 4.2** Agricultural figures for western Europe

		% of economically active population in agriculture		% total land used for agriculture	average size of farms (hectares)	% GNP from agriculture
		1960	1980	1980	1980	1981
EEC countries	Netherlands	10.8	5.6	56.7	15.6	3.8
	Belgium	8.0	3.3	52.0	15.4	2.3
	Luxembourg	15.4	5.2	75.8	27.6	1.7
	West Germany	14.2	6.8	53.0	15.3	2.1
	France	22.1	10.4	59.1	25.4	4.0
	Italy	30.8	16.6	58.1	7.4	5.8
	Denmark	16.0	6.8	62.9	25.0	5.4
	UK	4.0	2.6	77.2	68.7	2.0
	Eire	36.5	22.2	68.6	22.5	10.3
	Greece	55.8	31.4	56.0	4.3	17.8
Other western European countries	Spain	42.1	19.7	71.3	14.8	7.4
	Portugal	44.1	25.2	54.6	5.1	8.2
	Norway	19.7	9.1	3.7	4.6	4.6
	Sweden	14.1	5.2	10.1	11.2	3.5
	Finland	36.1	12.9	9.7	9.7	8.9
	Austria	23.8	10.7	43.3	9.4	4.6
	Switzerland	11.4	7.8	53.0	7.1	5.9
	Iceland	25.7	11.7	6.2	2.6	1.7

The farming hierarchy

specialised e.g. milk, potatoes	} personal needs less important than the demands of large urban markets
large, commercial – grain growing	
small-scale intensive – market gardening and fruit	
mixed farming – stock and fodder	} personal needs important, with some surplus for sale
hill farming – marginal land	
nomadic herding – subsistence	} personal needs dominant, little surplus for sale

△ **Figure 4.3** The farming hierarchy

▷ **Figure 4.4** Farming intensity in Europe

▽ **Figure 4.5** Arguments for, and against, the Common Agricultural Policy

Some achievements of CAP

Achieved a larger measure of self sufficiency. This reduces the costs and unreliability of imports.

Created higher yields due to input of capital for machinery and fertiliser

In NW Europe the average farm size has increased almost to the recommended level

Amalgamation of fields – in parts of France the number of fields has been reduced to one-eighth of the 1950 total

Production has changed according to demands, e.g., less wheat and potatoes and more sugar beet and animal products

Subsidies to hill farmers have reduced rural depopulation

Poorer farmers gain an opportunity to receive a second income by working in nearby factories ('five o'clock farmers') or from tourism

Higher income for farmers

Subsidies have reduced the risk of even higher unemployment in such rural areas as the Mezzogiorno (p 114)

Reduced reliance on crops imported from developing countries who themselves have a food shortage

A surplus one year can offset a possible crop failure in another year

Some problems still facing CAP

An increase in food prices, especially in the net importing EEC countries of West Germany and the UK

Creation of food surpluses – the so called 'mountains and lakes' (Figure 4.6)

Selling of surplus products at reduced prices to Eastern European countries (causes both political and economic opposition)

Increased gap between the favoured 'core' agriculture regions (Figure 4.4) and the periphery

Peripheral farm units still very small and often uneconomic

High costs of subsidies. 'Industrial' countries such as the UK object to 70% of the EEC budget being spent on agriculture

'Five o'clock farmers' spend insufficient time on their farms. In France 15%, and in West Germany 30%, of farmers have a second income.

Destruction of hedges to create larger fields destroys wild life and increases the risk of soil erosion

By reducing imports from developing countries the latter's main source of income is lost thus increasing the trade gap between the two areas

Figure 4.6 'Mountains' and 'lakes'

beef mountain

butter mountain

sultana mountain

grain mountain

EEC lake

milk

wine

olive oil

1982 harvest excellent, with high quality wines reaching a peak. To prevent the surplus depressing market prices the Commission allowed a short-time storage programme to aid wine growers in France, Luxembourg and West Germany.

1980–83, production rose while consumption fell.

Cheaper olive oil from Tunisia and increased production in Italy and Greece has led to a glut – and over-production will increase once Spain joins. Need for huge storage tanks – one near Athens contains 45 000 tonnes of olive oil. Paid for from European subsidies yet it maintains jobs in these poor areas, and stops youngsters moving to the city.

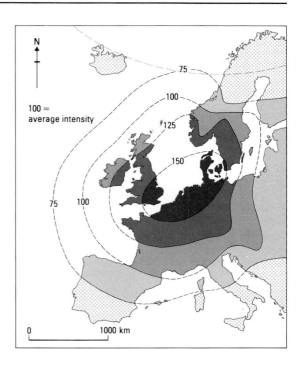

100 = average intensity

Farming in the EEC

The basic concepts for a common farm policy were set out in the 1957 Treaty of Rome as follows:

☐ To increase agricultural productivity

☐ To ensure a fair standard of living for farmers

☐ To stabilise markets

☐ To ensure reasonable consumer prices

These aims have replaced all existing national policies and often cause conflict between members. Together with the restructuring of farm units they still form the basis of the Common Agricultural Policy (CAP) in the mid-1980s. In 1968 it was noted that 75% of the farm sizes were under 10 hectares, and only 3% were over 50 hectares (Figure 4.2). With so many families employed in agriculture it was apparent that high standards of living were difficult to achieve.

Each member country also used to employ its own currency, and as exchange rates constantly altered, it was agreed that a new currency be introduced – the ECU (European Currency Unit). This was sometimes called the 'basket of currencies' with each country aligning itself to a set central valuation. A further complication is that farm prices are quoted in 'Green Rates' by which each country fixes its own level of support. Farm prices are fixed in units of account and then translated into national currencies at a certain exchange rate. For Britain, the exchange rate between it and the other EEC countries is the 'Green Pound'. In the early 1980s £1 sterling = £1.62 ECU.

How successful has the Common Agricultural Policy been? In all member countries there are 'pro-marketeers' and 'anti-marketeers' and trying to get a balanced interpretation is difficult. However, Figure 4.5 tries to show some of the arguments used by the 'pro' and 'anti' groups.

Mediterranean agriculture

Olives

The olive is often regarded as the yardstick of the Mediterranean climate. Its distribution is shown in Figure 4.7. The value of the olive is illustrated in a story concerning Athena and the sea-god Poseidon who both claimed the province of Attica and its chief city of Athens as their own. It was decided that both should give the Athenians a present, and the mortals would decide that whoever gave the more useful gift should have the province. Poseidon struck the earth, and a horse appeared. Athena drove her spear into the ground and an olive tree sprang up. Athena's gift was judged the better and she was given the province. Today an olive tree is preserved on the Acropolis itself.

northern limit of cultivation

major producing area

(3) world producer

◁ **Figure 4.7** Olive growing areas

▽ **Figure 4.9** Olive grove near Delphi. At its best a single tree can produce enough olives to yield 20 kg of oil when pressed.

△ **Figure 4.8** Olive trees near the Acropolis, Athens. There are approximately 500 000 000 olive trees in Europe, most grow in regular planted groves (Figure 4.9), the remainder are scattered over the countryside.

Why should the olive be so important?

☐ The fruit provides a food supply.

☐ The oil is used for cooking.

☐ The timber, resistant to fire, makes fine, hard, light-coloured furniture.

☐ It is a symbol of peace and victory ('to hold out the olive branch').

☐ It is used in making soap and toilet cream and in Portugal, in the sardine packing industry.

Why is it suited to Mediterranean areas?

It likes:

☐ Hot, sunny summers (no need for irrigation), and south facing slopes.

☐ An absence of frost, since although frost does not kill the tree, it does prevent its commercial use.

☐ Abundant moisture in late winter and early spring. (Moist cloudy summers make the oil too acidic for use.)

☐ Deep soils, but can survive easily in the thin, rocky soils typical of so many Mediterranean areas.

Europe produces 75% of the world's olive oil (the 'lake' of Figure 4.6), with Spain producing 33%, Italy 26% and Greece 14% of the world's total. The grey-green olive trees (Figures 4.8 and 4.9) are evergreen, producing white flowers in spring, and a purplish fruit in early winter.

Citrus fruits

Physical advantages of the Mediterranean

☐ Hot, dry, sunny summers – ideal for ripening. (The thick skin reduces moisture loss.)

☐ Mild winters – the crop is usually harvested November to May. Citrus plants prefer temperatures not to drop below −3°C.

☐ Deltaic lowlands provide alluvial soil for commercial production.

☐ Possibility of irrigation in drier areas (Figure 4.10).

Human and economic advantages

☐ Nearness to large urban markets of northern Europe, especially those with a high standard of living.

☐ Nearness to main roads and railways to transport the fruit fresh to these urban markets.

☐ Availability of a labour supply, especially in areas with low incomes and wages, to pick the fruit.

☐ Increased mechanisation, aided by EEC grants.

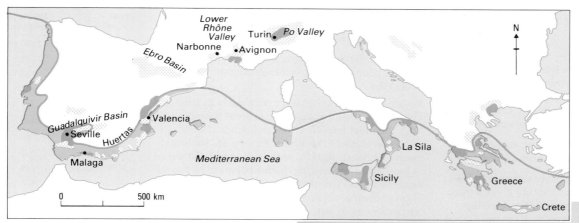

northern limit of oranges
irrigated areas
major orange growing areas
rice
lemons

◁ **Figure 4.10** Citrus fruits and irrigation in southern Europe

▽ **Figure 4.11** Irrigated orange groves near Vera, Almeria, Spain. If there was no irrigation, the area would support little vegetation.

▽ **Figure 4.12** Rice growing near Vercelli (Turin), Italy (bottom)

Oranges (Figure 4.10) grow best in the most southerly areas with Spain, then Italy and Greece the major producers. Bitter oranges (near Seville) sweet oranges and tangerines are grown.

Lemons are grown mostly in Sicily and Greece.

Grapefruits are only found in small quantities in parts of Spain.

Production of citrus fruits is increasing annually but is restricted by the long dry summer with its high evaporation rate, by large areas of poor soil and high land, and, in southern France, by the Mistral which lowers temperatures.

Irrigation

The traditional cereals, olives and vines of the Mediterranean lands complement the natural environment, but do not form the basis for a modern competitive agricultural economy. The major problem is one of water deficiency (Figure 7.1), especially in summer.

Spain The Huertas, (irrigated market gardens) have existed along the Mediterranean coastlands, where winter and spring rivers deposited alluvium, for several centuries. Recent schemes, unique in Europe, have integrated dam building (increasing storage areas) constructing new villages complete with modern services, and increasing irrigated areas with a result of increasing the range and volume of crop production (Figure 4.11).

France Tributaries of the Rhône such as the Durance and Verdun bring vast volumes of melt-water in spring to the lower Rhône valley, but almost dry up by late autumn. Attempts to regulate the flow have led to increases in the production of vines, early vegetables (primeurs) and, in the Camargue district of the Rhône delta, rice (Figure 4.10).

Italy Water from the Po and its many tributaries, and from springs have enabled the area around Turin to become the major rice growing region in Europe (Figure 4.12). In the south (the Mezzogiorno), several small irrigation schemes have been created to try to reduce rural poverty.

Greece and Yugoslavia have also increased their number of dams despite being in an earthquake area.

33

Vines

Conditions for growth

Temperatures Cold, short winters which strengthen root and stem growth and reduce pests. However, frosts in May are disastrous. Summers need to be warm (over 20°C) and sunny to increase the sugar content of the grapes.

Aspect South and south-east facing slopes are most favoured as they get maximum sunlight.

Precipitation Gentle rain in early summer helps to swell the grapes, but excess moisture gives a thin, watery wine, and encourages mildew. Hail is a major hazard, as occurred in parts of central France in 1983 when most of the crop was ruined.

Slope Slopes are preferable to flat land to aid drainage (Figure 4.13).

Soils must be well drained. The better ones include those found on limestone, valley gravels and sands, and loess (limon).

Labour A plentiful supply is necessary both to heavily prune the crop (vines grow rapidly) and to collect the harvest.

Figure 4.14 shows the major producers in 1980 and Figure 4.15 the location of these areas together with the most famous wines in Europe. Most wines produced in southern Europe are for local, everyday consumption, with more specialist wines in local areas – many of which happen to be found near the northern commercial limit of the vine. France, the major producer of both 'specialist' and 'vin ordinaire' is suffering from imports of cheaper wine from Italy – and the EEC's wine lake (Figure 4.6) will increase now that Greece has become a member and Spain and Portugal have applied for membership.

1980 winegrowers	(1000s of tonnes)
1 France	12696
2 Italy	11730
3 Spain	7748
4 USSR	5700
5 USA	4467
6 Turkey	3485
7 Argentina	3360
8 Portugal	1500
9 Romania	1486
10 Greece	1424
11 Yugoslavia	1313
12 Bulgaria	1200
13 South Africa	1130
14 West Germany	993

(**1**, **2**, etc. denote European countries)

◁ **Figure 4.13** These grapes are grown for champagne at Valleé de la Marne, France

△ **Figure 4.14** Major world wine producers, 1980

▽ **Figure 4.15** Wine growing areas of Europe

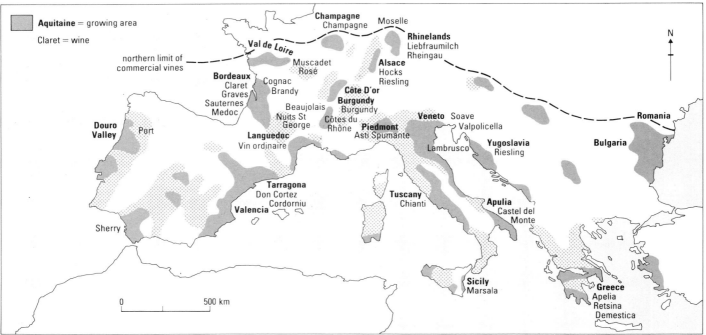

FARMING
Intensive cereals – Paris Basin

France is the most self-sufficient country in Europe as far as producing enough food is concerned, and 10% of the labour force is still employed in agriculture. France grows most wheat, barley and maize in Europe, and can usually export over 30% of her annual production to other EEC countries. The Paris Basin (Figure 4.16) followed by Aquitaine are the two major cereal growing areas. The region, or 'pay', of Beauce has over 90% of its land under cereals (Figure 4.16).

Advantages of the Beauce Region (Figure 4.17)

□ Summers are warm and sunny enabling cereals to ripen.

□ Winter frosts help to break up the soil.

□ Rainfall is light, under 750 mm, which is adequate for wheat and barley, especially as most comes in the growing season.

□ The almost level limestone plateau helps large scale mechanisation and transportation.

□ The limestone is covered by a thick deposit of limon. Limon is a fine, stoneless deposit believed to have been blown from non vegetated glacial margins in the ice age. It is capable of holding moisture yet rarely becomes waterlogged.

□ The large urban market of Paris is nearby.

Changes in farming in Beauce

Figure 4.18 shows part of Beauce in 1950 and 1980. In 1950 Beauce still showed some of the problems of many other agricultural regions of France (and indeed Europe) with numerous small farms, often too small to be profit-making, and individually scattered holdings. This fragmentation was a legacy of the Napoleonic Code where the inheritance (the farm) was divided equally between heirs. Villages in Beauce tended to be large, but not numerous, due to problems of water supply on the limestone. By 1980 a prairie type (i.e. hedgeless) landscape had evolved due to consolidation of farms due to policies of the CAP (page 31).

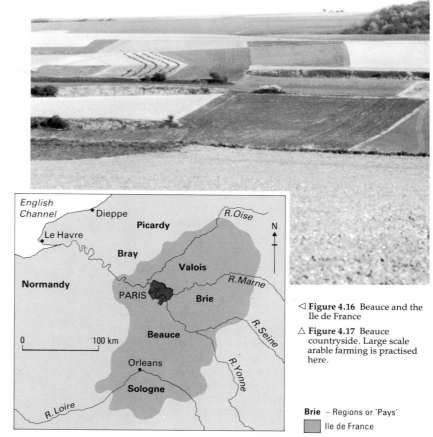

◁ **Figure 4.16** Beauce and the Ile de France
△ **Figure 4.17** Beauce countryside. Large scale arable farming is practised here.

Brie – Regions or 'Pays'
Ile de France

▽ **Figure 4.18** Changes in farming in Beauce. Describe and give reasons for the differences in: (*a*) the number of houses in the village (*b*) the ownership of houses in the village (*c*) the number and size of the fields (*d*) the road system

■▪■ houses for agricultural workers
▐▪▭ non agricultural workers houses
◇◇◇ new estate mainly for commuters
▱ dual carriageway
▭ country roads   ▨ fields

As a result of the Common Agricultural Policy there has been an increase in farm and field size, a decrease in the number of farms and farmworkers, an increase in the level of mechanisation, and an increase in yields due to improved fertilisers, quality of seeds and farming techniques. Many farms in Beauce now exceed 100 hectares (compare this with Figure 4.2) and output doubled between 1955 and 1980. This increase in production has continued following excellent harvests in the early 1980s, and the EEC have to give grants to keep prices paid to the farmer high. However, this increase in production, together with a slight fall in consumption has led to another 'mountain' (Figure 4.6).

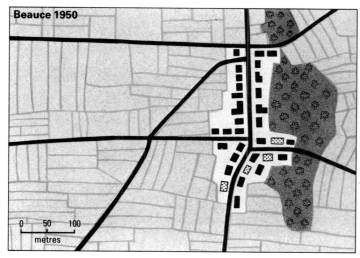

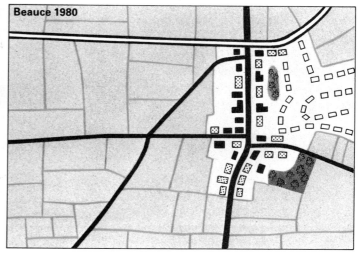

Intensive farming

The old polders of the Netherlands

Most of western Netherlands lies below sea level, but the majority of this area was reclaimed from the sea several centuries ago. These reclaimed areas are called polders, and now most of the area between Rotterdam and Amsterdam (Figure 4.19) lies between two and six metres *below* present day sea level. The landscape has, in the extreme west, a belt of sand-dunes which act as a natural defence against the sea (Figure 1.26). Inland of this lies a perfectly flat area drained by a series of canals which run between embankments and above the general level of the polders. The fields on the polders are bound by drainage channels and the excess water from the land is pumped, originally by windmills but now increasingly by diesel pumps, into the canals. Even now over 20% of the total area is water covered.

Many areas of these old polders are becoming increasingly urbanised. The Randstad (or Ring, Figure 4.19) conurbation has helped to raise the density of population in the Netherlands to 360 per km² – the highest density in Europe. Extra land is needed for this urban growth (for houses, factories and roads) and to feed its population. The expense of reclaiming land is enormous, and so the maximum use must be made of it to make it profitable – in agricultural terms this is known as 'intensive farming'.

Land use

There are three major types:

1 Dairying This is most intensive north of Amsterdam and is favoured by the mild winters, flat land, adequate and evenly spread rainfall providing lush grass, and the nearby large urban markets. Most of the cattle are Friesians (Figure 4.20), and although some milk is used fresh, the majority is turned into butter and cheese. The round Dutch cheeses are sold in the cheese-market at Alkmaar (Figure 13.3).

2 Horticulture under glass The area between Rotterdam and The Hague is a mass of glasshouses, with individual holdings making a profit on land averaging only one hectare. The costs of production are enormous due to:

□ Large, expensive glasshouses.

□ Operating oil-fired boilers to maintain high temperatures.

□ Sprinkler systems to provide water.

□ Computers, on the more modern holdings, to control heating, moisture and ventilation.

□ Facilities to cover plants in black plastic to retard growth in order to stagger the period of ripening.

□ Annual need to change the soil, and to use large quantities of fertiliser and manure.

□ Machinery to weed and behead dead plants.

□ Need for rapid transit to the local markets or for export overseas via Schiphol Airport (page 95).

◁ **Figure 4.19** Land use in the Netherlands

sand dunes

arable on the new polders

arable

mainly pasture

horticulture

'Randstad'

fresh water

△ **Figure 4.20** Dairying in the Netherlands, near Alphenad Rijn

Several crops a year can be grown varying from cut flowers in spring, to tomatoes and cucumbers in summer, and lettuce in autumn and winter. In recent years the number of smallholdings has declined as the urban area has expanded.

3 Bulbs The sandy soils between Leiden and Haarlem are used to grow bulbs. Tulips, hyacinths and daffodils in particular are grown on farms averaging 6–8 hectares in size. The sand dunes offer protection from the prevailing winds. Although the flowers have to be cut early in order to get them to market fresh, they also provide a huge seasonal tourist attraction (Figure 4.21).

Although the area under horticulture (both under glass and out of doors) is only 4% of the Netherlands, it provides a major export.

▷ **Figure 4.21** Tulip fields between Leiden and Haarlem

▽ **Figure 4.22** Aalsmeer – the largest flower auction in the world, in the heart of approximately 500 hectares of glasshouses

Aalsmeer auction mart

This is the largest auction mart in the world (Figure 4.22). The mart itself covers 45 hectares, and the buildings 30 hectares. Five mornings a week, 4000 growers bring their produce of flowers, potted plants and roses (Figure 4.23). For every kind of flower there is a special location. The growers place their flowers on awaiting carts which are numbered. By 07.00 hours the prospective buyers have inspected the flowers and go to the auction halls – each hall is capable of seating over 300 exporters, wholesalers, shopkeepers and street-traders (Figure 4.24). The buyers have a code disk with a number code on it, with which they can be registered on a computer. The auctioneer announces, over a loudspeaker, the name of the nursery from which the flowers come, the specific names of the flowers and details about their quality. The buyers sit with their hands on the pushbuttons. The auctioneer starts the clock and bidding begins. The hand of the auction clock goes from 100 (the highest price) to 1 (the lowest price). The first person to press the button is the buyer of that 'lot' of flowers. The art is not to bid too quickly (or you pay a higher price) or too slowly (for although prices fall, other bidders will get in first). The buyer can also, by microphone, indicate whether he wants the whole lot, or part of it – and bidding begins again. By 10.00 hours all the transactions have been made. The flowers are then prepared for transport by the buyers. Due to efficient organisation, the flowers reach the buyer within 15 minutes of their purchase. Such speed is essential if the flowers are to reach markets as fresh as possible. For overseas buyers, Aalsmeer is within 8 km of Schiphol Airport.

◁ **Figure 4.23** Inside the Aalsmeer auction mart, flowers and plants are stacked up for sale

▷ **Figure 4.24** Flower auction in progress in Aalsmeer

Intensive mixed farming

Denmark

Although Denmark today has a high agricultural output per person, the land, as shown in Figure 4.25, was not naturally fertile.

□ The terminal moraine was composed of clay and boulders and marked the maximum advance by the ice in glacial times.

□ Although the area to the west was sandy, it was low-lying with a high water table, giving rise to heath and marshland.

□ In the east was a more fertile boulder clay, but even this tended to be acidic, heavy, cold and prone to waterlogging.

Since the nineteenth century, much money and effort has gone into improving the latter two areas. Today the western areas are under coniferous trees and pasture land, and the east under cereal crops (Figure 4.25).

Danish farming before 1880
The relief (low and relatively flat), soils, and the climate, (winter frosts, warm sunny summers, rainfall below average) are similar to East Anglia, and Denmark used to be an important cereal growing area. Wheat and barley were the most important crops. The following factors led to changes in Danish farming:

□ Competition from much cheaper wheat grown on the American Prairies.

□ Invention (in Denmark) of the cream-separator which allowed the skimmed milk to be fed to the pigs, and the remainder to be used to make butter and cheese.

□ Rapid industrialisation and urbanisation of NW Europe (UK and West Germany) which led to an increased demand for fresh dairy produce.

Development of co-operative farming

The Danish farmers began to work together to get the maximum benefit from buying and selling on a collective basis and in bulk. Co-operative farming led to:

□ A highly developed system of small-scale farms which produced a standardised high quality product. The co-operatives collected the locally produced milk, eggs and bacon, prepared and then sold it. Government inspections guaranteed high quality to overseas buyers (Figure 4.26).

□ Introduction of scientific farming, with a heavy use of fertiliser and a rotation of crops.

□ Selective livestock breeding which produces the

(a) Danish red cow – which thrives on the relatively poor pastures. Denmark had one million milking cows in 1982. (b) Landrace pig – whose long back produces top quality bacon. Denmark had 9 million pigs in 1982.

Figure 4.27 shows how these figures have changed recently.

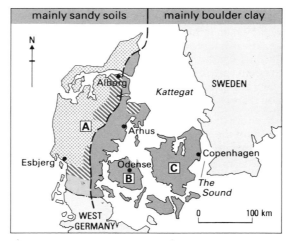

◁ Figure 4.25 Farming in Denmark

◁ Figure 4.26 Modern dairy plant with automatic butter-making machine, Fünen, Denmark

▽ Figure 4.27 Recent changes in Danish agriculture (Source of figures: Agricultural Council of Denmark)

	1960	1970	1980	1982
Number of farm units	196076	140197	114213	107500
Agricultural area, thousands hectares	3094	2941	2884	2876
Average area per farm unit, hectares	15.8	21.0	25.3	26.7
Full time workers	300000	161200	107700	102500
Hired workers	128300	34100	25400	23800
% of population in agriculture	16	9	6.8	6.1
Agricultural investments, £ million	56	83	370	230
Number of tractors	111300	174600	184400	176300
Number of combine harvesters	8900	42300	38800	38400
Number of horses, thousands	171	45	50	42
Number of cows, thousands	1438	1153	1082	1063
Number of pigs, thousands	6147	8361	9957	9348
Number of hens, thousands	9735	6330	4563	—
Cereals as % of agricultural area	46.7	59.1	73.0	74.6
Root crops as % of agricultural area	18.3	9.8	8.4	8.4
Grass as % of agricultural area	31.7	27.2	13.1	9.3
Urban area as % of total area	3.3	3.9	5.5	7.7
Gross agricultural income, £ million	282	395	982	1486
Export of agricultural products, £ million	390	547	2024	2624
Agricultural export as % of total export	54	31	28	28
Number of dairies	1350	—	—	175

□ Colleges to train and re-train young people and practising farmers.

□ Government help in the form of grants and low interest rates.

□ Links with such agricultural industries as bacon curing, brewing, milling, and the manufacture of butter, cheese and farm machinery.

Recent changes in Danish farming
(Figure 4.27)

- An increase in the average size of Danish farms and a decrease in the number of smaller farms.

- An increase in mechanisation.

- A shift of cattle and milk production from the east to the west (as well as fewer cows overall) and an increase in cereals in the east.

- A decrease in the agricultural workforce and a pronounced movement to the towns for jobs.

- Difficulty in getting labour for the twice-daily milking, leading to an increase in pig farming and cereal growing. In 1980 only 2% of school leavers went into farming.

- EEC membership has strengthened traditional markets with the UK and West Germany, and opened up new ones. 28% of Denmark's exports are agricultural products, and 66% of these go to the EEC.

- The EEC has provided the subsidies necessary to guarantee fixed prices for farm produce.

◁ **Figure 4.28** Farming in Denmark – the fields are bound by electric fences

△ **Figure 4.30** Modern Danish farms are still built around courtyards

A typical Danish farm on the island of Fünen

Figure 4.28 shows a view of farmland on Fünen, while Figure 4.29 shows the layout of one farm on the island, and Figure 4.30 the farm buildings. Despite its emphasis on dairy produce, two-thirds of Denmark is arable land (Figures 4.27 and 4.28). The land is divided into large fields, most of which are bound by wire fences not hedges. However, the wheat, barley, oats and rye, together with the tops of the sugar beet are all grown as fodder for the animals or for Danish consumption or use in industry (e.g. milling, brewing). Only a small proportion of the farm is actually under grass mainly because the grass is not of good enough quality. It is still fairly common to see the Danish red cow tethered, or at least limited to small areas of grazing ground. These animals are usually kept indoors from late September to late April and are fed on the fodder crops grown on the farm. Most farms are not large enough to store the large quantities of winter fodder needed and so when the cereals are harvested they are sent to the co-operatives for keeping until they are needed. Root crops and clover are also grown for fodder, although sugar is also obtained from the beet.

Figures 4.29 and 4.30 also show the farm buildings, and even modern farms are still built around the traditional courtyard. Notice the dwelling house on one side of the yard facing the cowsheds. The third side is usually occupied by accommodation for pigs and poultry and facilities to store some grain.

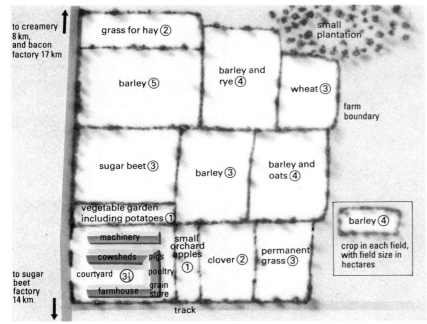

△ **Figure 4.29** Layout of a typical Danish farm on Fünen. There are 150 cows (120 Red Danish, 30 Friesian), 240 Landrace pigs and 220 hens. How big is the farm? Is this large or small for Denmark? What percentage of the land is arable? How does this compare with the national average?

Marginal farming areas

Transhumance in the Swiss Alps

Transhumance is the practice of pastoral farmers moving their herds and flocks to mountain pastures in summer and bringing them back to valleys for the winter. The herders accompany their animals and live in small huts on the 'alp' (Figure 4.31).

The Alpine farmers' year

Winter The weather is cold enough for the dairy cows to be kept in barns for up to six months. In previous years the farmer may have carved wood to make furniture, or toys and ornaments for the limited number of tourists. Today the luckier farmer may live sufficiently near to a ski-resort to become a ski-instructor.

Spring The cows calve in April–May, after which they are slowly taken to higher levels as the snow melts, and leaving the valley pastures for growing hay for winter fodder. Traditionally the cows were led uphill, with their decorated 'Queen', complete with bell, leading the way. Nowadays the animals are transported by truck.

Summer The cows move up to the alp – a plateau-like feature high above the glaciated valley, and on which lush, fresh grass grows. The milk they produce is turned into cheese.

Autumn After September the cows return to the valley, and the herders to their families. Any crops, such as the vine and fruit are collected, and a last cut of hay is made. By November the cattle are back in their barns and being stall fed.

Transhumance in the 1980s

The younger villagers prefer working in factories to spending half the year in isolation. It is often only the older generation who continue to take the animals to the summer pastures, and their numbers are decreasing. The EEC now provides money to hill farmers, but encourages them to clear, and farm, land only half way up the mountain. Here they can also grow hay (Figures 4.31 and 4.32), and visit the cattle each day, yet they can return to their village homes each night. Even so, the mountain farmers earn less than 30% of their lowland counterparts.

▽ **Figure 4.31** Transhumance in a Swiss Alpine Valley (bottom)

▽ **Figure 4.32** Swiss farmers grow and cut hay half way up the mountains, using power mowers which have been especially designed with extreme slope handling capabilities

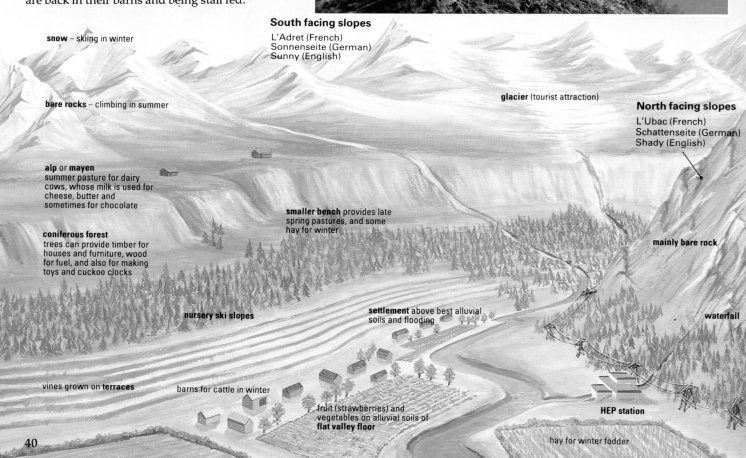

snow – skiing in winter

South facing slopes
L'Adret (French)
Sonnenseite (German)
Sunny (English)

bare rocks – climbing in summer

glacier (tourist attraction)

North facing slopes
L'Ubac (French)
Schattenseite (German)
Shady (English)

alp or **mayen**
summer pasture for dairy cows, whose milk is used for cheese, butter and sometimes for chocolate

smaller bench provides late spring pastures, and some hay for winter

coniferous forest
trees can provide timber for houses and furniture, wood for fuel, and also for making toys and cuckoo clocks

mainly bare rock

nursery ski slopes

settlement above best alluvial soils and flooding

waterfall

vines grown on terraces

barns for cattle in winter

fruit (strawberries) and vegetables on alluvial soils of **flat valley floor**

HEP station

hay for winter fodder

The Norwegian fjords

Fjords are not unlike Swiss valleys in appearance except that the valley bottoms have been flooded by the sea. Study Figure 4.33 and then answer the following questions by using pages 16, 18, 19, 20, 22, 26 and 40.

1 What are the following and how were they formed:
  fjord, saeter, hanging valley and delta.

2 Copy this land sketch. Then add to it, in appropriate places, the following:
  waterfall, an area of coniferous forest, bare rock, snow-line, tree-line, summer pastures, an area where oats, barley, hay and fruit can be grown.

3 Why can oats, barley, hay and fruit be grown so far north?

4 List the problems facing the farmer in this area.

5 List the advantages of living next to this inlet of the sea.

6 Describe and give reasons for the likely differences in land use between the two sides of the fjord (remember fjords run east-west).

7 Why are many saeters now either abandoned or used as summer chalets?

Traditionally many farmers living next to fjords turned to the sea in winter for extra income.

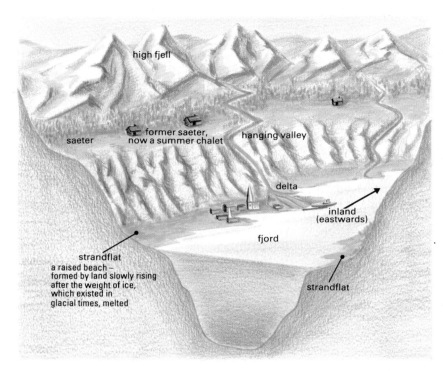

△ **Figure 4.33** Landsketch of a Norwegian fjord

Norway's modern 'farmer-fisherman'

'Nils Eriksen is at present making extensions to his farmbuildings, constructing a new farmhouse and tripling his number of cattle. His farm is at Grannes, some eight kilometres from Stavanger – the heart of Norway's oil industry. The Grannes farmstead lies in some of the best farmland in Norway but even so the climate of the area means that Nils continues the long established tradition among Norwegian smallholders who combine farm activities with a job on the sea. But whereas in the past these part-time farmers found fishing the supplementary source to their income, Nils is one of a growing group of Norwegians who have found new careers in the oil industry. Nils works on the Ekofisk oilfield, where he won a large prize from Phillips Petroleum for an invention which helped to increase production. It is with this money that he has been able to modernise his farm. Nils spends twelve days on leave at home followed by eight days on the rig – a time during which the farm is run by his wife and three children.'

◁ **Figure 4.34** Farming in the fjords, every piece of flat land is used

Norway

Norway is Europe's major fishing country. Four per cent are directly employed in fishing, with many more either part-time fishermen (see page 41), or working in allied processing industries. In the northern areas over 15% of the working population are fishermen.

Why has Norway turned to the sea?

Disadvantages of the land

□ Less than 4% can be cultivated, as most is mountain and tundra (Figure 4.2).

□ Gales, heavy rain and a short growing season also limit farming.

□ Limited mineral resources.

Advantages of the sea

□ Coastal areas are kept ice-free by the North Atlantic Drift. Even the Lofoten Islands have a January mean monthly temperature of 0°C.

□ The mingling of warm and cold water encourages the growth of plankton.

□ The shallow, offshore continental shelf allows sunlight to penetrate the water, which also encourages the growth of plankton.

□ The fjords provide deep, sheltered, natural harbours.

□ The Strandflat (Figure 4.33) provides land for small fishing villages and processing plants.

□ The Skerryguard (offshore islands) offer protection against the gales.

□ The cold climate helps to keep the catch fresh.

□ The midnight sun in summer provides longer hours of daylight.

△ **Figure 5.1** Fishing village in the Lofoten Islands, Norway

▽ **Figure 5.2** Changes in fishing

	Tonnage	World rank	Fishing vessels
1970	2856	4th	37 000
1978	2447	6th	27 000
1982	4300	5th	20 000

Recent changes

□ A decline in the tonnage of fish caught due to over-fishing in previous decades. New techniques such as echo-sounders and the use of floating factories have seriously depleted the numbers of cod and herring (Figures 5.2 and 5.3) while whaling has ceased. After the extension in 1977 of a 320 km (200 miles) fishing limit, the annual tonnage landed has increased.

□ A drop in the numbers engaged in fishing (Figure 5.2), especially those who were previously part-time fishermen.

□ Changes in the size of vessels. Even in 1970 75% of the vessels were under 10 metres in length and operated by one or two persons. Today vessels are larger and are dual purpose in terms of being capable of landing different fish.

□ Changes in the use made of the fish caught (Figure 5.4). There has been a decline in the demand for cod-liver oil, and an increase in the reduction of fish and in frozen fish.

□ A decline in the Mediterranean and east European markets.

□ Growth of co-operatives which help to maintain price levels, to plan export policies, to provide grants and, if necessary, to provide boats.

□ Although Norway rejected EEC membership, it did, in 1983, agree to link with member countries over fishing controls (see page 42).

Other Norwegian maritime activities

□ The fourth largest merchant fleet in the world.

□ Shipbuilding.

□ Oil, based upon the Ekofisk North Sea field which is located in Norwegian waters (page 53).

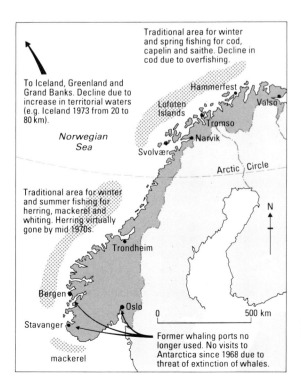

Traditional area for winter and spring fishing for cod, capelin and saithe. Decline in cod due to overfishing.

To Iceland, Greenland and Grand Banks. Decline due to increase in territorial waters (e.g. Iceland 1973 from 20 to 80 km).

Norwegian Sea

Hammerfest
Lofoten Islands
Valso
Tromso
Narvik
Svolvær

Arctic Circle

N

Traditional area for winter and summer fishing for herring, mackerel and whiting. Herring virtually gone by mid 1970s.

Trondheim

Bergen
Oslo

0   500 km

Stavanger

Former whaling ports no longer used. No visits to Antarctica since 1968 due to threat of extinction of whales.

mackerel

◁ **Figure 5.3** Changes in Norwegian fishing

▽ **Figure 5.4** What was done with the Norwegian catch in 1980

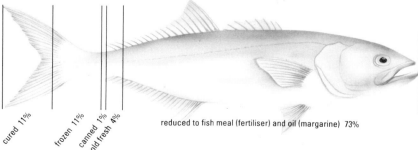

cured 11%   frozen 11%   canned 1%   sold fresh 4%   reduced to fish meal (fertiliser) and oil (margarine) 73%

The EEC Common Fisheries Policy (CFP)

After twelve years of discussion, an agreement was finally signed in January 1983. Initially to run for 10 years, the CFP created a 'Blue Europe' (as opposed to the so-called Green Europe for agriculture).

The 1970s – A decade of change

'Up to the end of 1976 fishing in the waters of the North Sea and the North-East Atlantic was a free-for-all, with scant respect for the conservation measures put forward by the North East Atlantic Fisheries Convention.' (European Commission) Fish stocks in the North Atlantic and the Norwegian Sea, especially of herring, could no longer sustain the degree of fishing inflicted upon them. The European distant water fleet virtually collapsed as Iceland, Canada, the Faeroes and the USSR extended their territorial limits to 320 km (200 miles), and the price of oil rose rapidly.

Elements of the Common Fisheries Policy

Stock conservation Viable stocks must be maintained, and those previously decimated must be rebuilt. Herring fishing had been suspended by member countries of the EEC between 1978–81 as stocks had become exhausted – but that was a voluntary decision. The CFP has set a total allowable catch for each year, which is divided between member countries to reflect traditional fishing activities. This was initially opposed by Denmark who had become a major fish landing country only since 1960. (In 1980 she had the ninth largest catch in the world). Of the total permitted catch of 1 280 000 tonnes, the UK was allowed 37%, Denmark 25%, West Germany 13%, France 12%, Netherlands 7%, Ireland 4% and Belgium 2%. 'In addition to the quotas are other conservation measures, relating to mesh sizes, access to certain grounds at certain times of year, regulations on the landing of fish and in some cases a total ban on catching. Many of these measures are already applied by member countries in waters under their jurisdiction on the basis of national legislation agreed at a Community level.' (European Commission)

Territorial limits These had led to earlier disputes (e.g. British–Icelandic 'Cod War' of 1974). It was agreed in 1983 that individual countries had exclusive fishing rights within 19 km (12 miles) of their shores (unless separate agreements had been made). EEC territorial waters were extended to 320 km (200 miles), and any member can fish here. An exception is a 'box' around the Orkneys and Shetlands extending 96 km (60 miles) where ships exceeding 26 metres in length can only enter with permission unless they are British or Danish.

Financial aid Subsidies are given to maintain fish prices, grants for building and modernising boats, and aid for temporary laying-up payments and long-term cutbacks.

Legal enforcement of policies through the European Court of Justice. All skippers must maintain log books and each country is obliged to take action against its own offending vessels. It may prove difficult to enforce the actual agreement.

Bilateral agreements

Agreements have already been reached between the Community and the Faeroes, Norway, Sweden and Canada allowing those countries to fish in EEC territorial waters and vice versa. Agreements are also being made with African countries such as Morocco, Guinea and Senegal. If Spain and Portugal join the Community the number of fishing vessels will increase by 75%, and a world fishing policy will become a step closer.

▽ **Figure 5.5** Fishing boats block the harbour of Thyboroen on the west coast of Jutland in the 'Cod War' of 1975

Scandinavia

Using all the information given on these two pages:

1 Describe how coniferous trees are planted, looked after and harvested.

2 In what ways has forestry become a 'highly scientific industry'?

3 Why are the cut trees being increasingly transported by road, and less by water?

4 What are the major uses of Scandinavian trees?

5 (a) Why is the world demand for Scandinavian wood products increasing? Do you think these demands are likely to be met?

 (b) If these demands are met what effect will this have on European forests?

6 Coniferous trees cover most of northern Scandinavia. The two major native trees are the Norway spruce and the Scots pine. Latterly such North American species as the Sitka spruce, Douglas fir and hemlock have been introduced.

 (a) Why do these trees grow well in Scandinavia? (see also Figure 2.15).

 (b) Why is less of Norway forested than Finland?

7 In which parts of Scandinavia can deciduous trees grow? What products can be obtained from these deciduous trees?

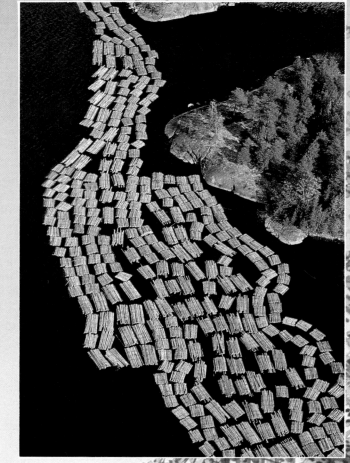

The tree seeds are sown in seedbeds. When the seedlings are 15–20 cm high, they are planted out in rows in another bed, to give them more room for growth.

When the seedlings are about 50 cm high, they are planted out in the forest in areas which have been cleared and ploughed. There are about 2500 trees per hectare. Fire look-out towers on hills are used to spot fires – the forest's worst enemy. Fires can be started by unguarded campfires, dropped matches etc. Trees can be treated with fertilizers and herbicides by spraying from the air.

The dead and lower branches are cut off. This reduces the risk of fire and stops knots from forming in the wood.

Forestry has developed into a highly scientific industry. To preserve supplies young trees have to be planted and encouraged to grow more quickly by spraying with fertilisers, often by air. There are strict controls of the selection of young trees, and their subsequent thinning and felling. Techniques have improved to combat insects and to control fires. The forester fells trees with modern lightweight chain-saws, and uses machinery which can uproot trees, remove branches and bark and cut them into standard lengths ready for transport out of the forest.

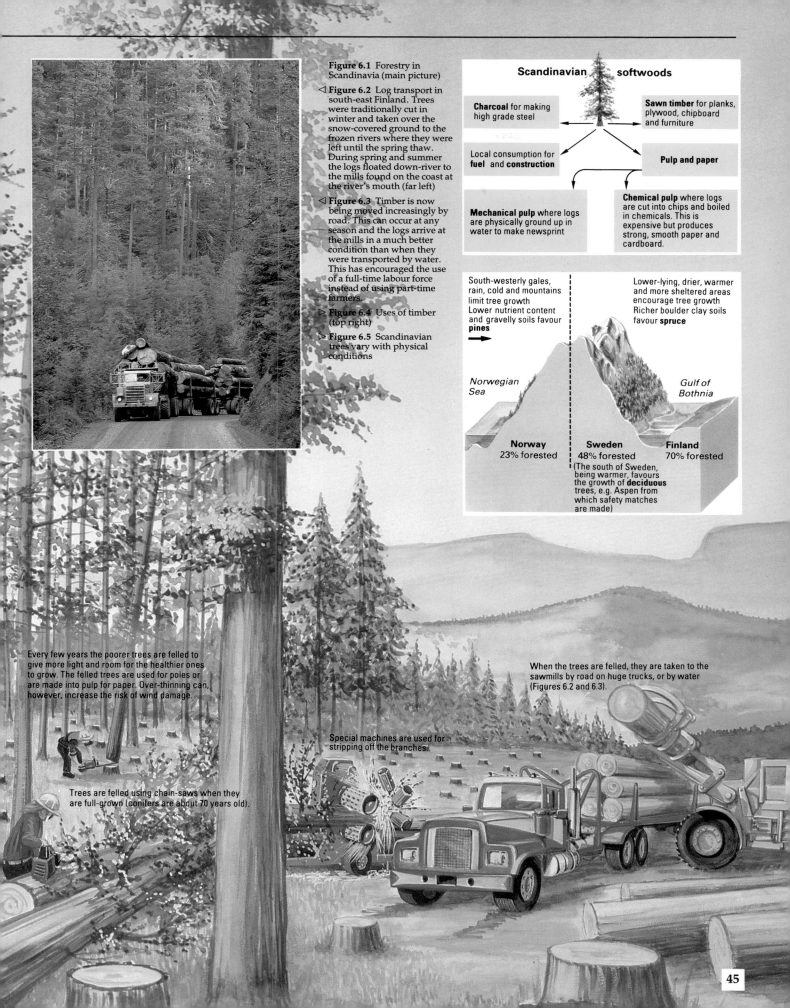

Figure 6.1 Forestry in Scandinavia (main picture)

◁ **Figure 6.2** Log transport in south-east Finland. Trees were traditionally cut in winter and taken over the snow-covered ground to the frozen rivers where they were left until the spring thaw. During spring and summer the logs floated down-river to the mills found on the coast at the river's mouth (far left)

◁ **Figure 6.3** Timber is now being moved increasingly by road. This can occur at any season and the logs arrive at the mills in a much better condition than when they were transported by water. This has encouraged the use of a full-time labour force instead of using part-time farmers.

▷ **Figure 6.4** Uses of timber (top right)

▷ **Figure 6.5** Scandinavian trees vary with physical conditions

Scandinavian softwoods

Charcoal for making high grade steel

Sawn timber for planks, plywood, chipboard and furniture

Local consumption for **fuel** and **construction**

Pulp and paper

Mechanical pulp where logs are physically ground up in water to make newsprint

Chemical pulp where logs are cut into chips and boiled in chemicals. This is expensive but produces strong, smooth paper and cardboard.

South-westerly gales, rain, cold and mountains limit tree growth. Lower nutrient content and gravelly soils favour **pines** →

Lower-lying, drier, warmer and more sheltered areas encourage tree growth. Richer boulder clay soils favour **spruce**

Norwegian Sea

Gulf of Bothnia

Norway 23% forested

Sweden 48% forested
(The south of Sweden, being warmer, favours the growth of **deciduous** trees, e.g. Aspen from which safety matches are made)

Finland 70% forested

Every few years the poorer trees are felled to give more light and room for the healthier ones to grow. The felled trees are used for poles or are made into pulp for paper. Over-thinning can, however, increase the risk of wind damage.

Trees are felled using chain-saws when they are full-grown (conifers are about 70 years old).

Special machines are used for stripping off the branches.

When the trees are felled, they are taken to the sawmills by road on huge trucks, or by water (Figures 6.2 and 6.3).

FORESTRY
Pulp and paper mills

Figure 6.6 shows the location of two towns in central Sweden – Sundsvall and Kramfors.

1 Why are there no trees on the mountains?

2 What is the tree-line? Why does it decrease in height northwards?

3 Why are the ice-formed lakes important?

4 The fall-line marks the junction between the older rocks of the Baltic Shield and the younger rocks near the Gulf of Bothnia. Why is this a good site for HEP stations? (page 56)

5 Why is HEP important to the pulp and paper industry?

6 Why is the chute no longer in use?

7 Why has a new road been built?

8 Why have the pulp and paper mills been built at Sundsvall and Kramfors?

9 What role does the Gulf of Bothnia play in the pulp and paper industry?

Figures 6.7 and 6.8 show the location of the major pulp, paper and saw mills in Norway, Sweden and Finland.

10 Accurately describe the distribution of these mills.

11 Account for this pattern.

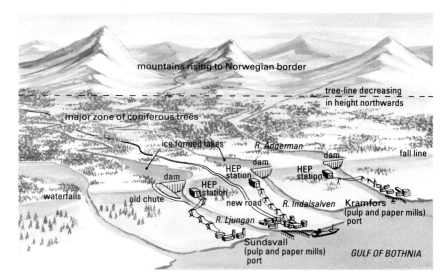

△ **Figure 6.6** Location of pulp and paper mills in central Sweden

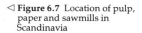

◁ **Figure 6.7** Location of pulp, paper and sawmills in Scandinavia

▽ **Figure 6.8** Timber and sawmill on the River Pielisjoki, Finland

Timber products – World ranking (1980)

	Sweden	Finland	Norway
Softwoods	5	6	–
Wood pulp (mechanical)	5	3	8
Wood pulp (chemical)	4	6	7
Newsprint (Figure 6.9)	4	6	9
Other paper	4	10	–
Sawn woods	6	8	–

Most of Scandinavia's exports go to north-west Europe. Norway's ports are ice-free and nearest to markets but it has fewer resources. Sweden relies mainly on the port of Gothenburg as the Gulf of Bothnia ports tend to be frozen for part of the winter, and are rather distant from world markets. Finland's ports lie on the warmer southern coast.

Problems facing forestry and the pulp and paper industry in Europe

Deforestation without adequate afforestation
Forests are a crop, but it takes many years to gain profit from the initial investment.

Fires This is the greatest single danger. Coniferous forests of northern Europe have a fire look-out service, but it is in the hotter, drier Mediterranean lands where bush fires, often, as in 1983, fanned by the Mistral, destroy land, crops and buildings (Figure 6.10).

Acid rain Rain turns acidic when sulphur and nitrogen oxides are released into the air from ore smelters, power stations and automobiles (page 116). When mixed with water vapour these pollutants can increase the acidity of rainfall by 4%. Pollutants from the UK and West Germany are slowly killing fish in Swedish lakes, and trees in Swedish forests.

Pollution from pulp and paper mills In non HEP paper and pulp mills, smoke is given off. Recent anti-pollution measures have tried to stop the release of waste from the chemical pulp process.

Demand for wood products far exceeds the European supply, even more so in the case of the EEC.

Competition from other land users such as farming in southern Sweden and Finland; recreation; reservoirs and urban development.

The EEC Forestry policy

In 1980 the Community's forests covered 20% of its total land surface and employed 1.4 million people. However, wood production had remained constant at around 80 million m³ per year which was only 40% of the Community's requirement. The balance had to be imported, making wood products second only to oil in the value of Community imports. By the time Spain and Portugal join the Community, the area under forest will increase, as will output, but demand will also be greater.

▽ **Figure 6.10** Holiday-makers watch the fire which destroyed 8400 hectares of the forest of Maures in southern France in 1979

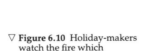

Aims of the EEC policy

'Forests should be protected and managed as a renewable resource to supply products and services which are essential to the quality of life in the European Community now and in the future.' (European Commission)

☐ To increase wood production by regenerating over-mature stands; improving species; applying fertilisers; giving protection against fire, storm and disease, and afforesting areas of land unsuitable for other purposes. Forests are one of the few major renewable raw materials.

☐ To make fuller use of all the harvested trees (e.g. roots, branches, resin) and to recycle wood products (e.g. paper).

☐ To encourage more efficient management, harvesting and marketing, especially by private forest owners, to reduce costs and increase revenues from wood products. In 1980 there were still over 2 million small woodland owners in the Community who accounted for 60% of the total forest area.

☐ To implement forest policies in conjunction with other land users such as agriculture, recreation, water supplies and urban–rural developments.

☐ To conserve and improve the nature and protection of the human environment so as to maintain the productivity of the forest, and to consider its landscape and wildlife. In afforestation, care must be taken to blend the forest in with the natural environment by avoiding 'straight-line' planting, by using different species within the same woodland, leaving summits clear for greater visual appeal, and adding the more attractive trees alongside roads and in valley floors.

☐ To conserve the habitats of animals and plants which are in danger of extinction.

☐ To give protection against erosion by water and wind, and against flooding and avalanches, especially in mountainous areas.

☐ To provide oxygen and to prevent the build-up of carbon dioxide in the atmosphere.

☐ To provide access for recreation on foot, free of charge, into as many forests as possible. Also to provide car parking and picnic areas, nature trails, information centres and horse riding facilities while trying to prevent damage, from those visitors, such as fire, erosion of footpaths, litter and vandalism.

☐ To ensure that adequate education and training facilities in forestry, including refresher courses, are available.

☐ To create employment and to improve the standard of living in rural areas.

☐ To provide financial aid when necessary.

Problems of water supply

Figure 2.2 showed the annual rainfall totals for Europe, yet the pattern of rainfall is usually more important than the actual totals.

□ Does the rain fall evenly throughout the year or is there a wet season (perhaps with too much moisture which returns rapidly to rivers and the sea) and a dry season (where water supply is insufficient for crops, animals and human activity)?

□ Does the period of rain coincide with the growing season – naturally the most important time for farmers?

□ Those areas with summer rain find the amounts less effective than if the rain had come in winter, because the higher summer temperatures increase the rate of evapotranspiration, (the loss of moisture from the ground and plants).

Figure 7.1 shows the balance between rainfall (precipitation) and evapotranspiration. Those areas where rainfall exceeds evapotranspiration have a water surplus, those where evapo-transpiration exceeds rainfall have a water deficit (Figure 7.2). Notice:

1 NW Europe (e.g. Norway) has a large water surplus. How can you explain this?

2 The area in central Europe with a water surplus. What is this area, and why does it receive a surplus?

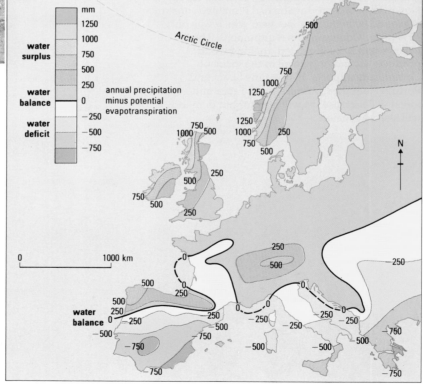

△ **Figure 7.1** Europe – the water balance; areas with a surplus or deficit of water

3 Most of southern Europe has a large water deficit. Give reasons for this.

4 The areas with the greatest surplus tend to be areas with a low population density, and so water has to be transferred to areas which are drier and more populated.

The Lower Rhône Valley

◁ **Figure 7.2** Southern Europe suffers from a deficit of water. Rivers dry up in summer months, leaving large expanses of barren land as shown here in Andalucia, Spain.

▽ **Figure 7.3** The Pont du Gard was a Roman aqueduct built in the first century A.D. to carry water over the River Gard to the city of Nimes (Figure 7.4)

Figure 7.3 shows one method by which the Romans tried to overcome the shortage of water in this area. Figure 7.4 shows the location of the Lower Rhône and three of its lower course tributaries. The problem of these rivers is their fluctuation in levels between summer and winter. Take Mirabeau on the Durance. The river rises in autumn as this is the wettest season. It falls in January and February as most of the precipitation in the upper basins (i.e. the Alps) falls as snow. However, following the rise in temperatures in spring, the snow melt can give rise to flooding in the lower valley. The mid-summer drought together with high evaporation rates means that the river level drops to expose large expanses of sands and gravels deposited as the spring floodwaters recede. The Rhône, with many more tributaries, has a much higher discharge but still shows the same pattern. The graph for Mirabeau should help you to understand why the Romans needed the Pont du Gard aqueduct!

Today the flow of both the Rhône and Durance has been controlled. Large dams hold back the spring melt-water, preventing flooding, and releasing it during the dry summer. Large areas are now under irrigation. The Crau (Figure 7.4) was previously extremely dry but now grows vines, fruit and provides rich pasture. West of the Rhône, intensive fruit and vegetable growing has replaced the single crop of the vine (monoculture).

The most recent innovation has been the introduction of a computer by the Compagnie Nationale du Rhône at Aix-en-Provence (Figure 7.4). '*The computer is essential in the economical control and distribution of water, considering the varying nature of the consumers – 116 municipalities, shipyards, farms, chemical plants and other industries – and the complexity of the conveying system.*' (*Geographical Magazine*)

Malta (See Figure 7.5)

1. Low average rainfall. (What was the average for the period 1967–80?)
2. The variability of rainfall. (What were the two annual extremes between 1967–80?)
3. The seasonal nature of the rainfall – coming when demand is at its lowest. (In which season does Malta receive rain?)
4. The often torrential nature of the rainfall. (How does this affect storage?)
5. Much of Malta is composed of limestone. How does this affect surface and underground 'reservoirs'?
6. Because summers have long periods of sunlight, high temperatures and strong winds, 80% of water stored in surface reservoirs is lost. Why?
7. Water obtained from underground reservoirs is 'hard'. Why is this? Hard water causes encrustation of pipes.
8. Demand for water from industry, agriculture and domestic sources has grown rapidly. By how much did it grow between 1967 and 1980?
9. As demand increases, more water is taken from underground reservoirs. How has this affected its salinity?
10. The World Health Organization recommends a safety level of 600 parts of chlorine per million (p.p.m.). Does Malta comply with this limit?
11. Until the rise in oil prices after 1973, Malta had hoped to overcome its problems by the distillation of sea-water. Unfortunately this process depends upon oil, and so has been abandoned.

▽ **Figure 7.4** Seasonal changes in water supply in the Lower Rhône Valley

▽ **Figure 7.5** Rainfall, water consumption and salinity data for Malta, 1967–80 (bottom) (Source of figures: Central Office of Statistics, Valletta)

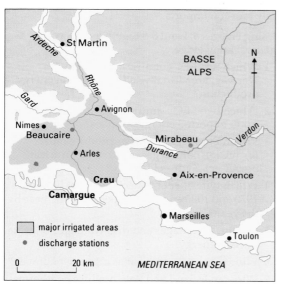

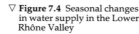

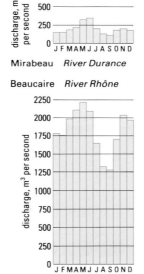

Mirabeau *River Durance*

Beaucaire *River Rhône*

Date	Annual rainfall (mm)	Total annual water consumption ('000 cubic metres)	Average annual salinity at 6 major pumping stations (chlorine ppm)	Maximum salinity recorded at any pumping station (chlorine ppm)
1967–68	412	15794	771	1070
1968–69	355	15794	853	1129
1969–70	688	16601	805	1236
1970–71	546	17978	861	1230
1971–72	542	17768	806	1321
1972–73	722	17414	741	1238
1973–74	304	18990	803	1164
1974–75	355	18240	958	1353
1975–76	697	19568	941	1401
1976–77	554	20753	948	1593
1977–78	330	22338	977	1646
1978–79	463	22378	936	1854
1979–80	617	22738	1063	2109

Production and consumption

Energy is vital for industry, agriculture and trade as well as for comfort in the home and for leisure activity. Figure 8.1. shows that Europe uses a far greater share of the world's energy than the population warrants. Indeed, most European countries, especially in the more industrialised and colder north and west, are amongst the highest users of energy per person in the world.

But Europe can no longer rely upon unhampered energy supplies. The Middle East War of 1973 seriously affected supplies of oil. Rises in the price of oil (which quadrupled in 1973–4 and doubled in 1979) have been a key factor in the world recession of the early 1980s. Figure 8.2 shows the major energy consumers in western Europe. The EEC is the world's largest single oil importer but over half of this oil comes from the three countries of Saudi Arabia, Libya and Nigeria. Oil accounted for 51% of the EEC countries' energy consumption in 1981 (it was 61% in 1973). Yet the oil bill increased eightfold in those years despite a fall in imports by 40%.

Imports fell due to:

□ Increase in domestic production (North Sea).
□ Changes to alternative forms of energy.
□ Conservation measures.
□ Fall in demand due to the recession.

The EEC's balance of payments, already 'in the red', could be worsened if:

□ Oil prices were forced to rise again.
□ The Dollar strengthened.
□ Other importing countries increased their demands.
□ Political unrest disrupted supplies.

Figure 8.3 shows the 'energy gap' in the EEC. Notice though that energy consumption has fallen since 1979 due to conservation ('Save It') measures, and since 1981 due to the worsening world economic position. The energy gap is the difference between the energy consumed and the energy produced. Primary production refers to energy produced by oil, gas, coal , nuclear fuels and hyro-electricity. Primary production has risen mainly due to the development of the North Sea oilfields. Figure 8.4 shows which EEC countries rely most on imports.

Using Figures 8.4 and 8.5 together with your general knowledge:

1 Which two EEC countries, together with Norway, are virtually self-sufficient in energy production?

2 Which two EEC countries are totally dependent upon imported energy supplies?

3 Which European countries produce most: (a) oil (b) natural gas (c) coal (d) nuclear power (e) hydro-electricity?

4 Which type of energy declined most between 1970 and 1980 and yet is expected to increase by the year A.D. 2000?

5 List the advantages and disadvantages of using nuclear energy.

6 Which country uses peat as a source of power?

7 Why can Iceland and Italy produce geothermal power?

8 Why do Norway, Switzerland, France and Italy produce significant amounts of hydro-electricity?

9 Which country has developed tidal and solar power?

10 Why should energy consumption depend upon economic growth (or be reduced by the recession)?

11 Which countries are likely to benefit from solar power?

12 What is meant by 'energy rich and energy poor' countries in the EEC?

▽ **Figure 8.1** Europe – population, and energy consumption, 1982

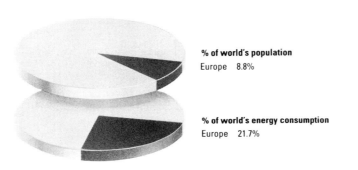

% of world's population
Europe   8.8%

% of world's energy consumption
Europe   21.7%

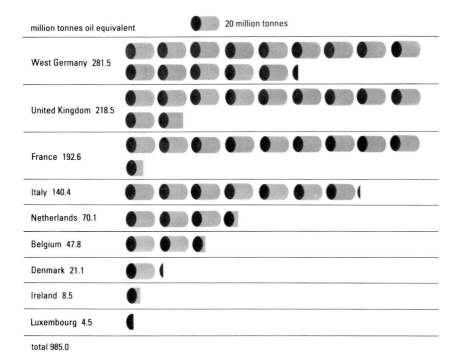

million tonnes oil equivalent   20 million tonnes

West Germany 281.5

United Kingdom 218.5

France 192.6

Italy 140.4

Netherlands 70.1

Belgium 47.8

Denmark 21.1

Ireland 8.5

Luxembourg 4.5

total 985.0

◁ **Figure 8.2** Major energy consumers in the EEC

The EEC Energy Policy

After several years of discussion this was finalised in 1980, and will be implemented by 1990. The difficulty in drawing up a common policy lay in the uneven balance of energy supplies. The main aims are:

□ Energy conservation measures which should mean that the growth in energy demand should be less than the general economic growth, e.g. if the annual economic growth is 1%, then energy demand should not grow by more than 0.7%.

□ That the level of oil consumption should be reduced to about 40% of the total primary energy used, as opposed to about 55% in the 1970s.

□ That the present level of gas consumption remains the same even though this may mean doubling the amount of gas imports by 1990.

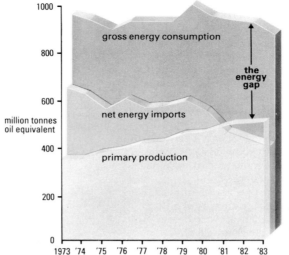

◁ **Figure 8.3** The 'energy gap' in the EEC

▽ **Figure 8.4** Which European countries rely on domestic energy supplies

Country	domestic energy supplies	0% 1970 100%	0% 1975 100%	0% 1980 100%
Denmark				
Ireland	(2, 8)			
United Kingdom	1, 2, 3, 4, (5)			
Luxembourg				
Belgium	(3)			
Netherlands	1, 2			
Italy	5 (1, 2, 4, 6)			
France	4, 5 (1, 2, 3, 7)			
West Germany	1, 2, 3, 4			
'The nine' members				

domestic energy supplies
1 oil
2 natural gas
3 coal
4 nuclear power
5 hydro-electricity
6 geothermal power
7 tidal and solar power
8 peat
(1, 3) = small amounts

imported energy   domestic supplies

□ That by 1990 three-quarters of primary energy requirements, especially in power stations, should be provided by coal or nuclear power. This would mean increasing the amount of coal needed from the 314 million tonnes in 1980 to 500 million tonnes by 1990. Nuclear power should also be developed because the European Commission states that it (the Community) *'cannot afford to ignore any source of supply because nuclear energy will increase industrial competitivity: a kilo of uranium generates as much electricity as 10 tonnes of oil (and as much as 600 tonnes when fast-breeder reactors come on stream) for a third of the price. The share of nuclear powered electricity generating should . . . double by . . . 1990. Development has to take into account health, safety and environmental needs, to which the Community devotes a substantial research effort.'*

□ The research into and the development of renewable sources of energy such as solar energy, hydro-electricity and wind, wave, tidal and geothermal power, although the realisation of their potential will only increase slowly. However, a recent report claimed that by A.D. 2000 the EEC could get 17% of its total energy from renewable sources (compared to 5% in 1983). This could include 4% hydro-electricity (the same as in 1980 as most sites have been developed) 4% from special energy crops (the production of energy from organic waste or biomass) 5% from the sun and wind and 4% from the tides and the waves.

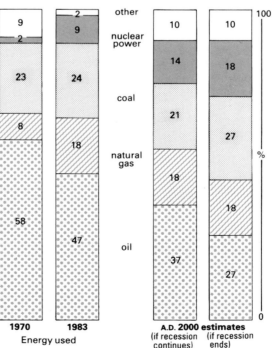

other
nuclear power
coal
natural gas
oil

1970 **1983** **A.D. 2000 estimates** (if recession continues) (if recession ends)
Energy used

◁ **Figure 8.5** OECD (Organisation for Economic Cooperation and Development) – changing uses of energy

□ A determined effort to save energy in homes, factories and transport, by proper insulation and improved techniques.

□ To pursue an energy pricing policy geared to attaining Community objectives.

Oil and natural gas

Figure 8.6 shows the location of the major oil and natural gasfields in Europe, and Figure 8.7 the major oil producers in western Europe. Until 1971 only West Germany produced a significant amount of oil, but this declined in the 1970s. During this time, however, the development of the North Sea oilfields led to a dramatic increase in production (to self-sufficiency) by the UK and Norway. Even so, in 1981 western Europe only produced 4.6% of the world's total oil, while at the same time consuming 22% of the world's oil production.

During the early 1970s most western European countries imported an increasing amount of oil as a basis for their economy and many new refineries and pipelines were constructed (Figure 8.8). However as world demand for oil has fallen, western Europe had, by the early 1980s, too much refining capacity. The fall in demand has resulted from:

□ The quadrupling of oil prices between 1973 and 1980.

□ A subsequent fall in demand for petrol and heating oil.

□ The economic recession of the early 1980s.

□ Conservation measures by countries trying to reduce their balance of payment deficits.

□ A switch to coal, natural gas and nuclear power.

Refineries have closed in Britain, France and elsewhere in Western Europe.

Oil and Norway

□ Drilling began in the North Sea in 1966. The Ekofisk field was discovered in 1969, coming into production by 1971 (Figure 8.6). The field, worked by Phillips Oil Consortium, was 350 km west of Stavanger, but separated from the mainland by the Norwegian trench which was too deep to lay down pipelines. As a result, oil was piped to Teesside (England). Norway became a net exporter of oil in 1975.

□ In 1977 two submarine gas pipelines took gas from the Ekofisk field to Emden in West Germany, and from the Frigg field to St Fergus, Scotland (Figure 8.10).

□ The most recent field is the Statfjord which sends its oil to Bergen by tanker.

□ 1980 was the year in which the legs of the Alexander Keilland broke in a gale and over 100 people were drowned as the oil rig overturned.

□ Peak production is expected in 1985 with 65 million tonnes of oil (75% from Ekofisk, 20% from Frigg and 5% from Statfjord).

□ With so small a local market over 80% of the oil and natural gas is exported. Although Norway only produces 2% of the world's oil, it accounts for nearly 25% of the country's GNP and over 40% of its exports by value.

△ **Figure 8.6** Oil and natural gas producers

▷ **Figure 8.7** Western European oil production 1971–83 (top right)

▷ **Figure 8.8** Oil in Europe (above right)

▷ **Figure 8.9** Oil platform in the Ekofisk oilfield

New discoveries are expected to be made north of 62°N, but problems include:

□ Gales

□ Deeper sea-bed

□ Long, dark winters

□ Icing up of oil rigs

□ Tracing possible oil spillage

□ Threat to fishing grounds

□ Distance from European markets

□ Distance from a workforce

The government is insisting that two rigs work near to each other, so that if there is a blow-out, the other can quickly drill at an angle and seal off the oilwell. Production is expected to fall slowly after 1995.

Country	1971	1976	1981	1983	(million tonnes)
Austria	2.5	1.9	1.3	1.2	
France	1.9	1.1	1.7	1.7	
Italy	1.4	1.1	1.7	2.2	
Norway	0.3	13.8	24.9	29.2	
UK	0.1	11.8	89.4	111.2	
West Germany	7.4	5.5	4.5	4.2	
Yugoslavia	3.0	3.9	4.3	4.1	
others	1.8	3.6	3.8	N/A	
Total	21.9	45.3	134.0	N/A	
World	2494.9	2954.3	2890.3	N/A	

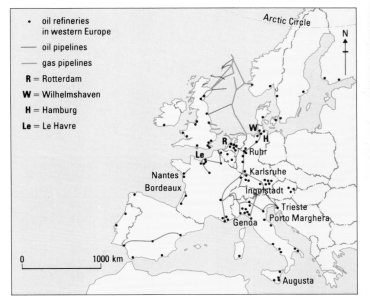

▽ **Figure 8.10** Norwegian oilfields and pipelines

△ **Figure 8.11** Oil platform in the Brent oilfield – similar platforms are found in other North Sea oilfields

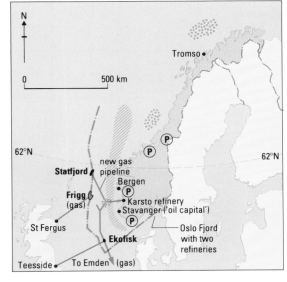

Coal

There are three stages in the formation of coal.

(a) **Peat** is composed of rotting vegetation and is used as a fuel in Ireland and Finland.

(b) **Lignite** (or Brown coal) lacks carbon and is the result of peat being covered by sediments and compressed. It is mined, usually by opencast methods, in West Germany and eastern Europe.

(c) **Coal** includes several grades (steam, bituminous and anthracite). The greater the carbon content, the greater the heat it produces. The major coalfields are shown in Figure 8.12. The output of coal reached its peak between the wars, and since then the number of miners, collieries and the total output has fallen. Significantly the amount of coal produced by each miner has increased. These figures are shown in Figure 8.13.

Causes of falling demand

□ Exhaustion of best and most easily accessible coalseams.

□ A labour intensive industry.

□ Competition from other types of energy.

□ More expensive to transport coal than its competitors.

□ Changing demand e.g. domestic use turning to oil and gas central heating, railways becoming diesel and electric.

□ Decline of 'heavy industries' such as steel, glass, shipbuilding, chemicals and engineering all of which used to use much coal.

□ Clean Air Acts aim to limit smoke in the atmosphere.

□ Modern power stations are constructed to use more than one type of fuel.

□ The costs of production are greater than in other parts of the world (West Germany's costs are twice that of South Africa and Australia) and so there is a threat of 'cheap' imports.

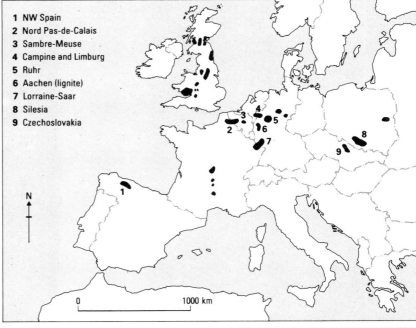

1 NW Spain
2 Nord Pas-de-Calais
3 Sambre-Meuse
4 Campine and Limburg
5 Ruhr
6 Aachen (lignite)
7 Lorraine-Saar
8 Silesia
9 Czechoslovakia

0 — 1000 km

	Coal production (million tonnes)			Number of significant collieries	Underground workers (000's)	
	1961	1971	1981	1977	1971	1983
West Germany	148	117	88	43	135.0	118.2
(Ruhr)	121	92	70	32	112.3	94.3
(Saar)	16	9	6	6	14.1	9.7
France	52	33	17	26	60	27.4
(Lorraine)	16	10	8	5	10.6	6.3
Netherlands	13	4	0	0	6.0	0
United Kingdom	187	135	109	242	221.0	163.0
Belgium	21	11	5	10	24.0	15.8
Total EEC	**430**	**312**	**240**	**324**	**473**	**324.7**

(a) in 1979 Czechoslovakia produced 28 million tonnes and Spain 11 million tonnes.

(b) in 1957 the Saar coalfield produced 3069 kg per man shift, and Lorraine 2500. By 1979 these figures had risen to 6634 and 4446 kg respectively.

△ **Figure 8.12** Coalfields in Europe (top)

△ **Figure 8.13** Coal production in western Europe

▽ **Figure 8.14** EEC coal consumption and production

Why is the EEC planning to increase coal production?

As Figure 8.5 shows the EEC aims to rely more on coal and nuclear power by A.D. 2000. This is mainly due to coal reserves in western Europe having an estimated life of 300 years (as opposed to oil's 30 and natural gas' 25). The price of coal did not rise as fast as that of oil in the 1970s, and the industry has become more mechanised and modernised.

But problems remain including:

□ Social problems resulting from pit closures.

□ It is still an ageing industry with costs and difficulties in mining coal increasing.

□ Uneven distribution of production with only West Germany and the UK being major producers.

□ Western Europe is using much more coal than it actually produces (Figure 8.14).

□ A strong pro-nuclear energy group.

□ Coal remains a 'dirty' fuel producing air pollution (smoke, dust) as well as creating noise, visual eyesores (despite modern conservation efforts) and increased traffic on the roads.

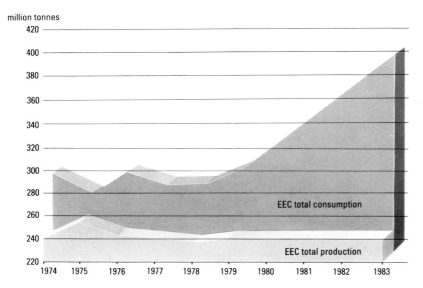

million tonnes

EEC total consumption

EEC total production

1974 1975 1976 1977 1978 1979 1980 1981 1982 1983

Nuclear power

Figure 8.15 lists some of the many arguments for and against the continued development of nuclear power in western Europe. Can you add any more to the list? What would *your* decision be?

The UK was the pioneer in developing nuclear power with eight stations open by 1962, and producing 13% of the total energy needs. It was through the Euratom Treaty of 1957 that members of the EEC pledged themselves '*To work together to use nuclear energy for peaceful purposes*', yet output by these EEC members remained negligible until the 1970s. Since then several countries, especially West Germany and France, have built numerous power stations and, as shown in Figure 8.16, the reliance upon nuclear power has increased considerably.

Location of nuclear power stations
(Figure 8.17)

□ Away from populated areas in case of accidents. (Give three examples.)

□ Away from areas with alternative forms of energy e.g. coalfields, oil refining ports. (Give three examples.)

□ Near large supplies of water which are needed for cooling purposes e.g.

   (*a*) on coasts, (give two examples).

   (*b*) on rivers, (give two examples).

□ On strong geological foundations to withstand the heavy weight of the power station.

□ On areas of flat land, ideally if the value of farmland is low, and where there is space for a possible second power station.

△ **Figure 8.15** The nuclear energy debate (top right)
▽ **Figure 8.16** Importance and growth of nuclear power
▷ **Figure 8.17** Location of nuclear power stations

For nuclear power

Oil and natural gas have limited reserves

Oil prices rose dramatically in the 1970s

Nuclear power likely to have the greatest cost efficiency

Uranium is the basic fuel, and as very little is needed transport costs are kept low

Low operating costs of power stations

Low labour intensity (i.e. low wages bill)

Clean form of energy (unlike coal)

Necessary to fill the gap between demand and production of energy in Europe

Large sums of money already spent on research

Against nuclear power

How safe is it? Public fear of radioactive leaks

A large conservationist lobby who claim one accident may kill many people and ruin the ground for centuries

Problem of waste disposal – plutonium stays radioactive for 200 000 years

In the long term should we be developing renewable forms of energy?

Expensive to build nuclear power stations

Cannot be used for two of industry's major demands: a) space heating b) transport

Early 1980s have seen a fall in demand for energy – means less need for new power stations

Money needed for further research better spent elsewhere

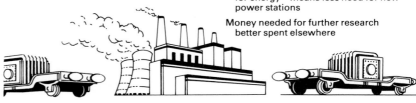

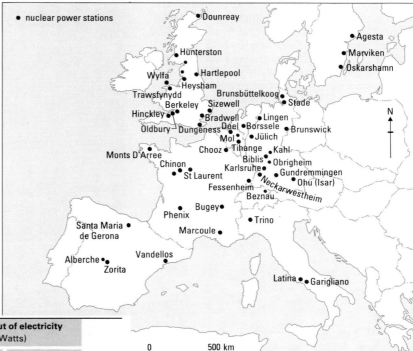

	% of energy from nuclear reactors, 1981	Output of electricity (GigaWatts)	
		1981	1990 (estimate)
Belgium	25.3	1.7	5.5
Finland	35.8	2.2	2.2
France	37.7	22.0	56.0
West Germany	14.6	9.9	25.0
Eire	0	0	0.6
Italy	1.2	1.4	5.4
Netherlands	6.4	0.5	0.5
Spain	4.6	2.0	12.7
Sweden	35.3	N/A	N/A
Switzerland	28.1	1.9	2.8
UK	12.7	6.4	12.3

(Nil in Norway, Denmark, Greece, Portugal, Luxembourg)

The EEC policy states '*The Community believes that, between them, coal and nuclear energy will be providing us with up to three-quarters of our electricity by 1990. The Community is well aware of the difficulties associated with public acceptance of nuclear power, and is particularly concerned to help resolve the health, safety and environmental problems associated with it.*' (European Commission) In 1979, nuclear energy accounted for about 3% of total energy consumption. In 1990, it should account for about 15%.

Water power

Hydro-electric power (HEP)

Hydro-electricity contributed only 4% to Europe's energy in 1980, a figure likely to fall now that the best sites have been utilised and alternative sources of power are developed. Most sites are either in:

(a) High mountainous areas such as the Alps, Apennines, the Massif Central, and Scandinavia (Figure 8.20).

(b) Along major rivers such as the Rhine and Rhône.

Norway

Norway is one of the richest countries with respect to hydro-electric resources in Europe. The vast mountain plateaus and their glacial lakes, together with the heavy precipitation, provide a natural potential for the generation of large and continuous supplies of HEP production throughout the year. River flow is lowest during winter and at a peak in late spring. A number of high altitude lakes and rivers have been turned into storage reservoirs by tapping lakes through submerged tunnels, and by building dams across rivers. Figure 8.18 shows some of the advantages for locating a hydro-electric power station in Norway. Many new, large, power stations have been built underground in rock caverns. Water is led to the turbines through tunnels which provide two big advantages:

(a) they increase the head of water

(b) they are hidden from view and so do not spoil the environment.

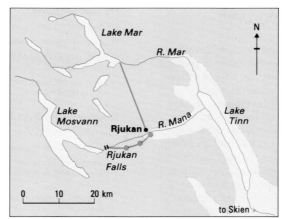

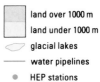

◁ **Figure 8.19** Norsk Hydro-Rjukan (Telemark)
▽ **Figure 8.20** The Hols I Hydro electric power station near Geilo, Norway

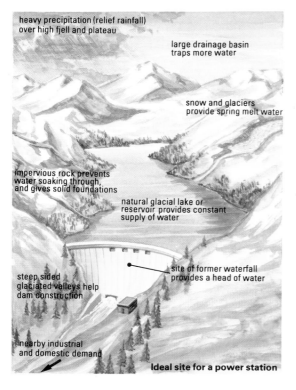

◁ **Figure 8.18** Requirements for the location of an upland HEP station

The cables from these stations, together with transformer sub-stations, are laid on extremely rough terrain, making installation and maintenance expensive.

1 Why does Norway receive heavy falls of snow and rain?

2 Why are river flows at their lowest in winter and highest in late spring?

3 How has tunnelling underground increased the output of hydro-electricity?

4 Using the land sketch in Figure 8.18 list at least six advantages of the site shown for the location of a hydro-electric power station.

The Rjukan HEP Scheme (Figure 8.19)

The Rjukan Falls plunge 300 metres, and attracted, in 1903, two businessmen who wished to manufacture a form of ammonia for use as a fertiliser. This process needed enormous supplies of cheap electricity. Water from the Mana river was diverted into a series of reservoirs. The newly formed Norsk Hydro Company produced more electricity than was needed, but electricity cannot easily be stored. So when demand was low, surplus power was used to pump water back up to the mountain reservoirs which was released again when demand increased. Although the production of fertiliser stopped in 1968, HEP is still produced here.

▽ **Figure 8.21** HEP scheme built by the Compagnie Nationale du Rhône at Avignon

▷ **Figure 8.22** Avignon – HEP on the Rhône

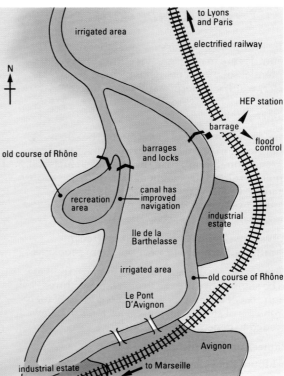

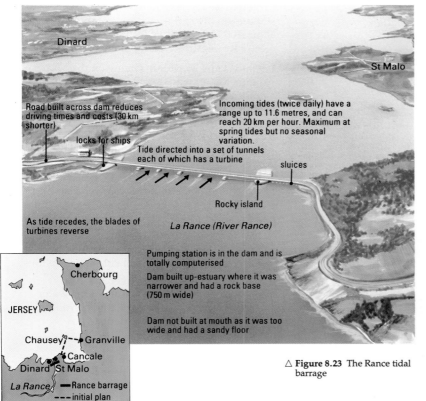

Road built across dam reduces driving times and costs (30 km shorter)

locks for ships

As tide recedes, the blades of turbines reverse

Dinard

St Malo

Incoming tides (twice daily) have a range up to 11.6 metres, and can reach 20 km per hour. Maximum at spring tides but no seasonal variation.

Tide directed into a set of tunnels each of which has a turbine

sluices

Rocky island

La Rance (River Rance)

Pumping station is in the dam and is totally computerised

Dam built up-estuary where it was narrower and had a rock base (750 m wide)

Dam not built at mouth as it was too wide and had a sandy floor

Cherbourg

JERSEY

Chausey — Granville

Cancale

Dinard St Malo

La Rance — Rance barrage
--- initial plan

△ **Figure 8.23** The Rance tidal barrage

The Rhône

The scheme was needed because:

☐ Seasonal variations in the flow of the river hindered navigation. The river was in flood in spring after snow melt in the Alps, and low in late summer after the drought.

☐ The speed of the river varied from slow, as it crossed flat basins, to fast as it passed through the narrow defiles between these basins.

☐ Increased need for energy during the 1950s and 1960s.

☐ Increased demand for water for industrial, farming and domestic uses.

One major scheme was built at Avignon (Figure 8.21). The advantages of this scheme are shown on Figure 8.22.

Tidal power

The Rance Tidal Barrage, built between Dinard and St Malo, was completed in 1967, and for over a decade was the only barrage of its kind in the world. It was meant as a prototype for a much larger barrage which was to be built across the bay of Mont St Michel (see inset on Figure 8.23). Using Figure 8.23 – what were the advantages of this site for a tidal barrage? How did it produce electricity? The larger project at Mont St Michel was never begun mainly because of an increase in nuclear power, an abundance of, then cheap, oil and natural gas, together with the problem of finding suitable sites and then the cost of building the scheme in the 1970s. Yet tidal power may still be a form of future energy. (A second barrage was built, in the early 1980s in the Bay of Fundy, Canada.)

Alternative sources

The European Commission and other non-EEC countries are making greater efforts to develop the potential sources of energy which are renewable: solar, wind, geothermal and wave power.

Solar energy

The amount of energy given out by the sun is enormous. In one day the earth receives far more energy from the sun than the total fossil fuels (oil and coal) already consumed, and in 20 days more than the total reserves of these fuels. Even in cloudy north-west Europe, a high energy demand area, there is a vast surplus of solar energy.

Advantages Renewable; pollution-free; no harmful side-effects; few conservation problems.

Disadvantages Research still in infancy; unlikely to be significant until the twenty-first century; high cost of development compared to fossil fuels; problems of storing surpluses; hectares of panels needed to generate electricity.

Pioneer projects include:

☐ Mount Louis, in the French Pyrenees – large mirrors concentrate the sun's rays to produce heat which can turn water into steam, which can then drive turbines to produce electricity (Figure 8.24).

☐ Adrano (Sicily) – a joint scheme financed by West Germany and France uses numerous solar panels (Figure 8.25), while in Denmark a village called 'Sol og Wind' has 27 houses and two community buildings heated by solar panels – but these panels cover 640 m² of land!

☐ Photovoltaic power generation is important as it can convert solar energy into electricity even when it is cloudy.

☐ At Bourriot-Bergonce (France) photo-electric energy is used to drive a pump which irrigates fields of maize.

☐ Biomass. This is living vegetable matter which can convert solar energy by photosynthesis into a chemical form of energy which can be used. Of 15 experimental schemes in Europe in 1983, two examples are the use of peat at Offaly (Eire) and flax at Plessis-Belleville (France).

△ **Figure 8.24** At Odeillo in the French Pyrenees solar energy is used to produce electricity

▽ **Figure 8.25** The 'Eurelios' solar power station at Adrano, Sicily. The installation was built with EEC funds as well as money from West Germany, France and Italy.

Geothermal energy

Holes are bored into hotter areas of the earth's crust. Cold water is pumped downwards and is heated by contact with underlying rocks, and turned to steam. It is then returned to power stations on the surface where, at temperatures of about 100°C it can drive turbines to produce electricity (Figures 1.22 and 8.26).

Iceland is ideally situated being on the Mid-Atlantic Ridge, where new rock is being formed at a point where the American plate is moving away from the Eurasian plate (page 8). Geothermal power has for some time been used in Reykjavik for central (space) heating, open-air swimming pools, and greenhouses. A controversial new power station is being drilled near Krafla in the north of the island, the site of an active volcano. Early tests ended after lava was seen erupting from one of the trial boreholes. However, trials began again in 1983 despite numerous problems which included:

☐ Possible damage to the power station by expected earthquakes and volcanic eruptions.

☐ The high temperatures, over 300°C at production levels, and acidity of the water damaging concrete casings, and corroding and blocking the boreholes at depths.

☐ High costs of developing and then producing energy.

Other areas suitable in Europe include Italy (Lardarello in Tuscany was the world's first geothermal power station) and SW France.

	Denmark	Sweden	West Germany	United Kingdom
tower height (m)	42	80	100	46
expected energy output per year (MWh)	1500	6800	12 000	10 500
location	Nibe, Jutland	Maglarp	Brunsbuettel	Burgar Hill, Orkney
date of operation	1979	1982	1982	1984

△ **Figure 8.27** Large wind turbines in Europe

◁ **Figure 8.28** Wind 'aerogenerator' turbine in Denmark

▽ **Figure 8.29** Proposed wave power in Norway

Wind power

This is seen to have an increasingly greater commercial potential. A number of European countries have developed prototype wind turbines (see Figure 8.28).

Although wind speeds tend to be higher in winter and so coinciding with times of peak demand surplus energy from gales cannot, as yet, be stored for use in times of calm. Nor can the eventual replacement of conventional power stations by wind turbines be envisaged. Studies in Sweden have shown that it could take as many as 1500 giant aerogenerators, each at least 60 metres in height, to take the place of one medium-sized nuclear power station. How will people react to all those structures placed on top of prominent hills and mountains?

Wave power

Waves are a renewable source of energy, and most storms occur in winter which is the time of peak energy demand in western Europe. As yet the problems of designing, constructing and maintaining huge structures in rough seas, together with finding an economic method of transforming the varying motions of waves into electricity still makes this a form of energy for the future.

Norway Norwegian engineers claim that they have perfected a way of focusing waves into a narrow funnel which increases their efficiency, and reduces costs of production to those obtained in conventional power stations. Mechanical devices (Figure 8.29) focus the waves in the same way as an optical lens focuses light waves. These devices would vary in shape and arrangement according to the shape of the coastline at the chosen site. The waves are then funnelled up a 'chute' which can cause the water to be 'lifted' by as much as 100 metres to reservoirs built on the mainland. Laboratory tests (done on models 1/1000th the size of the projected scheme) have been sufficiently successful for a full scale system of lenses and a chute to be built at Hakadal near Oslo (1983).

▽ **Figure 8.26** Geothermal power at Krafla, Iceland, the power station began operating in 1984

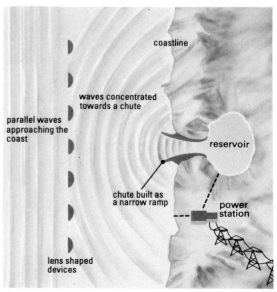

coastline

waves concentrated towards a chute

parallel waves approaching the coast

reservoir

chute built as a narrow ramp

power station

lens shaped devices

Iron ore in northern Sweden

Since the end of the nineteenth century the LKAB company (Swedish National iron ore mining company) have mined over 750 million tonnes of iron ore at Kiruna, Malmberget (Gallivare) and Svappavaara. It is estimated that over 3000 million tonnes remain untouched (Figures 9.2 and 9.3). At Kiruna and Malmberget the ore is mined underground and at Svappavaara by open-cast methods. The work is highly mechanised (Figure 9.1).

Advantages

Quality of ore At Kiruna the ore deposits form a strip 100 metres wide and 4 km long. Much of the ore is high quality magnetite, with an iron content of 60–70%.

Availability of ore The original workings were open-cast. However, by 1960 the 'mountain' had been changed into a series of large terraces extending down to the riverside (Figure 9.3). Since 1962 all mining has been underground.

Nearness of hydro-electricity The major HEP station is 96 km south of Kiruna at Porjus (Figure 9.2) and this is supplemented by numerous local schemes. Electricity is vital for the iron workings, the towns and the railways. Fast flowing rivers have numerous waterfalls, and the large natural glaciated lakes act as reservoirs.

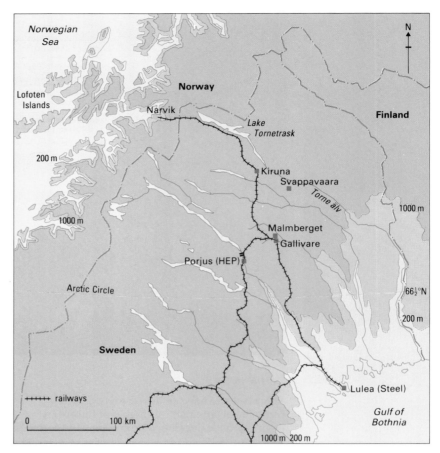

▽ **Figure 9.1** Mining at Kiruna has become highly mechanised

△ **Figure 9.2** Iron ore mining in northern Sweden

Problems

Transport In 1888 a railway line was built from the old mining centre of Malmberget to the port of Lulea on the Gulf of Bothnia. However, the Gulf freezes for five months every winter (Figure 2.13), and so in 1902 a railway line was built to Kiruna and then over the mountains to the Norwegian port of Narvik. The railway line was extremely difficult to build, and the cost of rail transport is very high. Despite being in the Arctic Circle, Narvik is kept ice-free by the waters of the North Atlantic Drift (Figure 9.4). Of the 30 million tonnes of ore which LKAB can produce each year, 25 million tonnes go to Narvik (in trains of 50 wagons, each wagon carrying 80 tonnes) and 5 million to Lulea. In 1982 an all-weather road was opened between Kiruna and Narvik.

Extremely cold winters where temperatures may fall to −40°C, making working conditions for employees, and the running of machinery, difficult. Snow may even remain on the ground until July.

Dark winters Being in the Arctic Circle, the sun does not rise for six weeks. All work has to be done under floodlights.

△ **Figure 9.3** Kiruna – Sweden. Iron ore used to be extracted from the surface creating terraces on the hillside. It is now mined underground and most is transported to the coast by rail.

Obtaining labour in such an environment. Wages are 25% above the national average, and the provision of housing and amenities has to be high to attact people from the south of Sweden.

Isolation from major areas of work, shopping, recreation, culture and development.

The falling world market for steel since 1975 and the recession of the 1980s.

Restructuring plan of 1983

In 1981 it was believed that steel production in Europe would grow, and LKAB made plans to sell 25 million tonnes of ore a year. By 1983 demand had fallen so much (see Figure 9.5) that only 15 million tonnes were needed for export. So LKAB, having been nationalised on 31 December 1982, issued a 'restructuring plan'. Some major points were:

☐ A reduction of output to 15 million tonnes in 1983, and to 11 millions in 1984.

☐ Concentrating production at Kiruna and Malmberget and closing the Svappavaara mine.

☐ Reducing the workforce by a further 1150 by 1984 (Figure 9.5).

☐ Requesting increased government aid for reconstruction of the company, and to lower rail charges.

☐ To open new levels at Malmberget in 1985 and Kiruna in 1990.

☐ To have periods of total shutdown in production. In 1983 there was a two-week lay-off in April, and eight weeks in the summer. With other enforced lay-off periods, workers at Kiruna lost 15 weeks pay.

☐ To transfer redundant employees to other parts of Sweden. Although the new road linking Kiruna and the south of Sweden may encourage tourists, at present iron ore mining is the only major occupation north of the Arctic Circle.

△ **Figure 9.4** The ice-free port of Narvik in Norway

▽ **Figure 9.5** Declining iron ore production and workforce

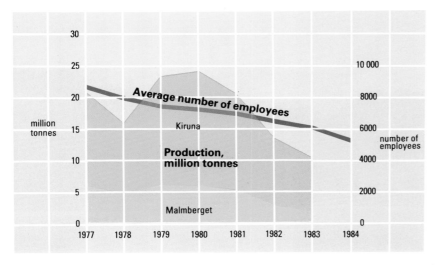

Coal

The Ruhr

Coal was first mined in the Ruhr Valley (Figure 9.6) in the thirteenth century, but was not mined on a large scale until the 1830s. Production reached a peak in 1938 when 127 million tonnes were produced. Since then output continually declined to 70 million tonnes in 1981 (Figure 8.13). Figure 9.6 shows the areas with the most pit closures, and Figure 9.7, how the area of mining has moved northwards between 1830 and 1980. Today the area covered by the Ruhr planning region is 80 km east to west, and 50 km north to south. It includes over twenty large towns and cities, and the whole conurbation includes over 6 million people. Figure 9.8 lists some of the advantages of the Ruhr as a coal mining area as well as some of the problems which it faces.

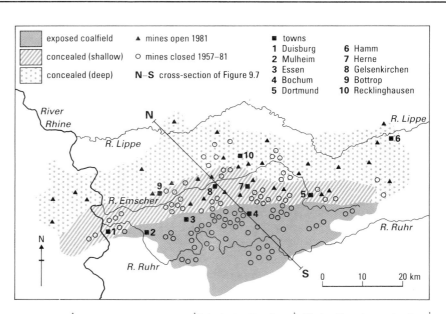

▷ **Figure 9.6** Coal mining in the Ruhr (top right)

▷ **Figure 9.7** Cross-section of the Ruhr coalfield (line of cross-section shown on Figure 9.6)

▽ **Figure 9.8** Advantages and disadvantages of coal mining in the Ruhr in the 1980s

▷ **Figure 9.9** A coal mining environment in France (bottom right)

Advantages

Centrally located within the EEC

Large proven reserves which should last up to three hundred years

Large variety (over 50 types) of coal being suitable for several purposes

New mines have a high level of productivity due to mechanisation

EEC policy of mid 1980s includes a greater reliance on coal by A.D. 2000

West German law requires 40 million tonnes of coal a year to be produced for electricity and 30 million tonnes for steel, giving a large, guaranteed market

Water transport by the Rhine and numerous canals (Chapter 12)

Disadvantages

The most easily obtainable coal is exhausted

Increasing depth of shafts with new coalfaces 1000 metres below the surface

Increasing depth means increasing costs of production

During the 1960s and 1970s many mines closed due to competition from the then cheaper imports of oil and natural gas

Decline continued in the early 1980s as the EEC policy gave a greater reliance to nuclear energy

Competition from cheaper coal from the USA and eastern Europe

Mine closures have led to large scale social problems where over 300 000 miners were made redundant between 1960 and 1980. Many towns, e.g. Bochum, had relied on mining as their major source of employment – 65 000 miners at its peak, only 200 in 1981

Problems of a 'scarred landscape' (Figure 9.9) with atmospheric and river pollution

Newer collieries are in semi-rural and rural areas, causing conflicts with conservationists and other rural land users

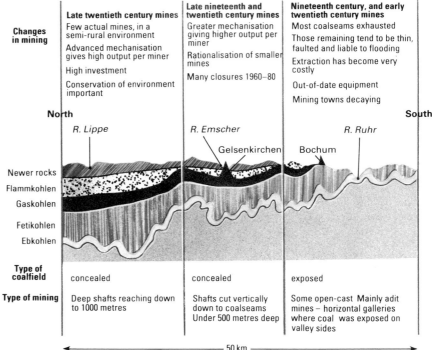

Lignite

Lignite or Brown coal is found in large amounts south-west of the Ruhr in the area between Aachen and Cologne. The coal is obtained using huge machines (Figure 9.10) and open-cast mining. Lignite is used for power stations, in the manufacture of briquettes, and as a raw material for the chemical industry. This mineral has been relatively crisis-free until the recession of the 1980s and its associated fall in demand for both steel and energy. However, even in 1981, lignite provided 10% of West Germany's energy requirements whereas 'hard' coal only provided 15%.

The Borinage (Belgium)

This area, in the extreme west of Belgium, forms part of the Franco-Belgian coalfield (Figures 8.12 and 9.11). Although relatively small in comparison to British coalfields and the Ruhr, it was an important mining area in the nineteenth century, with 60 pits operating in 1900. Unlike other coal mining areas it did not develop its own steel industry. After 1950, the output of coal declined rapidly, and the extract indicates some of the reasons for this decline.

The Borinage area '... *has experienced considerable economic decline and harsh adjustments have been necessary because of their over-dependence upon a single activity, coal-mining. Here there was little industrial development of any sort, and in 1953 coal-mining accounted for 56 per cent of employment. The seams of coal were almost exhausted, mines were very deep (over 1 kilometre) and in one particular colliery, Rieu De Coeur, galleries were specially refrigerated over one and a half kilometres below ground. As a small-scale producer (the Borinage produced 5.9 million tonnes in 1927, the peak year) it was a very high-cost coalfield. Not only was there heavy competition from oil and natural gas, but the increased cross-frontier competition and tariff-free conditions which arrived with the EEC meant that by 1958 Ruhr coal, even after being transported to Charleroi, was considerably cheaper. With the reduction in Atlantic freight rates, American coal could be sold at Charleroi for 841 B.f. per tonne, whilst Borinage coal cost 971 B.f. per tonne. Productivity was lower, production was small-scale and inefficient from many small pits, and Borinage coal could not be made competitive.*

The Borinage became a region of out-migration, mainly to Antwerp and Brussels and in the period from 1949 to 1962 the employment force actually fell from 67 973 to 38 344, a decline of 46 per cent. This rate of decline is very unusual in advanced industrial countries.' (Minshull, *New Europe*)

1 Using the extract and Figure 9.11:

   (*a*) How many pits were operating in the Borinage in: (*i*) 1951 (*ii*) 1961 (*iii*) 1981?

   (*b*) Why did coalmining decline so rapidly between 1951 and 1977?

2 Using any information on this double page spread, together with your own knowledge, describe the economic, social and environmental problems likely to result from the decline in coal mining in an area such as the Borinage.

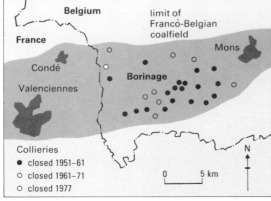

△ **Figure 9.10** Open-cast coal mining in the Ruhr. These machines are operated by five people and can mine as much coal in one day as 45 000 miners with picks and shovels (top)

△ **Figure 9.11** Colliery closures in the Borinage

Employment structure

Traditionally, industry has been broken down into three groups (primary, secondary and tertiary), to which, in the 1980s, a fourth group has been added (quaternary). Which of these are illustrated in Figure 10.1?

Primary industries extract raw materials directly from the earth or sea, such as farming, fishing, forestry and mining.

Secondary industries process and manufacture the primary products, for example steel, shipbuilding or furniture manufacturing. The construction industry also comes under this heading.

Tertiary industries provide a service and include shops, hospitals, schools and transport.

Quaternary industries provide information and expertise. This includes the new microchip and microelectronics industries.

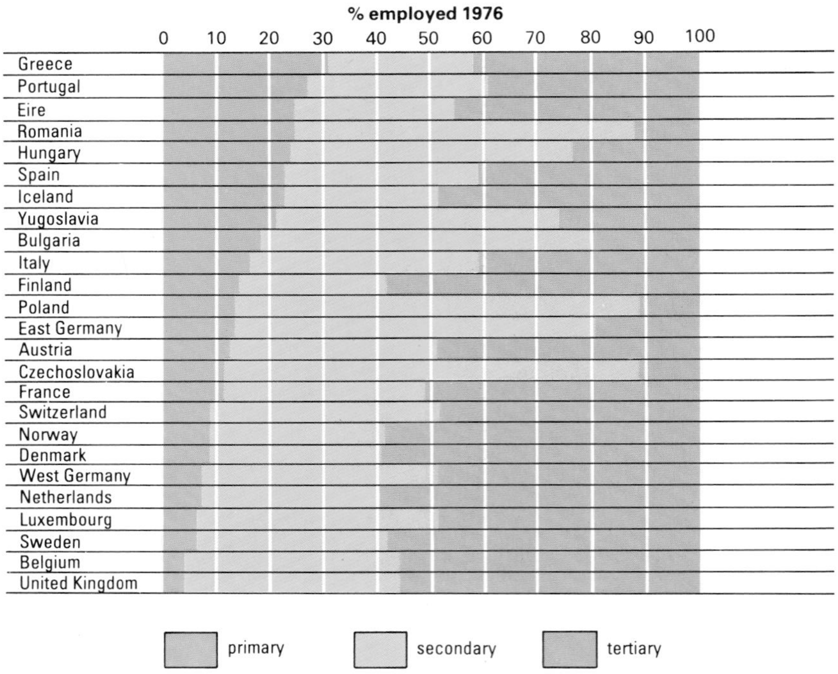

Employment structure in Europe

Employment figures can also indicate the level of development of a country (Figure 10.2).

1 Why do two Mediterranean countries have the largest percentage in primary industries?

2 Why do most eastern European countries also have large numbers employed in the primary sector?

3 What do you notice about the location of countries with less than 8% employed in primary industries?

4 Which seven countries have the largest percentage employed in secondary industries. What do you notice about their location?

5 Why do eastern European countries have so few employed in the tertiary section?

6 Why do countries around the Mediterranean Sea have relatively large numbers in the tertiary sector?

7 Does there appear to be any connection between the more developed countries in Europe and the numbers employed in tertiary industries?

8 What is the possible danger to a country employing a high percentage in the tertiary sector, and very few in the primary and secondary sectors?

% employed 1976

Greece
Portugal
Eire
Romania
Hungary
Spain
Iceland
Yugoslavia
Bulgaria
Italy
Finland
Poland
East Germany
Austria
Czechoslovakia
France
Switzerland
Norway
Denmark
West Germany
Netherlands
Luxembourg
Sweden
Belgium
United Kingdom

☐ primary   ☐ secondary   ☐ tertiary

△ **Figure 10.2** Employment structure in Europe

What else might graphs on employment structures show?

Graphs can usually only show selected data – hence figures can be distorted to suit a person's viewpoint. However, other data useful in discussing the employment structure of a country might include:

☐ Local or regional variations (Figure 10.3).

☐ Seasonal variations in employment (especially in tourist areas).

☐ Numbers unemployed (Figure 10.4).

☐ Ratio of male–female employment (and unemployment).

☐ The age groups within each sector (and those who are unemployed).

▷ **Figure 10.1** Palermo, Sicily. Study the photograph carefully. How many different types of employment and activity might be found here?

Employment structures in Italy

Look at Figure 10.3.

1 Name the two large islands.

2 Which part of Italy has the largest workforce? Can you account for this?

3 Which parts of Italy have the lowest workforce? How can you explain this answer?

4 Why are the highest percentage of primary workers found in the south?

5 Why do areas in the north have the highest percentage in secondary industries? Name two large inland cities and two large ports in this area.

6 Why are so few people engaged in tertiary industries in the south?

7 Why does the area (Lazio) on the west coast have the highest percentage in tertiary industries?

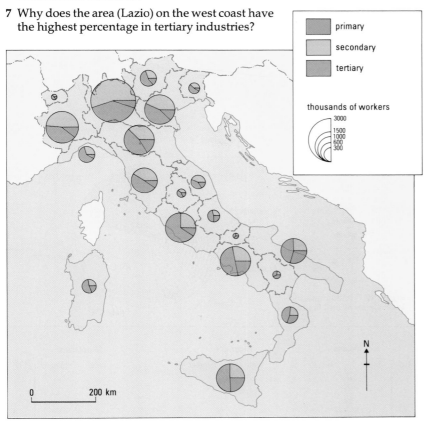

Rapid growth in unemployment in the early 1980s

According to the 1984 annual report of the EEC, *'This is the major single problem facing the Community, and one which is not likely to show any signs of improvement until at least 1986.'* This rapid growth is shown in Figure 10.4.

Two groups of unemployed causing most concern to the EEC countries are

(*a*) **Young people** As Figure 10.5 shows, by the middle of 1983, 5.4 million of the 12.3 million unemployed were under 25 years of age. Despite money being used from the Community's social fund, no real solution has been found. In Italy in 1983, over 75% of those without work were under 29 years old, and in the Netherlands 46% of school leavers were still unemployed 12 months later.

(*b*) **Women over 25** represented 45% of the unemployed in 1983. This group tends to be hard hit by recession, as traditional industries (e.g. textiles) decline and part-time work is curtailed.

Some causes of unemployment in western Europe

☐ Rise in the price of oil and natural gas.

☐ Rise in the price of other raw materials.

☐ A long term downturn in the industrial growth rate (first seen in late 1960s).

☐ An acceleration in the rate of inflation.

☐ Exhaustion of resources.

☐ Introduction of new machinery, including robots and computers.

☐ Fall in the demand for a product.

☐ Closure of firms due to inefficient management.

☐ Closure of firms due to extreme trade union activity.

☐ Closure of firms due to increased cost of wages.

☐ Closure due to old, inefficient working conditions.

☐ Rationalisation programme by larger companies.

☐ Competition from overseas.

☐ Lack of money for investment.

☐ Competition from rival products.

☐ Lack of government financial support.

☐ Redevelopment of inner city areas.

	% January 1977	% January 1981	% January 1983	% May 1984
total EEC	**5.2**	**7.0**	**9.0**	**10.5**
Belgium	7.5	12.8	12.9	18.6
UK	5.4	8.6	11.3	12.6
Denmark	6.3	8.4	9.5	10.7
France	4.8	7.2	8.9	12.0
Greece	0.8	1.7	1.8	3.7
Eire	9.2	10.0	11.5	18.8
Italy	6.4	8.3	9.6	10.1
Luxembourg	0.5	0.9	1.3	1.5
Netherlands	5.5	6.2	9.1	18.0
West Germany	4.0	4.3	6.5	9.1
Austria	N/A	N/A	N/A	4.7
Sweden	N/A	N/A	N/A	3.2
Norway	N/A	N/A	N/A	3.3
Spain	N/A	N/A	N/A	18.2
(Japan)	2.1	2.1	2.2	2.7
(USA)	3.8	6.2	9.7	7.5

△ **Figure 10.3** Regional employment structure in Italy, 1980

◁ **Figure 10.4** Unemployment in Europe

▷ **Figure 10.5** Youth and total unemployment in the EEC

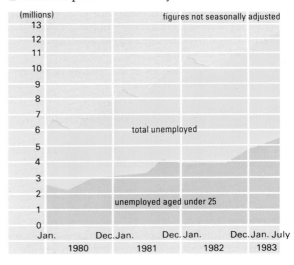

Foreign workers – minorities or guests?

Why were they accepted?

- In 1945, Europe needed large scale rebuilding after the Second World War. There were many more job vacancies than actual workers. Although the greatest shortages were in France and West Germany, even Switzerland, untouched by the war, needed extra labour.

- The increasingly affluent industrial countries took in foreigners from poorer parts of Europe (Mediterranean countries), and the Middle East; as political refugees (Eastern Europe) and from former colonies (especially North Africa).

- The postwar acceptance of guest workers (called *Gastarbeiter* in Germany) occurred at a time of economic growth in the host country. Migrants arrived to work in jobs which were better paid than at home. Initially most arrivals went into farming (95% of new arrivals in West Germany in 1965 went into farming for their first job), whilst others took 'dirty jobs' (e.g. dustmen) not wanted by the local inhabitants. Later many took unskilled jobs in factories (e.g. 5000 Turks in Fords car factory in Cologne, and 21 000 employed by Renault in France in the 1980s).

- Slow natural population growth in western Europe.

Who were these new arrivals?

By 1983 there were about 12 million migrants in western Europe, of which some 6 million were actual workers. Figure 10.6 shows the percentages of foreign workers in the EEC in 1980. However, it is France and West Germany who have received the most in terms of absolute numbers. In 1981 West Germany's 4.6 million *Gastarbeiter* accounted for 7.7% of the total population, while France's 4.1 million in 1979 gave the same percentage. Figure 10.7 shows where the migrants have come from. Many of these people came as migrants hoping to find temporary work and then return home, but later when their families arrived they became 'immigrants'.

For either **France** or **West Germany**, name the countries the migrants came from and give reasons why they should have left their home country. Figure 10.8 shows the age and sex structure of immigrants into France.

1 What do you notice about the balance between male and female immigrants?

2 What problems might this cause?

3 What do you notice about the age groups of the immigrants?

4 What are the advantages and disadvantages to a country receiving immigrants of these age groups?

'In reality this idea did not work. The German and French industries which had to invest money into the training of their new workers did not want to send them back so soon, and the foreign workers and employees who had become adjusted to the country and the style of life

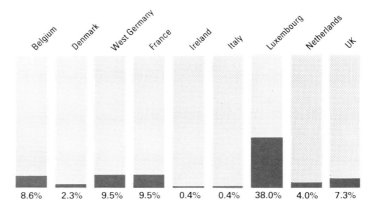

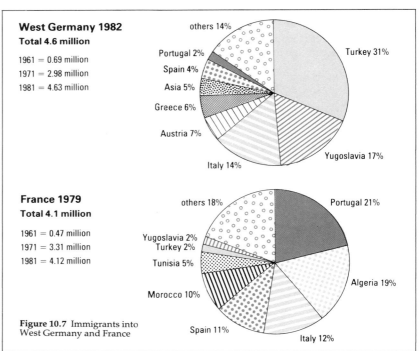

West Germany 1982
Total 4.6 million

1961 = 0.69 million
1971 = 2.98 million
1981 = 4.63 million

others 14%
Turkey 31%
Portugal 2%
Spain 4%
Asia 5%
Greece 6%
Austria 7%
Yugoslavia 17%
Italy 14%

France 1979
Total 4.1 million

1961 = 0.47 million
1971 = 3.31 million
1981 = 4.12 million

others 18%
Portugal 21%
Yugoslavia 2%
Turkey 2%
Tunisia 5%
Algeria 19%
Morocco 10%
Spain 11%
Italy 12%

Figure 10.7 Immigrants into West Germany and France

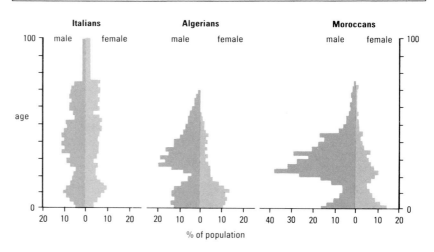

there wanted to stay longer and had their families follow them. In the end a concept of the employment market that was expected to bring advantages for both sides (manpower for an expanding economy and a reduction of unemployment in the home countries) has turned into a serious social and political problem for the West German and French governments.'

△ **Figure 10.6** Migrant workers in the EEC, 1980 (top)

△ **Figure 10.8** Age and sex structure of immigrants in France

Problems facing the immigrants

Housing Scarcity of adequate housing is a severe problem, with immigrants forming ghettos. In France the immigrants form shanty towns known as *bidonvilles*, bidon being the French word for a petrol can. *Bidonvilles* (Figure 10.9) are made from flattened cans, strips of plastic, planks of wood and any loose available material. Because they are illegal, they often lack electricity, sewerage or running water. Most *bidonvilles* have been removed, but several still remain around Marseilles and Paris. Some immigrant families and single men have been accommodated in high rise flats which lack sanitation, are damp and insect infested. However many immigrants, especially those who enter illegally, are prepared to live in poor accommodation in the hope of making enough money to send home.

Health Poor nutrition and lack of access to health care have marked effects on infant mortality and child diseases.

Education Many immigrants spent little time at school and a high percentage of North Africans 'leave' illiterate, and without skills. This makes employment difficult to obtain.

Jobs With this lack of qualifications, immigrants find only poorly-paid, dirty jobs, often with a high accident risk. In times of recession, it is the poorly skilled who are first to be laid off. Also the higher accident rate is due to the fact that many immigrants, coming from rural backgrounds, are not familiar with industrial work, and they often work long hours with tiredness reducing their concentration. In times of unemployment, immigrants with jobs may become victimised by members of the host country without jobs.

Language, religion and culture Although there may be a little integration with the local community (in Germany there are no *bidonvilles*) isolation, segregation and social tension tend to be the norm resulting from basic differences in language, culture and religion. Many immigrants are strict Muslims coming from rural regions, and the life in French and West German towns contrasts markedly with their former life.

Rights With language difficulties, it is hard for immigrants to secure rights such as sickness or unemployment benefits.

Maintaining links with home Most immigrants often only intend to stay two or three years, save up sufficient money and then return home. However, due to the high cost of living in the industrialised countries, many immigrants find it hard to save sufficient money to return.

△ **Figure 10.9** *Bidonville* in Nanterre, Paris. The French government decided to build 15 000 flats (like those in the background) in an attempt to abolish slums from the city.

The problem in the 1980s

As the number of new arrivals, and a high birth rate amongst existing immigrants increases the number of 'foreigners', a distrust of them is growing. These immigrants tend to live in, and around, the big cities and industrial centres. By 1983, 23% of the population of Frankfurt were foreigners and 18% in Paris. It is estimated that by 1990, 70% of pupils in Frankfurt schools will come from immigrant families.

In the early 1980s violent demonstrations against immigrants took place in Paris. Amongst EEC schemes are those to hold special immigrant training, to improve language, and to help repatriate immigrants wishing to return home. Two recent newspaper extracts stated:

'There is a growing tendency among parts of the German population to use foreign minorities as scapegoats. In the minds of some Germans it is the foreigners who cause the housing problem, who take away jobs from unemployed Germans, who cost the welfare state a lot of money, who use up the pensions paid for by the Germans, etc. Though there is little truth in those claims, people who feel insecure and threatened by economic depression are ready to believe them. . . . So an increasingly hostile attitude and demands to expel the foreigners can be observed among these groups of Germans.'

'France is preparing to expel nearly 20 000 unemployed immigrants and to tighten immigration restrictions on nationals of many Third World countries.

France has a tradition of keeping its door ajar to its ex-colonials. But recession, unemployment and rising crime conspire against all the best intentions. ''Two million unemployed are two million immigrants too many'' has become a slogan in Paris.' (*Sunday Times*, November 1982)

The steel industry

The locations of older industries such as steel were determined by physical factors (Figure 10.13). The three traditional major steel areas in Europe, the so-called 'heavy industrial triangle' based upon the Ruhr, the Franco-Belgian coalfield and Lorraine, were all raw material orientated.

△ **Figure 10.10** Steel works at Piombino, Tuscany, Italy

▷ **Figure 10.11** The decline in the steel industry

| | Steel production (million tonnes) | | | | | | | | | Employees | |
	1974	1976	1977	1978	1979	1980	1981	1982	1983	1977	1982
West Germany	53.2	42.4	39.0	45.0	46.0	43.8	41.6	35.9	25.7	214000	181000
France	27.0	23.2	22.1	23.1	23.4	23.2	21.3	18.4	13.5	149000	96000
Italy	23.8	23.4	23.3	23.7	24.2	26.5	24.8	24.0	17.4	97000	95000
Belgium	16.2	12.1	11.3	12.9	13.8	12.6	12.3	9.9	8.5	54000	43000
Luxembourg	6.4	4.6	4.3	4.5	4.6	4.3	3.8	3.1	2.2	20000	13000
Netherlands	5.8	5.1	4.9	5.5	5.8	5.3	5.5	5.4	2.5	22000	20500
UK	22.4	22.4	20.5	20.8	21.5	11.3	15.6	13.7	11.6	182000	79300
Denmark	0.5	0.7	0.7	0.7	0.8	0.8	0.6	0.5	0.4	5000	27000
Eire	0.1	0.1	0.1	0.1	0.1	0.1	0.3	0.2	0.1		
Greece	0.6	0.7	0.8	0.9	1.0	1.0	0.9	0.7	0.8		
EEC	**156.0**	**134.7**	**127.0**	**137.2**	**141.2**	**128.9**	**126.7**	**111.8**	**82.7**	743000	554800
USA	138.0	–	–	–	123.3	100.6	113.0	67.6		*EEC figures include Greece though it did not join the EEC until 1981.*	
USSR	–	–	–	–	149.1	149.1	148.9	147.0			
Japan	124.0	–	–	–	111.7	111.4	114.0	99.5			
World	**709.0**	**–**	**–**	**–**	**747.5**	**717.8**	**744.0**	**640.0**			

Nineteenth-century steelworks – A raw material location

The Ruhr had the advantages of:

□ Large amounts of high grade, easily obtainable coking coal (page 62).

□ Local deposits of clayband iron ore, and relatively nearby limestone outcrops.

□ Water transport provided by natural rivers (Rhine) and canals (Dortmund – Ems).

□ A growing local labour force, and market, which became skilled in the manufacture of steel and its associated industries.

The Franco-Belgian coalfield had similar advantages.

Lorraine, in NE France, was also based upon raw materials, but this time on large reserves of iron ore and limestone. Coal had to be brought from the Saar, and later, after the construction of the Moselle canal, from the Ruhr.

Post-war (1945) steelworks

As demand for steel continued to increase in the post-war years, several new works were opened. These were located on coasts on tidal water. Figure 10.10 shows the site of the Piombino works in Italy (see the map in Figure 10.12). Modern steelworks were built on coastal sites:

☐ Easier for import of iron ore from overseas (e.g. Spain, South America and North Africa) as local supplies became less and the demand for higher quality ores increased.

☐ Easier for the import of cheaper North American coal.

☐ Plenty of cheap, reclaimable land for the large steelworks with its harbour for bulk ore carriers, and its blast furnaces, strip mill and rolling mill.

☐ Improved communications with inland markets, and for easy export of finished steel.

☐ Increased intervention by governments who alone could finance large scale works, and who sought to bring jobs to areas of high unemployment.

An industry in a crisis – the 1980s

☐ The two oil crises of the 1970s led to a fall in demand of steel (increased energy prices, led to increased steel prices) – although European producers felt these were only temporary setbacks. In 1981 Europe had a capacity to produce 1 000 000 million tonnes, yet world demand was only 750 million tonnes (Figure 10.11).

☐ As world demand fell, so did prices and profits. Steelworks operated at a loss, resulting in the early 1980s in a closure of works and much unemployment.

☐ European ores are becoming exhausted, and the need to import from South America and North Africa has increased.

☐ There was a high level of over-manning in Europe.

☐ Open competition between the EEC, USA and Japan for a declining market.

☐ An increasing number of countries became steel producers. In 1950 there were 32 producers and in 1976, 76 producers. The greater the number of producers the greater the loss of markets to Europe, especially as these new producers came at a time of falling demand.

☐ The developing countries, with new equipment and lower wages, undercut the Europeans and they even began to find their own markets within Europe itself.

☐ Only the Dutch and Italian works were efficient. Whereas it took 8.3 hours to produce 1 tonne of steel in 1982 in Europe, it took only 5.9 hours in Japan.

☐ Many European sites were inland.

☐ High interest rates affected modernisation schemes.

☐ Plastics had taken over some of steel's market.

- ● main centres
- ● secondary centres

△ **Figure 10.12** The location of principal EEC iron and steel centres in 1982

The future As more countries developed their own steel industries, the European share of the world's market fell from 51% in 1966 to 18% in 1980. Despite heavy plant closures and labour shedding, financial losses continue. Even those governments who have heavily subsidised their steelworks have often only delayed the inevitable. High redundancy payments have been made by the EEC but alternative jobs are rarely found in areas where steel is virtually the only source of employment. The location of the 'slimmer' European steelworks is shown in Figure 10.12. Although signs of an increase in demand were seen by 1984, further reductions in both the number of steelworks and steelworkers are still likely in the mid 1980s. The future existence of the iron and steel industry in Europe depends upon its ability to compete in world markets – against the North Americans, Japanese, East Europeans and developing countries such as Brazil, South Korea and India.

Industrial location

Industry can be regarded as a system, which in its simplified form, can be represented in the following way.

Inputs ⟶ **Processes** ⟶ **Outputs**
(raw materials and   *(manufacture)*   *(end product)*
human factors)

In this model outputs minus inputs (costs) will equal profit (or loss).

Although a factory may be studied in isolation, it is often closely linked to other factories through the transfer of materials and products; for example, a car assembly factory needs parts from numerous associated firms.

Factors to consider in choosing a site for a factory

For the older established European industries, their location was often determined by physical conditions, but today other factors tend to be more important. Where many sites are available the firm or company will choose the most profitable one. This will be the site where the costs of raw materials, fuel and power, labour, land and transport are minimised, and where there is a large market for the product.

These factors are summarised in Figure 10.13 where they have been divided into a) physical factors and b) human and economic factors. Can you give a definition and an actual example of each of the eleven factors shown in this diagram?

In the late twentieth century the three major factors deciding industrial location are possibly the nearness to a large market, the availability of labour and government policy. In the nineteenth century it was physical factors such as the source of raw material (e.g. iron ore) and sources of energy (e.g. coal) which determined industrial locations. Figure 10.14 shows the major areas of traditional heavy industry in Europe.

physical factors

raw materials
power – energy
climate
natural routes
site and land

factory

human and economic factors

labour
capital
market
government policy
geographical inertia
economies of larger sized factories

△ **Figure 10.13** Location of industry

▽ **Figure 10.14** Major traditional heavy industrial areas in western Europe

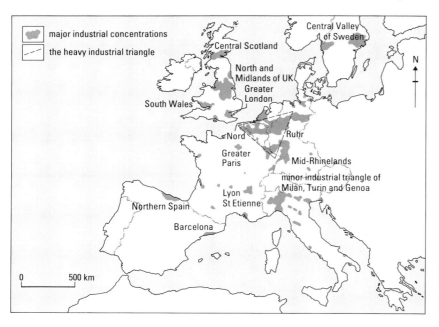

major industrial concentrations
the heavy industrial triangle

Central Valley of Sweden
Central Scotland
North and Midlands of UK
Greater London
South Wales
Nord
Ruhr
Greater Paris
Mid-Rhinelands
minor industrial triangle of Milan, Turin and Genoa
Lyon St Etienne
Northern Spain
Barcelona

N

0   500 km

Shipbuilding

Shipbuilding became established in those areas which had the following advantages:

□ Deep, wide, sheltered rivers or estuaries for the launching of ships (Figure 10.15).

□ Relatively steep river banks to allow the ships to slide into the river under gravity on launching.

□ Clay river bed to allow deepening (as the size of ships increased) and the construction of docks (to complete the ships after launching and to later repair or refit older vessels).

□ Nearby steelworks – a major raw material.

□ A large labour force – both skilled and unskilled.

□ Large areas of cheap, available land for the shipyards, for future expansion and for the many associated industries e.g. manufacture of rope, ships engines and boilers.

□ Areas with a large amount of ocean traffic.

Reasons for the decline in shipbuilding

□ World recession has led to a decline in world trade and in demand for new ships. There was 16% less cargo carried by sea in 1981 than in 1979.

□ Large overcapacity, especially in oil tankers. From 1973–78 the tanker fleet increased by 50% whereas oil transport only increased by 9%. Many specialised ships are now laid up.

□ The decline in NW Europe was delayed in the 1970s by the demand by offshore oil and gas companies, but new orders in the 1980s are few.

Textiles

The textile industry was the first 'industry' to be developed in Europe. Three areas in particular dominated (Figure 10.18), the Piedmont, Lombardy, Venetia region in north Italy; a zone extending from NE France through Flanders and into the Ruhr; and in Yorkshire and Lancashire in England. The early advantages which these areas usually possessed included:

□ Water power from streams and rivers (pre-industrial revolution).

□ Later the nearness or availability of coal as a form of energy (after the industrial revolution).

□ Soft, i.e. lime free, water as this gave a better lather when washing.

□ The nearness of such raw materials as wool (sheep on Pennines and Ardennes), flax (the Lys Valley in Belgium) and mulberry trees (silkworms in north Italy).

□ Ease of importing other raw materials such as cotton, and to export the manufactured cloth.

□ The inventiveness of the local people, especially the inhabitants of Flanders in the sixteenth century who were forced to flee to avoid religious persecution and who took their ideas and skills to safer parts of Europe.

□ Canals – as a cheap, convenient method of moving bulky materials.

- Fierce competition from the Far East and from eastern Europe where there are newer shipyards and lower salaries (Figure 10.16).

- In the early 1980s Japan broke the Quotas Agreement by which each part of the world agreed to build only a certain percentage of ships. This increased competition.

- Poor labour relations in several western European yards. Strikes and the inability to complete orders on time have meant a loss in orders and the payment of penalty clauses.

▽ **Figure 10.15** Location of shipyards (below left)

▷ **Figure 10.16** Decline in shipbuilding (gross tonnage)

▽ **Figure 10.17** A modern shipyard in western Europe. The ship being built is a freighter for India.

	1976	1978	1982
EEC ('The nine')	5140	3530	2525
rest of Western Europe	3146	2303	1760
(Western Europe)	(8286)	(5833)	(4285)
Japan	8349	6121	5811
World	22078	16547	14588

EEC – workforce of 200000 in 1976 fell to 100000 by 1981

The future is not bright. Despite the widespread closures and redundancies, giving a 30% cutback in output between 1976 and 1983, European yards are still at 30% greater capacity than is needed. This can only mean further yard closures and decline in labour force. The hope is for an increase in demand for more ships (since they have to be modernised or replaced sometime in the future).

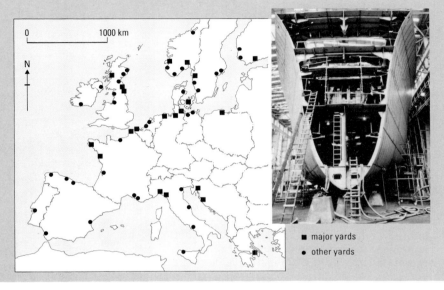

■ major yards

● other yards

There are two examples here of long established European industries – shipbuilding and textiles. When you have read through the accounts choose:

1 One area in Europe which is important for shipbuilding.

2 One area which is important for textiles.

For each area:

(a) Draw a labelled sketch map to show its location and the advantages of its site.

(b) Describe why the industry grew up in that location, and why it continued to grow.

(c) Give reasons why the industry in the area you have chosen has declined in recent years (the list on page 65 may give you some ideas).

(d) What steps do you think might be taken to either halt a further decline, or to introduce new jobs to the area?

Reasons for the decline in textiles

- Foreign countries began producing their own textiles, causing a loss in markets. These foreign countries, especially in the Far East, then took over other markets, and could even undercut European goods within Europe itself.

- Rise in the cost of raw materials, and several developing countries producing their own textiles had their own supply.

- Plentiful, and cheap labour in those developing countries.

- A slow growth in domestic consumption in Europe, partly due to a stable population, and people spending less on clothes.

- Out of date mills and machinery with too many small firms, and family-owned businesses.

- Recent modernisation in Europe (post 1975) has led to an improvement in machinery but this has meant fewer jobs.

- Growth of synthetic (artificial) fibres has led to the decline in demand for natural fibres, especially cotton and silk.

The future To allow time for modernisation and re-organisation, the EEC is negotiating import limitation agreements with some 30 low-cost textile producing countries. Also, firms are amalgamating to become more competitive. The need to maintain the industry is essential, as textiles are usually found in areas which already have high unemployment; and to support the chemical industry since 25% of their products include artificial fibres. The EEC Social Fund helps those who have been made redundant, many of whom are young people, older women and migrants. The future is not very encouraging, but modernisation and specialisation is making the textile industry more stable.

▽ **Figure 10.18** Location of textiles in the EEC

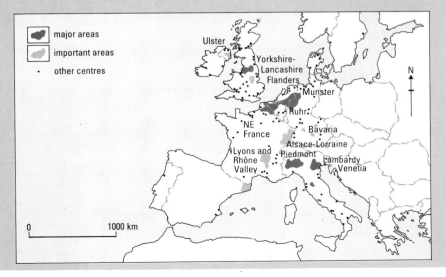

■ major areas

▨ important areas

· other centres

Ulster

Yorkshire-Lancashire

Flanders

Munster

Ruhr

NE France

Bavaria

Lyons and Rhône Valley

Alsace-Lorraine

Piedmont

Lombardy Venetia

0   1000 km

Switzerland

In 1983 Switzerland was second only to Japan as the most competitive country in the world in industry. Yet Switzerland has:

- No significant mineral deposits
- No fossil fuels (i.e. coal, oil, natural gas)
- Insufficient farming land to feed the population
- A land-locked location
- A small domestic market

'Footloose' industries: market and transport orientated

Because Swiss industries are not tied to the location of raw materials, they may be called 'footloose'. This term is applied to firms who have a relatively free choice of location. Many of these industries rely on skill or provide services for people and therefore are market orientated, and need good transport links by road or by air.

Precision industries 'Swiss technology is top technology'

'In many fields of the engineering and metalworking industries Switzerland plays a leading part internationally. This strong position, which was achieved in a tough world-wide competition, is the result of intense research and development. It is established again and again by outstanding features like quality, precision, technical and economic performances and an unparalleled observation of delivery times. In the long run a small country like Switzerland which has to export 70% of its production, can only exist due to technical peak performances. The client relying on an optimal service at any time is the first to profit from this achievement.' (V.S.M. Zurich)

As water was the only source of power available, numerous HEP stations were built. This in turn led to research and development in electrical engineering.

Switzerland made up for the lack of raw materials by processing and enriching those which were imported. Industry is therefore:

- Highly specialised.
- Capable of producing low material-content goods which need the maximum technology. The customer in other words is paying for the skill put into the product.
- Geared to producing precision goods of top quality and efficiency, and which need great accuracy (e.g. the new micro-analytical balance which has an accuracy of ±0.2 millionths of a gram).
- Aimed often at an individual customer, not for the mass market.
- Dependent upon competitiveness in quality and cost.
- Dependent upon selling that product.

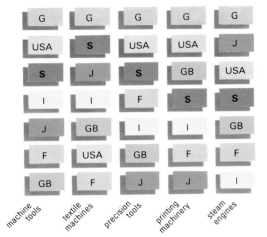

'With a population of approximately 6 million, Switzerland is one of the smallest industrial nations of the world. This country's share in world exports is roughly 2%. It may thus be all the more surprising that Switzerland ranks among the leaders in a variety of sectors of the engineering apparatus and metal industry.' (V.S.M. Switzerland)

G = West Germany
I = Italy
J = Japan
F = France
S = Switzerland
GB = Great Britain

Switzerland's industries include

Machines Swiss tools account for nearly 10% of the world market, and the country is a major producer of textile machinery (95% of which is sold abroad), machine and precision tools, and printing machinery (see Figure 10.19).

Watches These are manufactured in over 2000 factories, many being specialist component works, mainly in the Jura mountains in the north-west of the country. In 1982 45 million watches were made, of which 97% were exported. Yet even this industry, relying on skill and precision, was not immune to the recession of the early 1980s and exports fell by 12% in 1982 (Figure 10.20).

Transport e.g. mountain railways and aerial tramways.

Food processing With limited land use, agricultural products must be utilised to the full. Nestlé's named after its founder, have specialised in the processing of chocolate and condensed milk, and in tinned baby foods (Figure 10.21).

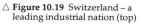

△ **Figure 10.19** Switzerland – a leading industrial nation (top)

△ **Figure 10.20** Watchmaker assembling parts of a watch dial at an Omega watch factory in Switzerland

▷ **Figure 10.21** Chocolate factory in Zurich

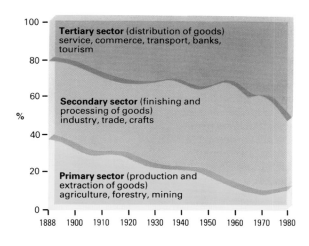

Tertiary sector (distribution of goods) service, commerce, transport, banks, tourism

Secondary sector (finishing and processing of goods) industry, trade, crafts

Primary sector (production and extraction of goods) agriculture, forestry, mining

◁ **Figure 10.22** Changes in Swiss employment structures

▽ **Figure 10.23** The Paradeplatz, Zurich – the financial centre of Switzerland

▽ **Figure 10.24** Mouth controlled microscope stand for microsurgery (bottom)

Growth of the service industry

As Figure 10.22 shows, the numbers employed in the tertiary or service sector increased from 23% in 1900 to 57% in 1980. This reflected the growth of:

- □ Industries with more managerial, clerical and distributive posts.
- □ Transport.
- □ Tourism and recreation, e.g. hotels, restaurants, ski centres etc.
- □ Banking and insurance associated with a developed country.

The Swiss banking industry

This grew as a result of Switzerland's lack of natural resources, causing the import of raw materials and the export of manufactured goods. This needed both banking facilities, as well as insurance. Swiss banks have gained an international reputation based upon confidence – confidence that transactions will be honoured, and that the identity of the investors will be kept. The three largest banks (which in reality are quite small, only coming between the top 30 and 60 in size in the world) are accurate in their transactions, offer a highly efficient service, are stable as a result of Swiss neutrality and have large foreign exchange departments. Figure 10.23 shows the Paradeplatz in Zurich – the 'home' of the so called 'Gnomes of Zurich'.

Quaternary Industries (page 64)

These include research and the new highly skilled electronics industries. Here too Switzerland has a leading role to play, especially with regard to medical technology, (Figures 10.24 and 10.25). Swiss companies have helped to engineer pacemakers, which enable those with heart disorders to lead normal lives, radiotherapy facilities for use in the fight against cancer, devices for counting red and white blood corpuscles for immediate analysis, apparatus used in microscopic surgery and the development of artificial joints for those who have rheumatic and arthritic complaints.

Opportunity for leisure and social activities help to decide the location of economic activities

Managers deciding where to locate a factory may be attracted to Switzerland because it has:

- □ A healthy climate with unpolluted air, especially favourable for good health (sanatoriums).
- □ Spectacular mountain and lake scenery.
- □ Opportunities for all the year recreation from walking and climbing in summer, to skiing in winter.
- □ An increasing demand for tourist and recreational based activities.
- □ Good educational amenities.
- □ Attractions for footloose industries.
- □ Good air and road communications (being in the heart of Europe).

▽ **Figure 10.25** Artificial finger joint – new parts moulded from silicone can be implanted into the body without rejection

The car industry – market orientated

This industry employed 1.5 million people in western Europe in 1982, working either in the making of component parts or in the assembly plants. Unlike the older, heavier industries, where physical factors determined their location (e.g. steel, ships), the car industry is 'market orientated', and it is found near to large centres of population. Rapid growth since 1950 has resulted from the development of the family car, and by 1980, one person in six in the EEC had their own vehicle.

The car industry consists of numerous component factories each making one specific part, (e.g. gearboxes, axles, sparking plugs, engines etc.). These parts are then taken to the assembly plant where they are put together as the car moves along a computer controlled conveyor belt or 'assembly line'. Each employee is responsible for one particular specialised job. This job has to be done in a given time before the car moves on down the line to have the next part added, and another car takes its place. This is an efficient but monotonous method of production. Greater efficiency is now achieved by using 'robots', but the increased mechanisation causes unemployment.

Assembly lines and mass production are dominated by a few large companies. Many small companies have had to amalgamate with larger companies for economic reasons. To increase their markets further, a large company in one country may link itself to a previous rival company in a different country to gain extra sales outlets. Some European car companies have had to be taken over by their government (e.g. Renault in France) in order to obtain extra finance, whilst others have become part of giant North American companies (e.g. Ford Motors and General Motors).

Figure 10.26 shows the major car producers in the world, and Figure 10.27 the location of the major companies in western Europe. Notice the concentration in four main areas – the English Midlands, the Paris region, the Ruhr valley and northern Italy. Recently the industry has had to face numerous problems, especially competition from Japan (see the growth of production in Japan in Figure 10.26) who are continually looking for new outlets, and possible amalgamations within Europe, and the recession which has depressed car sales. Many companies have had to close their smaller plants, and had to make large numbers of their workforce redundant in an attempt to become more competitive.

	USA	Japan	West Germany	France	Italy	UK
1971	8.6	3.7	3.7	2.7	1.7	1.7
1972	8.8	4.0	3.5	2.7	1.7	1.9
1973	9.7	4.5	3.6	2.9	1.8	1.7
1974	7.3	3.9	2.8	2.7	1.6	1.5
1975	6.7	4.6	2.9	2.5	1.3	1.3
1976	8.5	5.0	3.5	3.0	1.5	1.3
1977	9.2	5.4	3.8	3.1	1.4	1.3
1978	9.2	5.7	3.9	3.1	1.5	1.2
1979	8.4	6.2	3.9	3.2	1.5	1.0
1980	6.4	7.0	3.5	2.9	1.4	0.9
1981	6.3	7.0	3.6	2.6	1.3	1.0
1982	5.1	6.9	3.7	2.7	1.3	0.9

△ **Figure 10.26** Car output 1971–81 (in millions)

▽ Chrysler Co.
▼ British Leyland
○ Volvo
□ Saab
■ Ford Motor (USA)
◰ Opel
△ Daimler-Benz
▲ Volkswagen-Audi
★ Renault
◇ BMW
◆ General Motors
✳ Fiat Group
• car manufacturing towns in Europe

▽ **Figure 10.27** The European car industry

◁ **Figure 10.28** Volkswagen car factory at Wolfsburg

▽ **Figure 10.29** Outline landsketch of Wolfsburg

Wolfsburg – the Volkswagen car factory

Wolfsburg, located east of Hanover and near to the present-day frontier with East Germany, was chosen in 1937 to be the site for the, then new, factory for Volkswagen cars. The idea was to disperse industry from the Ruhr. Advantages of the site of Wolfsburg included:

□ Movement away from older industrial areas which had a lack of space and experienced congestion.

□ Land values are lower away from city centres.

□ Flat floor of the Aller valley was ideal for a large factory and for possible future expansion.

□ Large area of land needed for the assembly line, offices, power station, car parks for the 50 000 employees, storage areas for completed cars, and for the enlargement of the 'New town' of Wolfsburg.

□ Nearby water supplies from the river Aller and several reservoirs.

□ A 'greenfield' site near to large cities which provide a market and a workforce.

□ Nearby motorways (autobahns) for transport of materials.

□ Adjacent to a main line railway.

□ Adjacent to the Mittelland Canal which links the Ruhr with Berlin. The canal is used to carry bulky raw materials.

□ After 1945 the borders of Germany were altered so that although Wolfsburg now lies near to the East German frontier, it was able to employ many immigrants and refugees (see page 66).

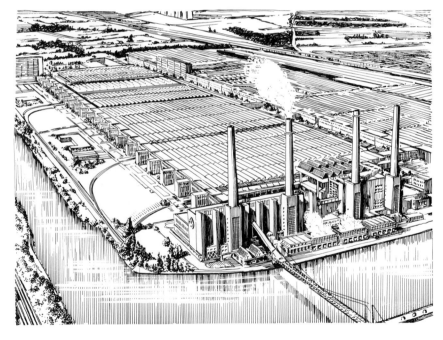

Figure 10.29 is a land-sketch of the Wolfsburg area shown on Figure 10.28. Copy and enlarge this sketch. On it label the following: Mittelland Canal; railway line; assembly line building; office blocks; power station; car parks; cars stored for transport; rural land; high rise and low rise accommodation for employees; flat valley floor of River Aller.

Norway
– adapting to change

In the 1920s Norway was western Europe's poorest country. The land was mountainous, the climate cold and wet, the soils thin. The Norwegians turned to the sea for their living, although even the sea was often inhospitable. By 1970 Norway was one of the more industrialised and better-off European countries, partly because the heavy rain and rugged mountains provided numerous HEP sites (page 56) giving Norway the world's highest production of electricity per person, and partly because of the development of fishing and a merchant fleet. By the 1980s Norway had a large trade surplus, mainly due, in the previous decade, to the discovery and development of gas and oil from the North Sea (page 53). Norway has used these three sources of energy to diversify and to modernise further her capital-intensive industries. The skill of the people, the small domestic market and the specialisation of industry have enabled Norway to become a net exporter. The country has very few labour disputes, in January 1984 had only 3.1% unemployment, was a member of EFTA (Figure 1.2) and had trade agreements with the EEC.

Changes in maritime activities

The Norwegian merchant fleet ranked seventh in the world in 1980. It serves a world market with 90% of its tonnage trading between other nations and never visiting a home port. This, together with the local fishing industry, has led to the growth of a large shipbuilding industry. The Norwegian shipbuilders have taken the advantage of traditions stretching back more than a thousand years; the numerous sheltered, deep-water fjord-side yard sites; and a stable, skilled workforce. The industry has a world-wide reputation for reliability, and has been quick to introduce new ideas and to meet changing demands of customers. Recently, the shipowners have moved away from the large tankers and bulk carriers (now less in demand) towards smaller but technically sophisticated vessels like gas tankers, chemical carriers, ro-ro ships (roll on – roll off) and specialised units for the offshore oil industry. Norway's maritime activities cover the whole range of activities from design, construction, and repairs to shipbroking and insurance.

Recently the shipyards have turned to the challenge of constructing oil rigs and producing platforms together with supply vessels for the exploration and exploitation of North Sea oil and gas reserves. Figure 10.31 shows one main yard with both its traditional dock area, and its new extensions. Norway had, in 1982, constructed 39 drilling rigs, with the newer models increasingly constructed to search for oil in deeper and more hostile waters. The Haug Esund Mekaniske Verksad As yards (Figure 10.31) have 1000 metres of quay, and 2.5 hectares (6 acres) of their 12 hectare (30 acre) site under cover. It has a dry dock

and a floating dock. In recent years it has built bulk carriers, oil tankers, refrigerated cargo ships, a chain-laying crane barge, a fish processing ship, a coastguard ship, as well as oil rigs and oil platforms – all signs of its adaptability.

Another change, described on page 41, is how the traditional farmer–fisherman of the fjords is becoming a farmer–rig worker. Aquaculture (fish farming) has also become a new growth industry since 1970 (Figure 10.32). The main fish bred are the Atlantic salmon and the salmon trout, although shellfish are also being introduced. The first farms bred trout in fresh water ponds, but these froze in winter and so the present farms are in the warmer, unpolluted fjords, where winter temperatures rarely fall below 3°C. Large quantities of fish scraps from the traditional fishing industry provide fish bait at economic prices. The present day fjord farmer–fisherman is highly trained and skilled.

Figure 10.30 Norwegian built tanker (inset)

△ **Figure 10.31** Haug Esund Mekaniske Verksad As yard, Norway

▷ **Figure 10.32** Fish farm on Hardanger Fjord, Norway

Changes in land-based activities

Industrial growth has mainly resulted from the abundance of HEP (page 56). It is this cheap, renewable form of energy which has resulted in the construction of ten aluminium factories. Aluminium is a metal constantly making new inroads into industrial production, transport and the home. Other chemical industries, such as the one in Figure 10.33 are located, like the aluminium factories, on areas of flat land in the fjords, confirming that Norway 'is an industrialised society in a non-industrialised landscape', i.e. a high percentage of the population are employed in industry. Naturally, such industrial sites make the import of raw materials and the export of the finished product easy by water transport.

Norway is also adapting quickly to the changing world by developing a highly skilled electronics industry. Norway tends to lead the world in products linked to maritime activities. One product is the cryptographic encoder–decoder for the transmission and reception of signals via telephone and radio channels – a vital link with merchant ships, oil rigs and fishing vessels, as well as with isolated rural communities on the mainland. Figure 10.34 shows the control room of a Norwegian North Sea oil platform. The Norwegians are also producing anti-submarine weapons, and laser range-finders for the defence of their fjords; sophisticated underwater acoustics for the location of fish; equipment for combating oil spills and drilling gear. Norwegians are facing the future by adapting to new innovations, and producing highly skilled, reliable products.

▷ **Figure 10.33** Flat land is a scarce resource in Norway – every available square metre is being used here at Høyanger for industry (above right)

▷ **Figure 10.34** Control room of an oil platform in the Frigg field

Urban growth and patterns

In 1960 30% of the world's population lived in urban areas. By A.D. 2000 the world's population will have doubled, and half will be living in large cities. In Europe, especially in western Europe, the drift from rural areas to the towns has been going on for several centuries. Now most countries have over 70% of their population living in urban areas (Figure 11.1).

Why people move into cities

- More and better paid jobs
- Better housing
- Better services such as schools, hospitals and libraries
- More entertainment
- Better transport facilities
- The work-place is nearer, thus reducing time, distance and cost from home
- Better shopping facilities

Can you add to this list? And what do you think are the problems of living in large cities?

Urban models

It has been suggested that towns do not grow in a haphazard way, but that they show certain generalised characteristics. For example, Burgess (Figure 11.2) suggested that most towns grew outward in a concentric pattern, whereas Hoyt (Figure 11.2) thought a 'wedge' shape was more typical of their growth. A model is a theoretical framework which may not actually exist, but which helps to explain the reality.

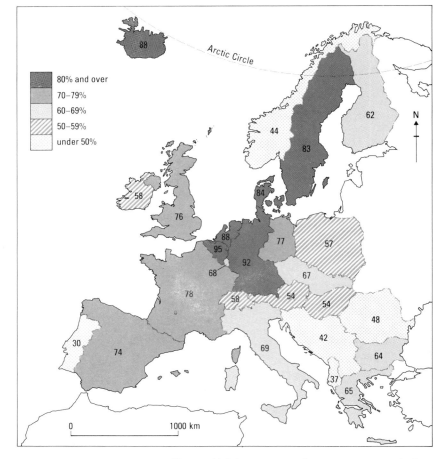

△ **Figure 11.1** Percentage of population living in towns and cities

▽ **Figure 11.2** Two urban models

Figure 11.3 is a transect drawn across a typical, but not an actual, German city.

- What is meant by the term 'Central Business District' (CBD)? What types of land use can be found there? Why?
- Why are new large shopping centres and offices replacing small shops in the part of the city built in the nineteenth century?
- Why is the railway station near to, but not in, the city centre?
- Why is the high cost housing found on the edge of the city?
- Where would you expect nineteenth century industry to be found? Why has this changed in the late twentieth century?
- What is meant by the term 'commuting zone'?
- Why have flats and shopping centres been built in the commuting zone?

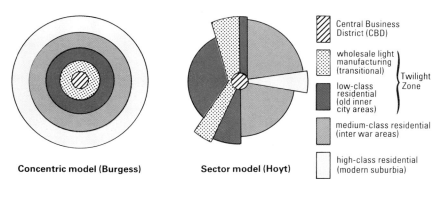

Concentric model (Burgess)   **Sector model (Hoyt)**

Central Business District (CBD)

wholesale light manufacturing (transitional) } Twilight Zone

low-class residential (old inner city areas) }

medium-class residential (inter war areas)

high-class residential (modern suburbia)

▽ **Figure 11.3** Transect to show structure and change across a typical German city (after T.H. Elkins)

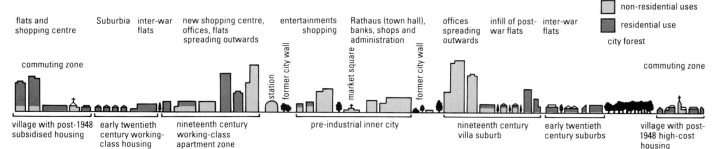

Urban problems

High land values, especially in the CBD. In many large cities large companies are having to leave these expensive sites and are moving to 'greenfield sites' with more space and cheaper rates.

Traffic congestion caused by large numbers of commuters and shoppers travelling to the city centre by public and private transport. Congestion is highest at morning and evening rush hours, and it is increased by the narrow, unplanned streets, and the lack of car parks.

Pollution This includes noise and air pollution resulting from traffic and industry. Older areas experience vandalism and litter.

Urban decay As Figure 11.4 shows, many older parts of cities, built in the nineteenth century, have become run-down and suffer from a lack of amenities. Throughout Europe there is still a shortage of bathrooms, indoor toilets (Figure 11.5), running water and garages.

Rising unemployment resulting from the decline of older industries which had been located in inner city areas in the last century. The influx of immigrants (guestworkers) and refugees have added to this problem.

Crime is higher in larger urban areas.

Cost of services As the more wealthy move away from the more central areas, those remaining have less money to pay for public services, and yet are often those who need these extra services (e.g. hospitals).

△ **Figure 11.4** Naples – this view gives an idea of the chronic overcrowding and decay in the city

Look carefully at Figure 11.6 which is a view of an old established industrial town. What do you consider to be the major environmental problems facing the inhabitants? What possible solutions may be put forward by planners?

Home ownership

In most of Europe people tend to live in flats rather than owning their own homes (Figure 11.7), yet home ownership is looked upon as a status symbol – even in the communist countries in the east. Recently the ambition of many city dwellers has turned to buying or renting a second home in the country. Sweden, where 22% of the inhabitants have a second home, heads the list.

▽ **Figure 11.6** Lille – the crowded factories with no room to expand, the haphazard distribution of buildings and the railway are typical of an old industrial landscape

Germany	84.6%
France	69.7%
Italy	57.6%
Netherlands	71.3%
Belgium	53.7%
Luxembourg	78.0%
United Kingdom	98.7%
Eire	63.6%
Denmark	90.4%

△ **Figure 11.5** Percentage of houses in EEC countries with indoor toilets in 1971

▽ **Figure 11.7** Home ownership in Britain and West Germany

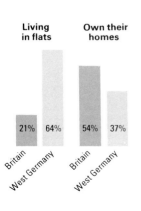

Living in flats: Britain 21%, West Germany 64%
Own their homes: Britain 54%, West Germany 37%

Modern and traditional housing

Modern Many European cities have undergone a lot of rebuilding since 1945 – some due to war damage, others to replace old housing and abandoned industry. In most cases new buildings have been in the form of flats, usually several stories high (Figure 11.8).

Traditional housing was usually built as a response to climatic factors or the availability of raw materials. Several types are shown in Figure 11.9 and you could add more.

▷ **A**
▽ **B**

Figure 11.8 Modern European housing, **A** is in Paris, **B** is in Marseilles

△ **A**
▷ **B**
▽ **C**

Figure 11.9 Traditional European housing

A is in the Lofoten Islands and like other places near the Arctic Circle (e.g. Iceland) the houses are usually made of wood.

B is the traditional house of southern Norway. The wood comes from the local coniferous forest, and the turf on the roof acts an an insulation against cold, windy winters.

C In Amsterdam, there is a contrast. Here houses have had to be built on piles driven into the former lake beds.

D shows a Swiss chalet. Wood, from local forests is the major building material, and the steep roof is a response to the heavy winter snow falls.

E is typical of areas around the Adriatic sea (e.g. northern Italy and coastal Yugoslavia). Houses are built of local stone, of which there is an abundance.

△ **D** (top)
△ **E**
◁ **F**

F illustrates typical Mediterranean-type houses, on a Greek island. The thick stone walls (stone is again found in excessive amounts locally) shutters, and shady courtyards are suited to the hot summer sun, and give protection from the local strong winds. They are painted white to reflect some heat, and the flat roofs indicate a lack of rainfall.

Distribution of population

In Europe Using Figure 11.10 and an atlas,

1 Which areas are sparsely populated because they are: (a) too cold (b) rather dry (c) too mountainous (d) lacking in rich soils?

2 Which areas are densely populated because they have: (a) reliable rainfall (b) moderate (i.e. not extreme) temperatures (c) rich supplies of minerals or energy (d) rich soils (e) flat land (f) major communication lines (g) outlets to the sea?

cities ■ over 1 000 000 population

● 500 000–1 000 000 population

• 100 000–500 000 population

people per km²

    100 and over
    50–99
    10–49
    1–9
    1 or less

△ **Figure 11.10** Distribution of population

▽ **Figure 11.11** Land use in Hanover, West Germany

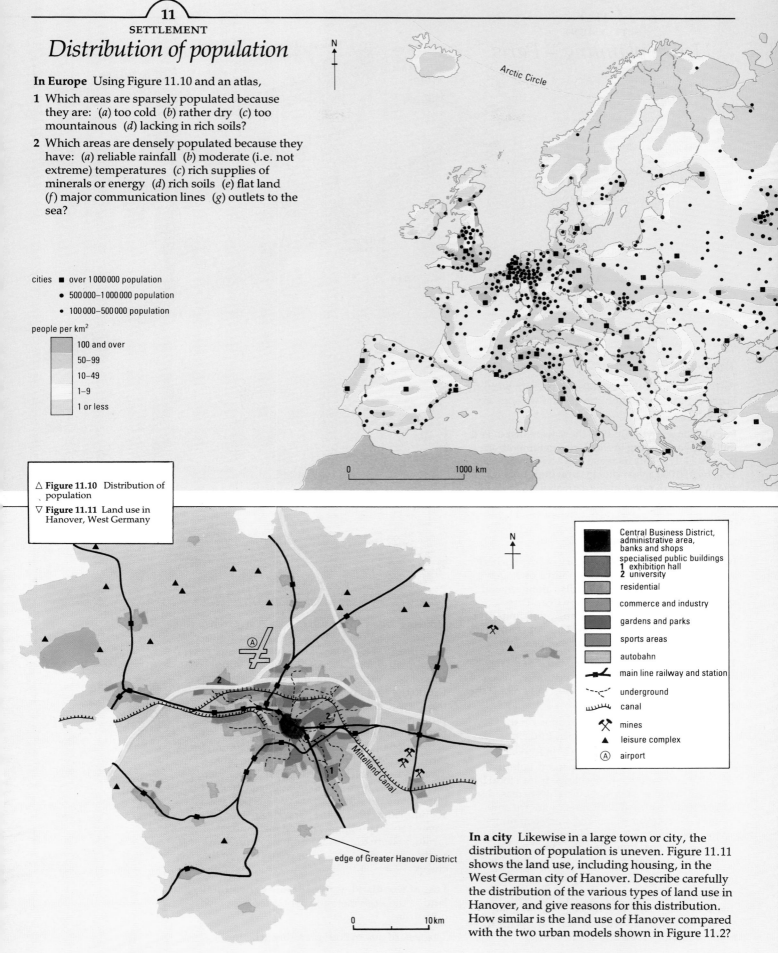

0   1000 km

Central Business District, administrative area, banks and shops

specialised public buildings
1 exhibition hall
2 university

residential

commerce and industry

gardens and parks

sports areas

autobahn

━━ main line railway and station

- - - underground

⊔⊔⊔ canal

⚒ mines

▲ leisure complex

Ⓐ airport

Mittelland Canal

edge of Greater Hanover District

0   10km

In a city Likewise in a large town or city, the distribution of population is uneven. Figure 11.11 shows the land use, including housing, in the West German city of Hanover. Describe carefully the distribution of the various types of land use in Hanover, and give reasons for this distribution. How similar is the land use of Hanover compared with the two urban models shown in Figure 11.2?

Urban planning – Paris

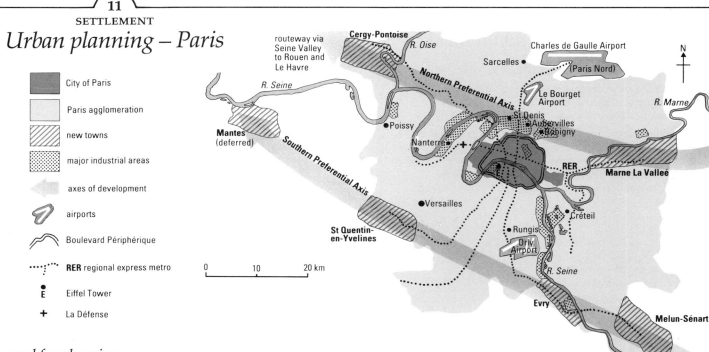

City of Paris

Paris agglomeration

new towns

major industrial areas

axes of development

airports

Boulevard Périphérique

RER regional express metro

0   10   20 km

E Eiffel Tower

+ La Défense

The need for planning

Paris, like many other established cities in western Europe, has grown haphazardly and without any planning.

Population growth By 1980 there were just over 8 million people living in the Paris agglomeration (Figure 11.12). This increase had accelerated after 1954 by 150 000 a year due to rural depopulation, a rise in the birth rate and the arrival of 'guestworkers' (page 66). The pull of Paris was accompanied by a decline in towns and villages in the surrounding area, leading to what has been called, the 'French Desert'.

Industry The nineteenth century industries had been located in the inner city suburbs of St Denis, Aubervilles and Bobigny, and also along several stretches of the River Seine. However, these industries were set in old, cramped buildings and caused considerable pollution. This concentration of industry has itself led to a further problem . . .

Traffic congestion It was estimated that by the mid 1970s there were 12.2 million journeys each day on public and private transport in Paris. Of the estimated 3 million commuters:

(a) 35% used cars causing congestion on the narrow city centre roads, noise and air pollution, accidents and parking problems.

(b) 50% travelled by public transport. Suburban commuters often had to change from a local bus to the metro or a second bus. This increased the congestion at rush hour times at metro and main line strations, making some commuter journeys up to 2 hours in length. Improvements in roads only added to the cost of public transport.

(c) 15% walked to work, filling the pavements.

Congestion is increased as many suburban dwellers have to travel across Paris to another suburb for work – added to which Paris is the focal point of France's road and rail network.

Housing Many inner suburbs form an extensive 'Twilight zone'. In 1970 over 89% of the houses were pre-1914, 50% lacked a w.c. and many others were small and lacked adequate water supply or sewerage. Despite the overall shortage of houses within the agglomeration, the population living in the 'City' itself fell by 11.6% resulting in many properties becoming empty and vandalised. A post-war method to try to increase the accommodation available to new arrivals and for those evicted in slum clearances was to build 'Grands Ensembles' (Figure 11.13). These were often 5-storey high-rise flats, and were built as huge estates in suburban areas. This policy was abandoned in 1972 as the 'Grands Ensembles' created social problems, lacked recreational facilities, were too distant from work (increasing traffic congestion) and often were built 'on the cheap'.

Loss of woodland, waterside and agricultural land as the agglomeration continued to sprawl outwards.

The lack of any overall planning schemes.

The Schéma Directeur

This was a planning solution published in 1965 and revised in 1969 and 1975. Its main proposals included:

- Preserving the historical cultural centre by limiting the height of office blocks, making the narrow boulevards traffic-free, and maintaining older buildings.

- Establishing 'suburban' nodes with commerce, administrative, cultural and public buildings. The aim was to decentralise offices, and to re-invigorate the inner suburban zone. The hope was to reduce traffic congestion in the city centre and to create employment foci in the inner suburbs. The most notable achievement is La Défense (see Figures 11.12 and 11.14). This node has one high office block; numerous smaller office, cultural and administrative developments; is linked by the metro; and is next to the new university. Other nodal points include Rungis (with its large food market), Poissy, Créteil, St Denis, Bobigny and the new Charles de Gaulle airport (Figure 11.12).

◁ **Figure 11.12** Paris region with the new towns along the preferential axis

◁ **Figure 11.13** The serpentine 'Grands Ensembles' near Pantin, France (below left)

▽ **Figure 11.14** La Défense – a new suburban node offers employment outside the city centre

▽ **Figure 11.15** Evry new town (bottom)

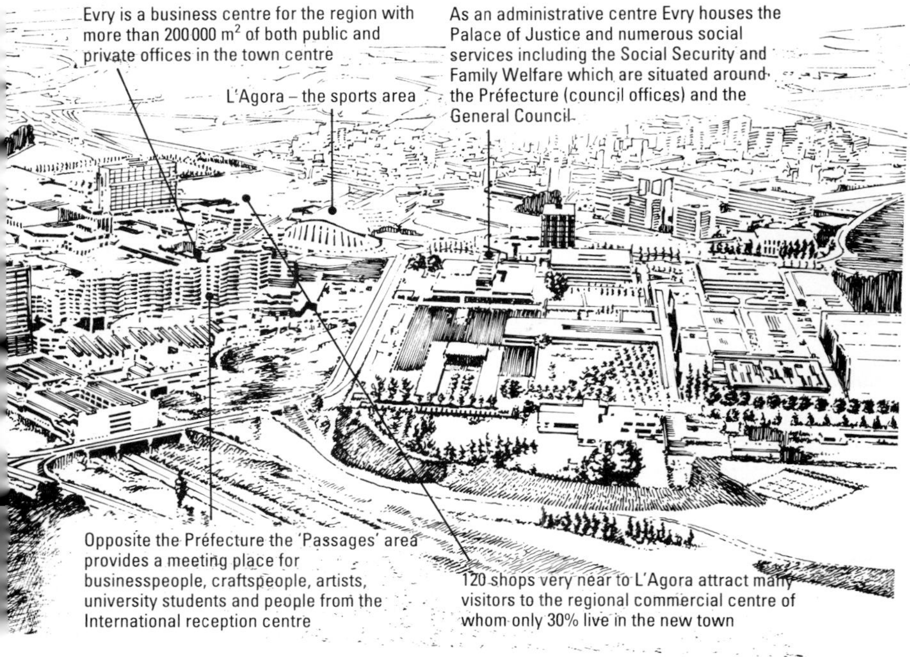

- The Réseau Express Régional (RER) which is a new express metro using surface suburban routes and going underground in the city centre. Figure 11.12 shows the first section, and it is planned to add two north–south links. In time it might cover 260 km, and link both airports and the new towns (page 88).

- Building 800 km of new motorways and urban expressways. This included three ring motorways:

  (a) The Boulevard Périphérique (Figures 11.12 and 12.4) which, already completed, forms an inner ring road.

  (b) The Rocade de Banlieve (an outer ring road) some 15 km out.

  (c) The Autoroute Interurbaine de Seine et Oise at 20 km from the city centre.

- To house the increasing population, six new towns (later reduced to five) were to be built. However, it was decided that instead of having a ring of new towns around the city (as in the case of London) which encouraged concentric growth, development should take place along two preferred axes – one on either side of the River Seine (Figure 11.12). Each new town would eventually have 300 000 to 800 000 inhabitants, and be linked to the 'City' by the RER.

  Figure 11.15 shows the layout of Evry new town. This was built to rehouse people displaced by slum clearances in central Paris, and to provide homes for the continuous increase in the capital's population. Industrial areas were built so that the inhabitants did not have far to travel to work, and cheaper types of housing were built nearest to these industrial areas. Industry was also placed near to the River Seine, main roads and the RER. The CBD, which would include several higher rise buildings, would have a modern pedestrianised shopping centre, considerable office development and three major car parks. The town would have its own community and medical centres, together with indoor and outdoor recreation amenities.

Present day concerns over the plan

- The Charles de Gaulle airport and its routeway to the Rhine has detracted from the preferential axis.

- A decreased rate of growth of Paris means the new towns need not exceed 200 000 inhabitants and one may not be built.

- The green belt has been lost in parts to developers.

- An increased demand for single family houses rather than for blocks of low flats.

- Demand for fewer motorways and better public transport.

- The loss of whole districts of inner Paris to the builders.

- The increasing height of office blocks in the CBD.

Evry is a business centre for the region with more than 200 000 m² of both public and private offices in the town centre

L'Agora – the sports area

As an administrative centre Evry houses the Palace of Justice and numerous social services including the Social Security and Family Welfare which are situated around the Préfecture (council offices) and the General Council.

Opposite the Préfecture the 'Passages' area provides a meeting place for businesspeople, craftspeople, artists, university students and people from the International reception centre

120 shops very near to L'Agora attract many visitors to the regional commercial centre of whom only 30% live in the new town

Randstad Holland

'Randstad Holland' is a collective term for a large number of towns lying close to each other in the west of the Netherlands. Although Figure 11.16 shows its location, there is no official boundary. Recently the Dutch have included a rich area of agricultural land, 'The Green Heart' as a part of Randstad. Randstad means 'The Ring, or Rim, City', and is a horseshoe shape of urban areas stretching from Dordrecht through Rotterdam, Delft, The Hague (the seat of government) Haarlem, Ijmuiden and Amsterdam (the capital) to Utrecht. As these towns grow, they are slowly joining together to form a conurbation with increasingly less open space between them. Figure 11.16 also shows the population growth of Randstad Holland.

Problems

- □ The rapid growth in population from 0.75 million in 1850 to about 6 million in 1980. This area covers 16% of the Netherlands, but houses 43% of its population. In 1978 the population density of the Randstad was given as 1049 people per km² – one of the highest in the world.

- □ A rapid rise in the birth rate between 1950 and 1970.

- □ An increase in immigrants either from former Dutch colonies in south-east Asia, or as 'guestworkers' (page 66). Many have been housed in the type of accommodation shown in Figure 11.17.

- □ The decay of housing in older cities, especially those properties which needed foundations sunk into the wet polders.

- □ Suburbanisation, as people are beginning to move out of the larger cities and into medium-sized centres surrounding these cities. Between 1970 and 1980 Amsterdam lost 15%, Rotterdam 16.7% and The Hague 18.7% of their population. Young people able to buy cars are the main age-group moving outwards and increasing the urban sprawl.

- □ An increase in traffic congestion, especially at rush hours, as most of the people moving out of the cities to live, still have to commute to work within those cities. This has also led to new metros and motorways being built.

- □ The growth of industry is taking over more agricultural land. It is claimed that Rotterdam itself needs an extra 6000 hectares a year.

- □ The concentration of industry has resulted in air and river pollution.

- □ More land has been lost to Schiphol Airport, and more is threatened by the demand for a second airport.

- □ As more towns, motorways and airports are built, the amount of land used for agriculture and recreation decreases. At present 40% of the Netherlands' agricultural produce comes from 'The Green Heart'.

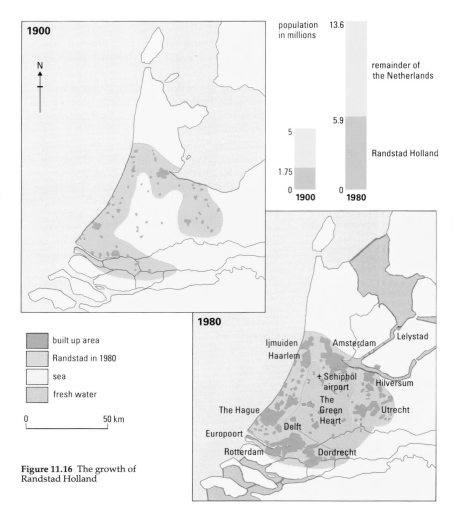

Figure 11.16 The growth of Randstad Holland

- □ A decline in the quality of life. Motorways and electricity pylons are visual eyesores and pollution increases ecological problems.

- □ The demand for 'fresh' water has resulted in the use of underground supplies which, in places, has resulted in salt infiltration.

- □ As there is no 'centre' to Randstad, it is difficult to produce a plan for the whole region.

△ Figure 11.17 Part of the Bijlmermeer housing estate in south-east Amsterdam

Lelystad – A new town on the polders

Lelystad is the capital of Eastern Flevoland the third completed Dutch polder, 1950–57, (a polder is an area of land, usually lying below sea level, which has been reclaimed from the sea).

Why was Lelystad built?

- [ ] As the administrative centre of Eastern Flevoland.

- [ ] To take overspill population from Amsterdam, partly people who had lived in slum property, and partly those who wished to live in a more rural environment.

- [ ] To reduce pressure by urban developers upon 'The Green Heart'.

- [ ] To provide jobs in an attempt to reduce the concentration in Amsterdam, and to reduce commuting from Lelystad into Amsterdam.

- [ ] To provide recreation amenities for the polder and Amsterdam.

△ **Figure 11.18** The new town of Lelystad

▽ **Figure 11.19** Structure plan of Lelystad

▽ **Figure 11.20** Neighbourhood unit – Lelystad (below right)

- shops and offices
- industrial sites
- residential areas in neighbourhood units
- main roads
- proposed railway
- parks and open space (mainly urban fringe)
- The Agora – theatre, swimming pool, library, sports centre, restaurant
- † crematorium and cemetery
- water
- pedestrian/cyclist bridges

The layout

In 1960 the task of building a medium-sized town in a short period of time in an area of swampy reed beds seemed unreal. Among the aims of the planners were – *'The creation of a living climate in which the inhabitants could combine the advantages of life in a smaller settlement (house with a garden at a price or rent within people's means, recreational facilities within a short distance of the dwelling, few or no 'environmental problems') with the advantages of life in a larger city (good communications, high level of services, better job opportunities).'*

The first houses, three storey dwellings, were completed in 1967, and by 1981 it had a population of 43 220 (see Figure 11.18). Figure 11.19 shows the planned layout of the new town. It is being built to try to segregate traffic from pedestrians. Each district is separated from another by main roads at a somewhat lower level, e.g. Houtribdreef and Polderdreef (Figures 11.18 and 11.19). The inhabitants cross these dividing roads by means of bridges built for pedestrians and cyclists.

The town was planned in four neighbourhood units situated around an elongated central area, and each divided into sub-neighbourhoods of 5–6000 inhabitants. The density of housing is low, usually less than 30 dwellings per hectare (Figure 11.20). The blocks of dwellings are grouped along narrow streets and small squares where there is little, or no, traffic. By 1981 80% of the dwellings built were single family houses with gardens and garages. The population structure is typical of a 'pioneer community' with a predominance of young adults (25–35 years) and young children (0–10), and relatively few older youths (15–25 years) and elderly people. The birth rate is higher, and the death rate lower, than in the remainder of the country.

At first jobs in the service industries seemed plentiful (e.g. the offices of the Polder Development Authority) but the most recent arrivals are now having to commute to Amsterdam for work. Both a main line railway and a motorway are planned to link Lelystad with the capital. A striking feature of the plan is the phased construction, making it possible to stop further expansion if necessary without giving the impression of the town being incomplete. Indeed the rapid fall in the birth rate after 1970 in the Netherlands suggests that Lelystad may only grow to 75 000 not the initially planned 100 000.

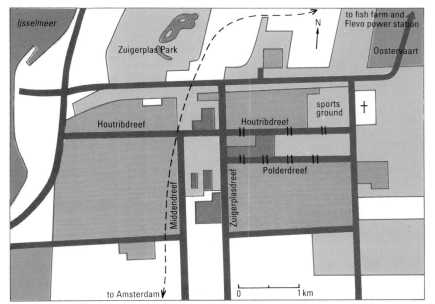

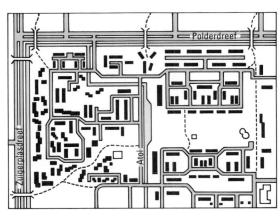

Motorways

Motorway building as we know it began in Germany in the 1930s. Today these autobahns (Austria and West Germany), autoroutes (Belgium and France), autostradas (Italy), autosnelweg (Netherlands), autopistas (Spain), and autoestrada (Portugal) have been linked across international boundaries to form the 'E' or Euroroute network as shown in Figure 12.1. (This system is not yet recognised by all European countries.)

Notice how these routes link up:

□ Major conurbations and cities

□ Major industrial areas with important ports

□ Eastern and western Europe

While they tend to avoid:

□ The centres of urban areas

□ High land areas (although the E25 and E35 do cross the Alps)

□ More rural and less densely populated areas

Motorways increase the accessibility of areas which can lead to an increase in economic activity:

□ By making journeys faster for the long-distance lorry driver, the tourist and the commuter.

□ By allowing larger, and therefore more economic, lorries to operate.

□ By attracting new industries, especially at interchange points.

□ Reducing accidents and congestion by having no on-coming traffic, no severe bends, no road junctions and by using several lanes.

▽ **Figure 12.1** The Euroroute motorway network

▷ **Figure 12.2** The Bolzano Brennero motorway, Italy

However, motorways do:

□ Take up much land – both urban and farmland. A one kilometre stretch of motorway takes up, on average, 16 hectares of land.

□ Have high construction and maintenance costs.

□ Still suffer from congestion during maintenance, and at their ends during peak periods.

□ Suffer from serious pile-ups especially in times of extreme weather conditions.

Figure 12.2 shows part of an autostrada in Italy.

West German autobahns

The rapid growth of motorisation in West Germany would not have been possible without many extensions and improvements to the road network. The length of the autobahn network has more than trebled since 1950 (2100 km in 1950, 7500 km in 1980). This gives Germany, after the USA, the largest motorway network in the world and there are no tolls to be paid on the autobahns.

Figure 12.3 shows the volume of traffic on the major West German autobahns.

1 Where do the routes numbered 1–8 lead to?

2 (a) Describe the major pattern illustrated by the map.

(b) Give reasons for your answers.

3 What do the West Germans mean when they refer to the concentration of autobahns 'in the Frankfurt cross'?

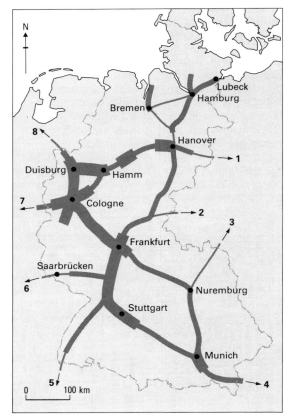

◁ **Figure 12.3** West German traffic flows

Road traffic – vehicles per day

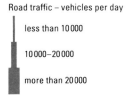

less than 10 000

10 000–20 000

more than 20 000

Urban transport

Some problems

Congestion caused by private cars, service lorries and public transport can cause havoc in cities. This problem is naturally increased during rush hour peaks. Transport is also responsible for noise and fumes, which are particularly serious near urban motorways.

Lead pollution from engine exhausts can lead to brain damage and mental retardation.

Because of heavier traffic in the city accidents occur more frequently between cars, other forms of transport and pedestrians. In addition the amount of land given over to roads and car parks means less space in the city.

Urban motorways (Figure 12.4) are also making us wonder if towns are designed for cars or for people. Some people think that urban motorways are a blessing because they help the flow of traffic, they make driving easier, they reduce congestion in inner-city areas, and they reduce accidents by segregating cars from pedestrians. Other people think, on the other hand, that they take up valuable land, their construction results in the demolition of buildings, they are expensive to construct, they increase noise and air pollution to residents living nearby, and they devalue adjacent housing.

Commuting

The daily movement in all urban areas of Europe shows a distinctive pattern of two peak periods of high intensity associated with the movement to work in the morning, and home again in the late afternoon. A commuter is a person who lives in a smaller town or village surrounding a larger town or city, and who travels to that larger town or city for work. The increase in car ownership and the improvement in road networks has led to more commuters living at an increasingly further distance from their place of work. This has, in turn, led to increasingly larger commuter 'hinterlands' surrounding the larger cities.

Figure 12.5 shows commuters into and out of Mulheim which is in the Ruhr district of West Germany. How well does it agree with the expected pattern of commuting?

1 The greater the distance to travel, the fewer the commuters (compare Dortmund and Recklinghausen with Essen and Duisburg). How far is it between Dortmund and Mulheim?

2 Mulheim has a net loss of commuters to surrounding larger cities. Give three examples.

3 Mulheim has a net gain of commuters from surrounding smaller towns. Give three examples.

4 People will travel further if there are good communications. Why do some inhabitants of Mulheim work in Cologne which is 65 km distant?

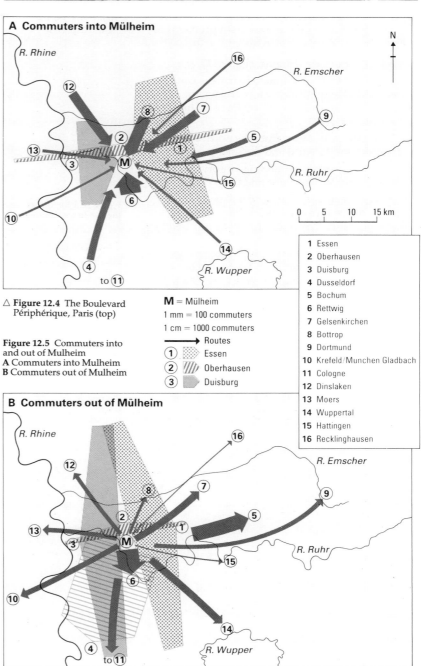

△ **Figure 12.4** The Boulevard Périphérique, Paris (top)

Figure 12.5 Commuters into and out of Mulheim
A Commuters into Mulheim
B Commuters out of Mulheim

M = Mülheim
1 mm = 100 commuters
1 cm = 1000 commuters
→ Routes
① Essen
② Oberhausen
③ Duisburg

1	Essen
2	Oberhausen
3	Duisburg
4	Dusseldorf
5	Bochum
6	Rettwig
7	Gelsenkirchen
8	Bottrop
9	Dortmund
10	Krefeld/Munchen Gladbach
11	Cologne
12	Dinslaken
13	Moers
14	Wuppertal
15	Hattingen
16	Recklinghausen

Paris
– an attempted solution

Urban motorways

Napoleon Bonaparte, in the early nineteenth century, built a road network which radiated outwards from the Arc de Triomphe in Paris. However, by the early 1960s the increase in cars and lorries had led to acute traffic congestion within the capital as all the routes met in the city centre. Major improvements were essential to help the economic and social life of the city. The first major scheme was the construction of the 'Périphérique' which was an inner-ring road surrounding the centre of the old city – 'Paris Ville' (see Figures 12.4 and 12.6). The Périphérique was built in the 1960s and greatly reduced the volume of traffic, together with the associated problems of noise, fumes and accidents in the city centre.

The A86 'L'autoroute Urbaine' (Figure 12.6)

The volume of traffic continued to increase and so it was decided to build a new motorway link, encircling the eastern parts of Paris. The two main aims were:

(a) To link the motorways from the north and south (Autoroutes du Nord and du Soleil).

(b) To link the rapidly expanding airports of Roissy-Charles de Gaulle and Orly.

The A86 between the A1 and A6 will be 36 km in length, and parts are expected to have 60 000 vehicles per hour. The route should be finished by 1987.

Figure 12.6 also shows the major motorways radiating outwards from Paris. Try to find out to which parts of France the following roads lead: A1, A4, A6, A10 and A13. Using Figure 11.12 (page 82), how do these motorways link up with the five new towns surrounding Paris?

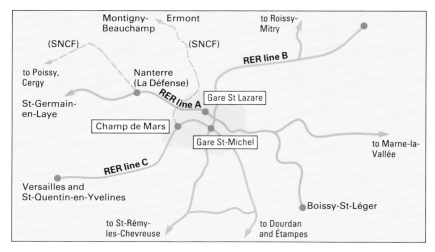

△ **Figure 12.7** The RER – Réseau Express Régional

The RER (Réseau Express Régional)

This is a high speed, electric underground system (Paris already had a Metro) aimed at linking the north and west of Paris with the south and east, and the north and east with the south and west. By the mid 1980s the system should have linked with both the existing underground system and also with the state-run railways (SNCF). The RER will consist, intially, of three lines, numbered A, B and C (see Figure 12.7). The RER is aimed to link:

□ New centres of commerce such as La Défense (page 83) and the new food market at Rungis. Trains from La Défense (Nanterre station) take only 5 minutes to reach the city centre by travelling at speeds of up to 96 km per hour (Figures 12.8 and 12.9).

□ The two large airports of Orly and Charles de Gaulle with each other, and the city centre.

□ The five new towns surrounding Paris. A branch of line A goes to Marne-la-Vallée and, with the SNCF to Cergy-Pontoise; line C reaches St Quentin-en-Yvelines, Evry and Melun-Sénart (see Figure 11.12).

□ With the state-operated railways (SNCF). By 1984 links had been made with:

(a) Cergy-Poissy and the RER line A at Nanterre station.

(b) Montigny-Beauchamp and the RER line C at Champ de Mars station (Figure 12.7).

▽ **Figure 12.6** Motorways and the A86 in the Paris region

———— Périphérique
—A1— autoroute (motorway)
—A86— A86 complete
- - - - A86 under construction
· · · · · A86 proposed
✈ airport

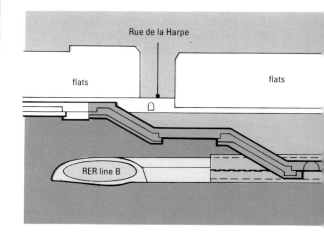

△ **Figure 12.8** RER station –
Auber, Paris

▽ **Figure 12.9** RER train at
Auber station

▽ **Figure 12.10** Plan for the new
'Gare St Michel' (bottom)

Present and future plans

☐ By 1985 it is hoped to operate between 24 and 30 trains per hour on each RER line (Gare St Lazare alone is expected to handle 16 000 travellers per hour).

☐ The building of a new station at Saint-Michel where lines B and C cross at different levels, and where there is a SNCF station (Figure 12.10). Here some 45–50 trains per hour will carry shoppers, office workers and tourists. Different levels and exits will be linked by escalators and moving pavements. The location of the station coincided with the site of the original settlement of Paris, and archaeologists are hoping for discoveries during the excavations.

☐ A line going around the outskirts of Paris – the equivalent of an outer ring road.

☐ The development of an aerotrain.

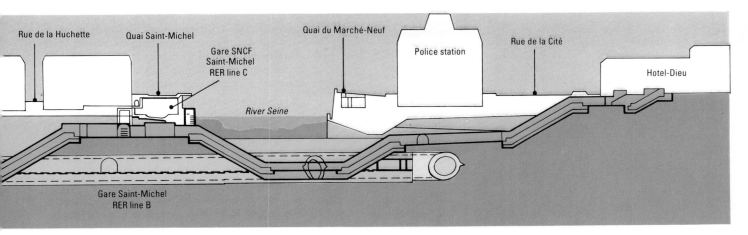

Rail

Trans-Europ Expresses (TEE) and Inter-city trains

These link most major urban centres in western Europe and provide a regular, fast and clean journey, which cuts across national frontiers.

▽ **Figure 12.11** Trans-Europ-Express routes   ▷ **Figure 12.12** A Trans-Europ-Express train

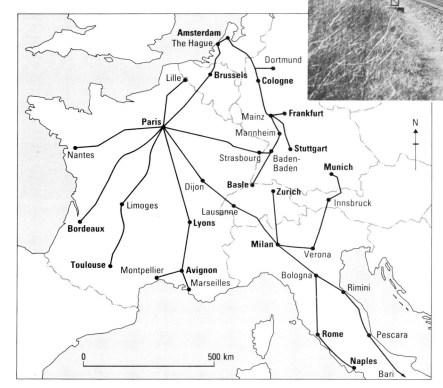

Using the map in Figure 12.11, locate the following TEE services:

Beethoven	Amsterdam	→Frankfurt
Edelweiss	Amsterdam	→Zurich
Rembrandt	Amsterdam	→Stuttgart
Erasmus	Amsterdam	→Innsbruck
Aquitaine	Bordeaux	→Paris
Merkur	Copenhagen	→Karlsruhe
Rheingold	Amsterdam	→Milan
Ligure	Milan	→Marseilles
Le Résseau	Geneva	→Barcelona
Roland	Milan	→Bremen
Le Capital	Paris	→Toulouse
Mistral	Paris	→Nice
Parsifal	Paris	→Hamburg
Mont Blanc	Hamburg	→Geneva
Romulus	Rome	→Vienna
Le Cisalpin	Paris	→Milan
Catalan-Talgo	Geneva	→Barcelona
Prince Eugen	Hamburg	→Vienna
Chopin	Moscow	→Vienna

The Mistral, for example, has dining cars, bars, hairdressing salons, shops, reclining seats, and air conditioning (Figure 12.12). This train takes its name from the cold wind which also travels down the Rhône valley at high speeds (page 20).

'Europole' – the train of the future?

The scheme favours a 'Hovertrain' propelled by a sound-proofed turbo jet on a cushion of air. Each carriage would carry 80 passengers. However, despite its technical, economic and political advantages, this scheme has yet to gain public support. Its advantages would include:

☐ Linking up administrative centres within the EEC i.e. Strasbourg (Seat of European Parliament), Brussels (headquarters of the European Commission) and Luxembourg (Court of Justice and European Investment Bank). The journey from Brussels to Strasbourg via Luxembourg would take 103 minutes.

☐ Linking Basle (which hosts meetings of world bankers) and Geneva (United Nations Economic Commission for Europe).

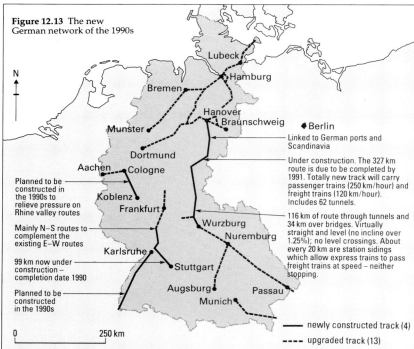

Figure 12.13 The new German network of the 1990s

Berlin
Linked to German ports and Scandinavia

Under construction. The 327 km route is due to be completed by 1991. Totally new track will carry passenger trains (250 km/hour) and freight trains (120 km/hour). Includes 62 tunnels.

116 km of route through tunnels and 34 km over bridges. Virtually straight and level (no incline over 1.25%); no level crossings. About every 20 km are station sidings which allow express trains to pass freight trains at speed – neither stopping.

Planned to be constructed in the 1990s to relieve pressure on Rhine valley routes

Mainly N–S routes to complement the existing E–W routes

99 km now under construction – completion date 1990

Planned to be constructed in the 1990s

—— newly constructed track (4)
- - - - upgraded track (13)

0 ___ 250 km

- It could stimulate economic activity in parts of Europe suffering most from economic and social decline – Liège (Belgium), Metz and Nancy (France). It could also create activity in the Ardennes and Alsace.
- The elevated monorail would use little land, and reduce track maintenance to a minimum, since there would be no contact with the train and so no friction.
- Hovertrains can cope with steeper gradients than conventional trains.
- The EEC have the money in their regional funds, while the balance would be easier to pay as several countries would be involved.
- Future extensions could be from Strasbourg to Frankfurt (reducing pressure on the overcrowded German rail system in the Rhine Valley) and to Brussels and London (linked by the Channel Tunnel). Europole could be in operation before 1990, but only if first of all it can gain public support.

French railways (SNCF)

The construction of the TGV (Train à Grande Vitesse – very high speed train) and track began in the 1970s (Figure 12.14). A new line was laid between Paris and Lyons, but bypassing Dijon which was on the existing route. The new electric railway, on which a world rail speed record of 380 km per hour (237 miles per hour) was achieved during trials in February 1981, is designed entirely for passenger trains (freight still goes via Dijon). There are no level crossings and no tunnels, and the line follows the land contours similar to a motorway. The southern section was opened in September 1981, and the northern section in September 1983. The distance of 422 km (300 miles) between Paris and Lyons is covered in 2 hours. There are 18 services a day on this, the world's fastest passenger service, and the present day maximum speed of 270 km per hour is likely to be increased as the TGV and the track prove themselves. Each TGV has first and second class accommodation and a bar. Meals are served at passengers own seats in two of the first class cars. Normal fares apply at off-peak times, but on busier days and times a supplement is charged. Each coach is supervised by a stewardess.

Routes These are shown in Figure 12.15.

Advantages of the TGV

- Boost to France's image as an advanced technological country, and especially to SNCF.
- SNCF after years of loss-making have a route making a considerable profit.
- High speeds mean the journey from central Paris to central Lyons is quicker than by air.
- Improved standards of comfort.
- Helps decentralisation from Paris, with Lyons in particular benefitting.
- The construction of 109 new trains together with possible future export orders, has led to an increase in employment.
- Reduces congestion on main roads, and reduces reliability upon the often trouble-torn road haulage industry.

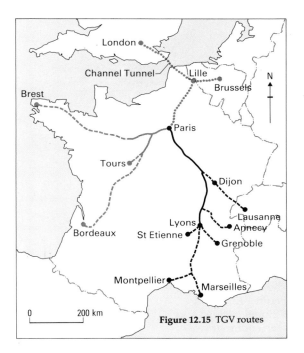

1 New track and high running speeds are only found on the Paris-Lyons section, but TGV have extended their journeys to Marseilles and Montpellier (under 5 hours to the Mediterranean), to Grenoble (3½ hours to the Alps) and Switzerland.

in use 1984 (Sud-est)
— new track
----- TGV on existing track

2 The now accepted 'Atlantique' extension which will include 300 km of new track, will eventually reach Brest, Tours and Bordeaux. The journey to Bordeaux would take 3 hours compared to the 6 hours in 1950.

accepted 1984 (Atlantique)
— new track
----- existing track

3 A possible north-east extension to Lille and Brussels and, if the Channel Tunnel is built, to London.

future proposals (Nord)
·········

Figure 12.15 TGV routes

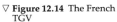
▽ **Figure 12.14** The French TGV

Disadvantages of the TGV

- A time of recession and a shortage of money, therefore fewer people may use it.
- High costs for the new trains.
- Environmental and ecological opposition.
- Many kilometres pass through high quality farmland yet no stations.
- Opposition from air companies who are being undercut both in terms of times and costs by TGV.

The SNCF, after years of losses and redundancies, have created for themselves a new image. In 1983 over 4000 jobs were created, 4 lines re-opened, car parks built at stations, new rolling stock built and better family bargains introduced. Unlike most countries in Europe, France is seeing the railways increasing in traffic, both freight and passenger.

Water transport

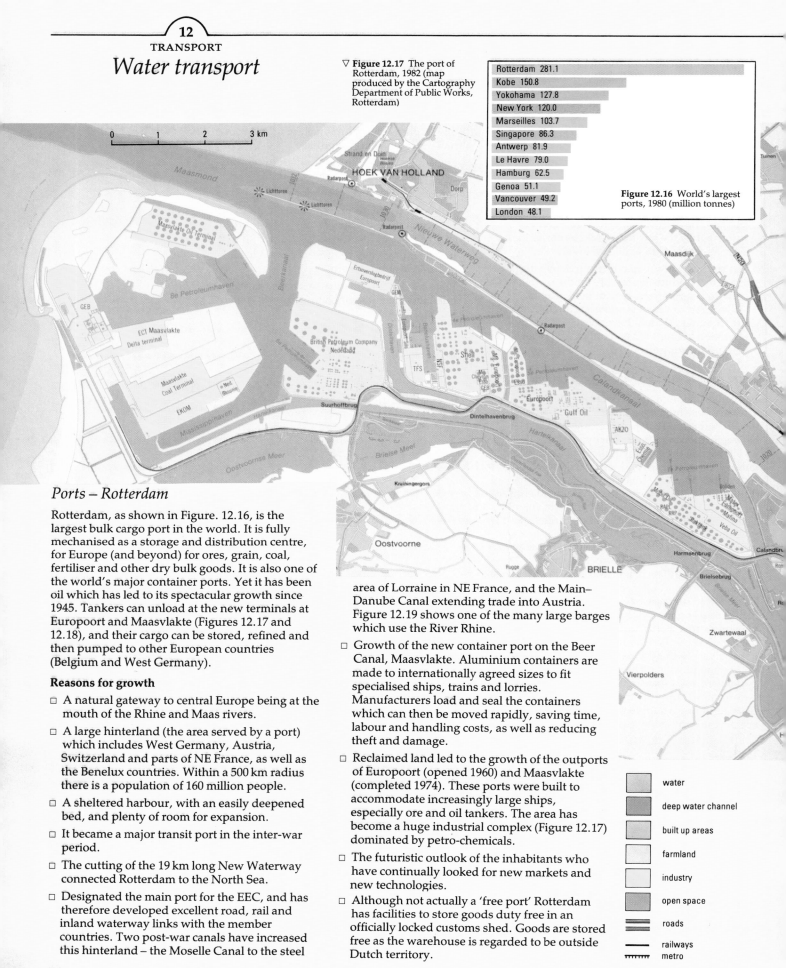

▽ **Figure 12.17** The port of Rotterdam, 1982 (map produced by the Cartography Department of Public Works, Rotterdam)

Port	million tonnes
Rotterdam	281.1
Kobe	150.8
Yokohama	127.8
New York	120.0
Marseilles	103.7
Singapore	86.3
Antwerp	81.9
Le Havre	79.0
Hamburg	62.5
Genoa	51.1
Vancouver	49.2
London	48.1

Figure 12.16 World's largest ports, 1980 (million tonnes)

Key:
- water
- deep water channel
- built up areas
- farmland
- industry
- open space
- roads
- railways
- metro

Ports – Rotterdam

Rotterdam, as shown in Figure. 12.16, is the largest bulk cargo port in the world. It is fully mechanised as a storage and distribution centre, for Europe (and beyond) for ores, grain, coal, fertiliser and other dry bulk goods. It is also one of the world's major container ports. Yet it has been oil which has led to its spectacular growth since 1945. Tankers can unload at the new terminals at Europoort and Maasvlakte (Figures 12.17 and 12.18), and their cargo can be stored, refined and then pumped to other European countries (Belgium and West Germany).

Reasons for growth

□ A natural gateway to central Europe being at the mouth of the Rhine and Maas rivers.

□ A large hinterland (the area served by a port) which includes West Germany, Austria, Switzerland and parts of NE France, as well as the Benelux countries. Within a 500 km radius there is a population of 160 million people.

□ A sheltered harbour, with an easily deepened bed, and plenty of room for expansion.

□ It became a major transit port in the inter-war period.

□ The cutting of the 19 km long New Waterway connected Rotterdam to the North Sea.

□ Designated the main port for the EEC, and has therefore developed excellent road, rail and inland waterway links with the member countries. Two post-war canals have increased this hinterland – the Moselle Canal to the steel area of Lorraine in NE France, and the Main–Danube Canal extending trade into Austria. Figure 12.19 shows one of the many large barges which use the River Rhine.

□ Growth of the new container port on the Beer Canal, Maasvlakte. Aluminium containers are made to internationally agreed sizes to fit specialised ships, trains and lorries. Manufacturers load and seal the containers which can then be moved rapidly, saving time, labour and handling costs, as well as reducing theft and damage.

□ Reclaimed land led to the growth of the outports of Europoort (opened 1960) and Maasvlakte (completed 1974). These ports were built to accommodate increasingly large ships, especially ore and oil tankers. The area has become a huge industrial complex (Figure 12.17) dominated by petro-chemicals.

□ The futuristic outlook of the inhabitants who have continually looked for new markets and new technologies.

□ Although not actually a 'free port' Rotterdam has facilities to store goods duty free in an officially locked customs shed. Goods are stored free as the warehouse is regarded to be outside Dutch territory.

Land use – Rotterdam to Maasvlakte

Most industrial activity takes place along the south bank of the New Waterway (Figure 12.17). Eemhaven has become a container basin, while west of Pernis are the huge oil refineries belonging to Shell and Chevron. Botlek grew as the shipbuilding and repair port and although the tonnage launched has decreased considerably, new chemical industries and grain storage facilities have increased. A large modern refuse processing plant has been built on the north bank of the Botlek harbour processing both town, industrial and chemical wastes. Around Rozenburg the land was only one metre above sea-level and suffered from frequent flooding. Today it has been raised to 5 metres, though much has since been removed for docks.

Between Maasluis and Brielle are four parallel waterways, each with a well-defined function (see also Figure 12.18).

(a) The New Waterway acting as a fast highway for ocean-going ships from Rotterdam.

(b) The Caland Canal giving access to Europoort.

(c) The Hartel Canal for inland shipping from Europoort and the hinterland rivers of the Waal, Rhine, Maas and Scheldt.

(d) The Brielle lake which is exclusively recreational.

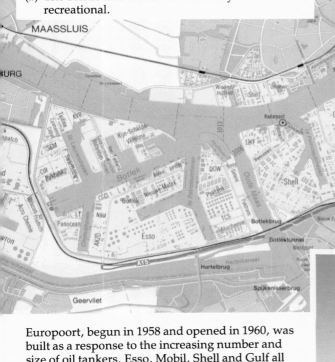

Europoort, begun in 1958 and opened in 1960, was built as a response to the increasing number and size of oil tankers. Esso, Mobil, Shell and Gulf all have refineries here. A deep-dredged channel (the Maasmond) allows large tankers to enter the port. Maasvlakte was completed in 1974 and has an electricity generating station, a trans-shipment depot for iron ore and coal, an oil terminal, a container terminal and a liquid gas plant. However, due to environmental objections, the long commuting distances, and the recession in the world's steel industry, the plan to build a second Dutch iron and steel works here has been shelved.

△ **Figure 12.18** (Top) Europoort and Maasvlakte looking north-west. On the left is the recreational area of the Brielle Lake (Brieise Meer) and next to it the Hartel Canal. Notice the refineries, and on the right the Caland Canal. In the background is Maasvlakte with its electricity power station and oil terminal. You should be able to identify these features on the map of Rotterdam (Figure 12.17).

◁ **Figure 12.19** Coal carrying barges on the Rhine, Rotterdam

Inland waterways

▽ **Figure 12.20** Inland waterways

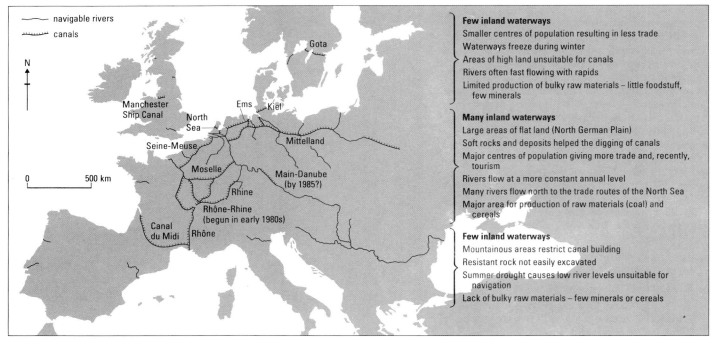

Figure 12.20 Inland waterways

Legend:
- —— navigable rivers
- ⌐⌐⌐ canals

N

0 — 500 km

Map labels: Gota, Manchester Ship Canal, North Sea, Ems, Kiel, Mittelland, Seine-Meuse, Moselle, Main-Danube (by 1985?), Rhine, Rhône-Rhine (begun in early 1980s), Canal du Midi, Rhône

Few inland waterways
- Smaller centres of population resulting in less trade
- Waterways freeze during winter
- Areas of high land unsuitable for canals
- Rivers often fast flowing with rapids
- Limited production of bulky raw materials – little foodstuff, few minerals

Many inland waterways
- Large areas of flat land (North German Plain)
- Soft rocks and deposits helped the digging of canals
- Major centres of population giving more trade and, recently, tourism
- Rivers flow at a more constant annual level
- Many rivers flow north to the trade routes of the North Sea
- Major area for production of raw materials (coal) and cereals

Few inland waterways
- Mountainous areas restrict canal building
- Resistant rock not easily excavated
- Summer drought causes low river levels unsuitable for navigation
- Lack of bulky raw materials – few minerals or cereals

The major canal building period in Europe was in the late eighteenth and early nineteenth centuries (Figure 12.20). Following that, canal transport declined in the face of competition firstly from the railway and later by road.

Increasing importance of inland waterways

- ☐ Despite its slowness and inflexibility of routes, water transport remains much cheaper than road, rail or air. It is most cost-effective for moving bulky goods which are non-perishable, and give little profit in comparison to their weight.

- ☐ The increase in road and rail charges following the rise in oil prices of the 1970s.

- ☐ The development of large 4400-tonne barges which can be propelled by 'push-barges'. Each barge can carry the equivalent of 110 railtrucks or 220 twenty-tonne lorries. These larger barges have also reduced labour, fuel and loading costs. Figures 12.21 and 12.22 show Rhine traffic.

- ☐ European agreements to increase canals and navigable rivers so that large sized barges can eventually travel between the Mediterranean Sea, the North Sea and the Black Sea.

Recent improvements

- ☐ The Rhône–Saône was mainly canalised in the 1950s and 1960s but only became fully operational in 1983.

- ☐ The Moselle Canal linking the Ruhr coalfield with Lorraine's iron ore.

- ☐ Rhine–Main–Danube project should be completed in 1985 with the final stretch being between Nuremberg and Regensburg.

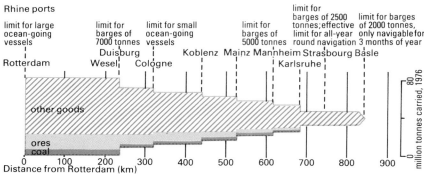

Rhine ports

limit for large ocean-going vessels — Rotterdam

limit for barges of 7000 tonnes — Wesel / Duisburg

limit for small ocean-going vessels — Cologne

limit for barges of 5000 tonnes — Koblenz

limit for barges of 2500 tonnes; effective limit for all-year round navigation — Mainz Mannheim / Karlsruhe / Strasbourg

limit for barges of 2000 tonnes, only navigable for 3 months of year — Basle

other goods

ores
coal

Distance from Rotterdam (km): 0, 100, 200, 300, 400, 500, 600, 700, 800, 900

million tonnes carried, 1976 (0–80)

△ **Figure 12.21** Traffic on the Rhine (middle)

△ **Figure 12.22** Barges of several nations dock at a pier on the Rhine on journeys between points as far apart as Rotterdam and Basle

- ☐ Rhône–Rhine Canal. Approval was given in 1982 to build a 229 km section linking these two major waterways and so allowing the new 4400-tonne barges to sail the 1580 km between Marseilles and Rotterdam. This link between Dôle and Mulhouse will have 24 locks, 17 ascending the 158 metres from the Rhône, and 7 descending the 106 metres to the Rhine.

Tourism Although the canals of Amsterdam and Venice were mainly used for commerce, they now benefit greatly from tourism. Other canals (e.g. Canal du Midi) are being re-opened.

Air transport

Schiphol Airport

In the Middle Ages, when the Haarlemmermeer (Haarlem lake) was still an arm of the sea, the extreme north-east was funnel-shaped, causing gales which wrecked many ships. It was given the name 'Schipshol' meaning 'Hell of ships'. In 1573 a naval battle took place here between the Dutch and the Spaniards. The lake was drained in 1852 into a fertile polder, and part of the flat area of land was officially opened as Schiphol Airport in 1963.

☐ It has been built on a large expanse of flat land with ample room for its continual expansion (a second terminal building is scheduled for 1989), and with clear views for aircraft landing.

☐ It is in the centre of the Randstad conurbation (page 84) in which six million people live. It is only 10 km from Amsterdam and 70 km from Rotterdam.

☐ It was adjacent to the A4 highway which has since been diverted around the airport to make more space; turned into a six lane motorway; and taken under the runways through a 500 metre tunnel.

☐ The opening of a new railway from Amsterdam to Schiphol (1978), and The Hague (1981).

☐ The airport has relatively few days of fog, snow and high winds, which means delays due to adverse weather conditions are limited.

☐ It is sufficiently distant from large urban areas to reduce noise and air pollution, and the risk of accidents.

☐ It is a long way from other airports reducing traffic control problems.

The airport has become, with Frankfurt and London Heathrow, one of the three largest in Europe. Figure 12.23 shows the layout and expanse of the airport. The terminal buildings contain banks, insurance companies and exchange offices. It has large car parks and restaurants not just for the flight passengers, but for the 1.5 million tourists who just visit the airport each year. Nearby are three large hotels and several companies depending to a large extent on Schiphol for transport by air of their products. In 1980 it was estimated that 200 000 people earned a living either directly or indirectly from the airport. There are also public bonded warehouses.

Public bonded warehouses

The opening in 1964 of a public bonded warehouse, the first 'bonded zone' at any international airport, has helped to turn Schiphol into a major distribution and trading centre for airfreight. '*The importance of these public warehouses is that foreign firms, mainly from outside Europe, which have business interests in Europe, North Africa or the Near East, can set up a central store for spare parts in the public bonded warehouse at Schiphol for their goods which have been airfreighted to Schiphol in bulk. They do not import these goods into the Netherlands and consequently do not have to pay any import duties. Within certain limits the goods may be processed, provided there is no actual manufacture, and they can immediately be delivered by plane to the required destination abroad once a call for delivery has been received by telephone, telex or cable. The goods concerned are mainly high-grade such as computer parts, cameras etc.*' (Schiphol Airport Authority)

Growth in air passengers

passengers in millions

Paris	1974	1982
Orly-Sud	7.4	7.4
Orly-Ouest	5.2	8.9
Charles de Gaulle 1	2.5	7.0
Charles de Gaulle 2	–	6.2
Le Bourget	1.7	–
Total	**16.8**	**29.5**

Schiphol (Amsterdam)
passengers in millions

1969 3.4

1979 10.1

1989 35 (estimate)

◁ **Figure 12.23** Schiphol airport, Amsterdam

Traditional patterns

Markets

Open markets are still a typical feature of European life, and remain an important method of shopping in many European cities as well as in most smaller towns and villages. Shoppers usually find that the goods on sale in such markets are cheaper than in larger shops because:

☐ Often the produce is sold direct from a local farm or small factory.

☐ Stallholders have lower overheads, not having the rates or rent of the city centre shop, or its large volume of stock, nor counter or checkout assistants.

Advantages

☐ The relative cheapness compared to city centre shops.

☐ The selling of low order goods, many of which include fresh fruit and vegetables.

☐ Shoppers can compare quality and price.

☐ Usually open six days a week.

☐ They provide a personal service, especially with many stalls being small family concerns. In a small community they provide an important social meeting place.

☐ They are often in accessible locations.

Location These markets are likely to be found in the centre of small towns in the old market square (Figure 13.1), or in older inner city areas adjacent to the CBD of larger cities (but just outside it to take advantage of cheaper land). In older market towns they do add to the atmosphere of the settlement but can lead to increased traffic congestion on market days.

△ **Figure 13.1** Open air market, Bruges, Belgium

▷ **Figure 13.2** The flower market at Singel, Amsterdam

▽ **Figure 13.3** Alkmaar cheese market

Specialist markets also exist in larger towns. In Amsterdam and the surrounding region examples include:

- Waterlooplein or 'Flea Market' where a large second-hand market sells everything from clothes and household goods to furniture, books and records.
- Singel flower market (Figure 13.2) where freshly cut flowers from the local polders and glass-houses are sold.
- Alkmaar cheese market (Figure 13.3).

Local shopping and tourism

In many parts of Europe, the relatively recent growth in tourism has increased the potential income for local shopowners. As a result many stallholders and shopkeepers, especially in the drier, sunnier southern parts of Europe, have combined the selling of local produce with local crafts.

Figure 13.4 is a view from the Rialto Bridge in Venice. Traditionally this was the major market for the Venetians, but with so many tourists visiting the bridge, many shops have turned to selling glasswear, clothes and other handmade goods.

Figure 13.5 was taken in Split in Yugoslavia. Here the remains of the walls of Diocletian's Palace (a Roman emperor around A.D. 300) divide the market into two parts. On one side of the wall is the traditional market selling locally grown fruit, vegetables and flowers, whereas on the other side are stalls selling mainly leather goods and hand-carved wooden ornaments, made locally, to tourists.

Local craft shops The growth of tourism in an area such as Rhodes, a Greek island off the south-west coast of Turkey, has led to the increase in the manufacture of local handicrafts which in turn has led to the increase in craft shops. Rhodes was famous in Roman times for producing ceramic tiles, which decorated the floors of large houses and public buildings. Today ceramics are still made in small workshops, and sold to tourists from the shops (Figure 13.6). Socrates Street, in Rhodes town, has many open-fronted shops selling jewellery of gold and silver worked by local craftsmen, and the ceramics and vases produced in small factories.

◁ **Figure 13.4** Shops near the Rialto Bridge, Venice

▽ **Figure 13.5** Open air market in Split, Yugoslavia (below)

▽ **Figure 13.6** Tourist shops in Socrates Street, Rhodes town

City centres

The main advantage of the city centre is its accessibility, since it forms a junction of all the main roads from the suburbs and the surrounding towns and villages.

In recent years, partly as a result of increasing traffic congestion where these routes met, many old towns and city centres have been transformed into traffic-free pedestrian precincts. Precincts are created for the convenience, safety and comfort of the shopper. The streets are often tree-lined, and contain flower beds to make them more attractive, and seats for the weary to rest.

Chief characteristics of the city centre

- The large variety of shops and the goods they sell, and their large volume of stock.

- The high land values which increases competition between shops for sales, and often leads to a development of two or three stories to save space.

- Large multi-functional department stores and nationwide supermarkets both needing a rapid turnover of stock.

- Many specialist shops selling high order durable goods, such as shoes, clothes, jewellery, electrical and furniture goods which generate high profit margins. These 'comparison' goods are bought less frequently, but customers like to be able to choose between various styles and prices.

- The presence of commercial functions such as banks and building societies, as well as service functions such as travel agencies, cafés and hairdressers.

- The cheaper priced supermarkets and specialist shops mean people will travel from a large trade area (even beyond the city boundary) but perhaps only weekly or monthly.

Redeveloped city centres

Some cities have totally rebuilt their shopping centres in the CBD – most of these being over 50 000 m². Many of these centres such as La Place des Halles in Strasbourg, Le Polygone in Montpellier and in such new towns as Evry, are multi-functional. That means that as well as shops, a wider range of economic, recreational and social functions are found making this the major area of tertiary employment in the city.

Figure 13.8 Lille town plan (Reproduced under licence to Chas. E. Goad Ltd., Hatfield, England) This shows a plan of the shops in one of the main streets.

1 Why has the Rue de Béthune been blocked off at each end?
2 Which shops or firms are multi-national?
3 Can you classify the buildings under headings such as: department stores, specialist shops, commerce and entertainment?

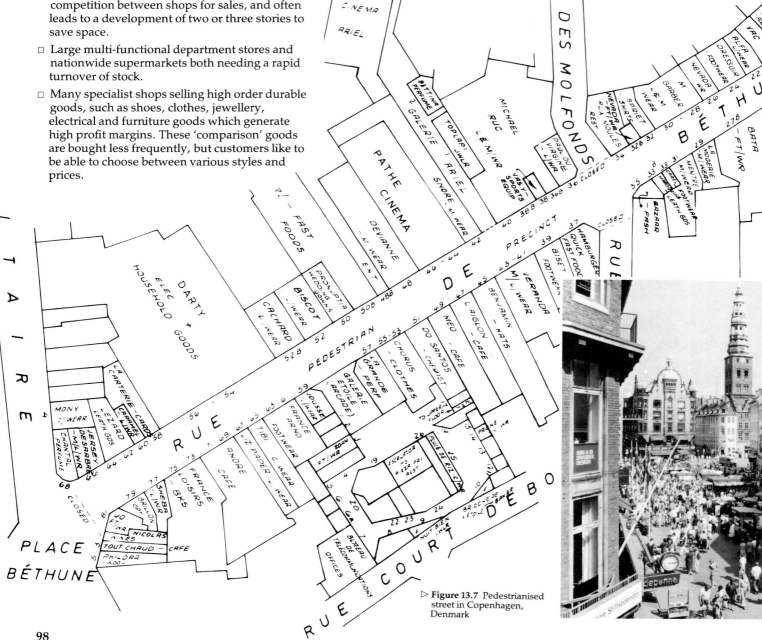

▷ **Figure 13.7** Pedestrianised street in Copenhagen, Denmark

Hypermarkets

▽ **Figure 13.9** Large Carrefour hypermarket, with parking for hundreds of cars, France

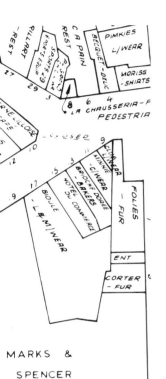

A hypermarket is a large shopping centre, usually built on one level, and never less than 30 000 m² of floor space. It is usually situated on the edge of a large city, and is aimed at motorists by trying to attract them from the congested city centres (Figure 13.9). The first hypermarket was opened in France in 1960, and by 1980 there were over 300 of them. The largest is on the outskirts of Toulouse. It was opened in 1972 with car parking for 4000 cars, and 60 checkouts. French hypermarkets were originally developed as a single store, but during the 1970s this changed and by 1980 most new and existing developments consisted of a large supermarket as the main tenant, with perhaps 10 to 30 smaller specialist shops and services within the centre.

What does a hypermarket provide?

Hypermarkets will have most of the following features:

□ A large volume of stock

□ A wide range of goods

□ A warehouse type of layout in a single-storey building

□ Large trolleys for bulk buying

□ Competitive prices

□ Numerous cash checkout points

□ Restaurants, play areas, rest rooms and perhaps even a petrol station

Where are hypermarkets built?

Some of the main location factors in determining where hypermarkets are built are shown in Figure 13.9. Notice the following:

□ Out of town location where rates and rents are lower allowing for the larger floor area and the cheaper prices.

□ Plenty of space for possible future expansion.

□ Large amount of cheap land available for large, free car park.

□ Out of town site to avoid opposition from CBD shopowners.

□ Near to several large urban areas for customers.

□ Next to a main road, or ideally next to a motorway intersection for easy delivery of goods and access for shoppers. This avoids local traffic congestion (as in the CBD) and increases the trade area of the hypermarket.

Sun, sand and sea
The traditional long-stay resort

Benidorm

This is regarded as the most popular European resort. Various holiday brochures describe it as follows.

Location On the Costa Blanca, 'The White Coast', 40 km and one hour's coach drive, north of the regional capital and airport of Alicante (Figure 14.1). The original settlement was a small, white-walled fishing village set on a small headland which separated two extensive beaches. These two long, curving sandy beaches are known as the Levante (to the north) as this is the one over which the sun rises, and the Poniente (to the south) which is where the sun eventually sets. Behind the resort rise steep, rounded hills covered in orange and lemon groves.

Climate (Figure 14.2) Summers are both hot (what is the average daily maximum temperature in July?) sunny (how many hours of sunshine are expected in an average July day?) and dry (how much rain is likely to fall in July and August?). Although winters are wetter, they are still mild (what is the average daily temperature in January?)

Accommodation The beaches are fringed by modern, high-rise hotels (Figure 14.3), most of which have their own restaurants, bars, swimming pools and sun terraces. Behind the hotels are self-catering villas, and in the surrounding countryside, campsites.

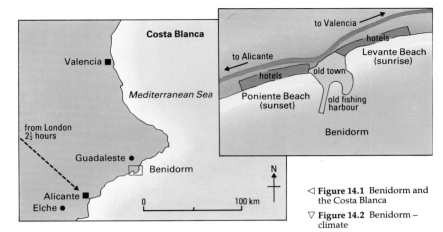

◁ **Figure 14.1** Benidorm and the Costa Blanca

▽ **Figure 14.2** Benidorm – climate

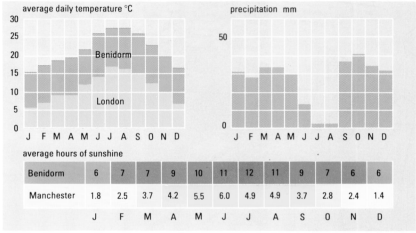

	J	F	M	A	M	J	J	A	S	O	N	D
average hours of sunshine												
Benidorm	6	7	7	9	10	11	12	11	9	7	6	6
Manchester	1.8	2.5	3.7	4.2	5.5	6.0	4.9	4.9	3.7	2.8	2.4	1.4
	J	F	M	A	M	J	J	A	S	O	N	D

▽ **Figure 14.3** Benidorm

Nightlife Illuminated shops attract tourists in the cool of the evening. Numerous bars provide flamenco and disco music; wine and beer; Spanish and other European food. A highlight is the weekly 'medieval night'. There are several nightclubs.

Shopping Local bazaars, boutiques and shops offer everything from fine clothes, leather goods and ceramics, to wickerwork and perfumes.

Surrounding countryside (Figure 14.1) The 'Lemon Express' is a miniature railway which takes tourists through some of the many local vineyards and olive, orange and lemon groves. Inland are numerous small, whitewashed villages still untouched by tourism. Alicante, with its old harbour and weekly market, is best seen from the heights of the Santa Barbara Castle. Its museum of twentieth century art contains an outstanding collection of paintings.

Eleche is noted for its palm gardens, the largest in Europe, planted over 2500 years ago by the Carthaginians.

Guadalest has a Moorish fortress, built 600 metres above sea level, and perched on a pinnacle of rock, like an eagles nest, from which the village is named.

Safari Actana attracts visitors to see its wild life.

Algarve

This tourist area lies on the south-facing coast of Portugal and like Benidorm, has grown in an area of Europe with a previously low standard of living. Along this coastline of spectacular cliffs and sandy bays, of cobbled streets separating whitewashed houses, and of architectural styles reflecting the Moorish history, lies the present day resort of Albufeira.

Albufeira has developed from a small fishing port. Although the sun and the sandy beaches attract many visitors, the region is advertised as one for active pursuits, especially golf and tennis.

Accommodation consists of both luxury hotels (Figure 14.4) and self-catering apartments (Figure 14.5).

☐ What are the advantages of staying at the hotel? And the advantages of using the apartments?

☐ Describe the physical attractions of the site of the hotel? What amenities have been added to the hotel?

☐ The apartments are set back from the coastline. Why is this? What amenities do they have?

☐ Figure 14.6 shows the cost of accommodation at the hotel and at the apartments. Which is cheaper? Why is this? Why do prices at both vary between different seasons?

☐ What does BB and half-board mean? Why is this often preferable to full board?

Hotel & Board Arrangements	AURAMAR (BB)		OLIVEIRAS APTS (SC)	
Nights in hotel	7	14	7	14
Departures on or between				
1 Nov.–7 Nov.	155	210	–	–
8 Nov.–21 Nov.	147	193	–	–
22 Nov.–10 Dec.	128	–	–	–
11 Dec.–17 Dec.	–	–	–	–
18 Dec.–24 Dec.	–	–	–	–
26 Dec.–31 Dec.	–	–	–	–
1 Jan.–25 Jan.	–	–	–	–
26 Jan.–9 Feb.	141	185	103	121
10 Feb.–7 Mar.	149	196	111	132
8 Mar.–21 Mar.	159	209	121	145
22 Mar.–14 Apr.	171	220	133	156
15 Apr.–30 Apr.	183	–	145	–
1 May–10 May	231	349	–	193
11 May–17 May	239	360	–	213
18 May–28 May	258	385	–	230
29 May–7 Jun.	257	384	–	230
8 Jun.–21 Jun.	266	396	–	235
22 Jun.–28 Jun.	271	410	–	261
29 Jun.–12 Jul.	283	421	–	261
13 Jul.–12 Aug.	298	441	–	288
13 Aug.–26 Aug.	282	427	–	261
27 Aug.–9 Sep.	279	416	–	235
10 Sep.–30 Sep.	260	390	–	230
1 Oct.–31 Oct.	238	359	–	193

◁ **Figure 14.6** Comparative costs. Prices are for November 1983–October 1984. Oliveiras prices apply (per person) to three people sharing a one-bedroomed apartment. Auramar prices apply (per person) to two people sharing a room with two or three beds, with kitchenette, bath, w.c. and balcony

▽ **Figure 14.4** Hotel Auramar, Albufeira (below left)

▽ **Figure 14.5** Oliveiras Apartments, Albufeira (below right)

HOTEL AURAMAR

This modern aparthotel stands in attractive gardens in a quiet position overlooking a cove. It's a two minute walk down a slope to the sandy beach, and from here a pleasant 25 minute stroll along the sands takes you into the centre of Albufeira. Alternatively for a small charge you can take the hotel bus. The Auramar stages regular entertainment with dancing and folklore shows and nearby there's a lively disco. Breakfast ingredients are supplied so you can enjoy them in the privacy of your room.

● large pool ● sun terrace ● gardens and lawns ● air conditioning throughout ● all bedrooms have a kitchenette ● pleasant open-plan bar-lounge ● dining room overlooking sea ● snacks available in self-service snack bar ● two tennis courts ● dancing and entertainment in nightclub most nights ● souvenir shop ● children's pool ● cots, highchairs available

Our opinion 'Ideal for people of all ages, including children, looking for a comfortable beach holiday in an easy-going atmosphere. Many people find the kitchenette a useful bonus.'

● Hotel bedrooms: 282

OLIVEIRAS APARTMENTS

These smartly furnished, terraced apartments are built around an attractive central pool and terrace area with a children's playground and snack bar, just under two miles from the centre of Albufeira, and 10 minutes from the Vilanova complex. The nearest shops and a discotheque are also about ten minutes walk away, and the bus stop for the town centre is 100 yards away. The many facilities of the nearby Hotel Montechoro can be used by our clients, although there is a charge for tennis, squash, sauna and use of the pool.

The apartments have one, two or three bedrooms (including one double bedroom in each apartment) a lounge/dining room (most with an extra single divan bed), and a fully equipped kitchen or kitchenette. Three bedroom apartments are duplex with the third bedroom reached by a spiral staircase. Most of the apartments have an internal balcony.

No lift

Maid Service: daily except Sundays and Public Holidays

Grocery pack included

Growth of tourism

The earliest resorts were spa towns, which the more wealthy visited to 'take the waters'. Today, the most popular resorts are on the coast (Figure 14.7). Long-stay resorts have sandy beaches, long hours of sunshine and limited rainfall, together with good access to major urban areas by road, rail or air. Short-stay resorts (possibly even day trip resorts) are also usually found on coasts, and lie near to large urban areas. Cultural and historic resorts tend to be inland, and are usually found in capital cities, in older settlements with castles and cathedrals, or in areas of previous civilisations. The mountainous areas of Europe, especially those with heavy snowfalls, are ideal for winter sports.

1 Describe and give reasons for the distribution of the six types of resort shown on Figure 14.7.

2 Can you find out where the following tourist areas are located? The Algarve, Costa Blanca, Costa Dorado, Costa Del Sol, Costa Brava, Côte D'Azur, Alps, Tyrol, Ligurian Riviera, Languedoc-Roussillon, Loire Valley, Rhine Valley.

Recent growth in tourism, and changes in holiday patterns

☐ Greater affluence resulting from higher salaries.

☐ Greater mobility with more car owners and an increase in charter flights.

☐ Improvement in transport systems with better motorways, improved airports and inter-country rail routes.

☐ Longer holidays, earlier retirements and more leisure time.

☐ People taking more than one holiday a year.

☐ An increase in short-stay (mini break) holidays – i.e. spending three nights or less away.

☐ A desire to travel further afield, to look for more unusual and more energetic holidays, and to see different cultures and ways of life.

☐ Growth of package holidays.

☐ Increase in advertising.

☐ Changing attitudes of people who feel an annual holiday to be a 'right' rather than a reward for working.

☐ Tourism is less affected by the recession than many other industries.

☐ An increase in self-catering holidays – villas, camping, caravans, and time-share holidays.

☐ Increasing encouragement, including financial, by national governments and the EEC.

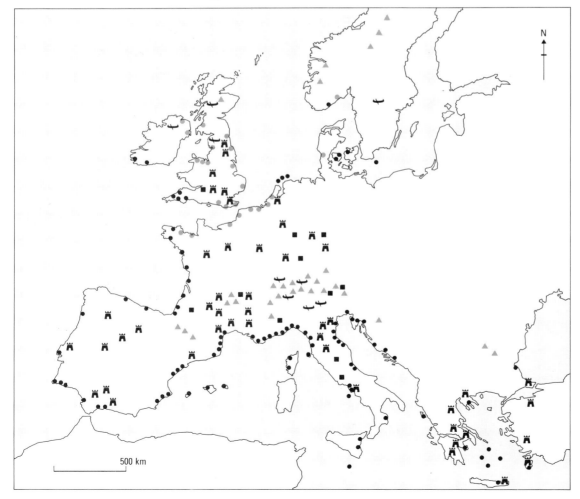

◁ **Figure 14.7** Location of various types of European resorts

Ħ historic – cultural
▲ mountain and winter sports
● long-stay coastal
● short-stay coastal
⌣ lakes
■ spas

500 km

Tourists arrivals and departures in western Europe see Figure 14.8.

□ Italy, Spain and Greece have many tourists because of their hot, dry, sunny summers and their mild winters.

□ Italy, Portugal, Spain and Greece have sandy beaches and warm seas.

□ Italy, Switzerland, Austria and Scandinavia attract skiers.

□ Italy, Greece and the UK offer cultural and historical holidays.

□ France and West Germany are more affluent and so many of their inhabitants travel abroad for their holidays.

□ Spain, Portugal, Italy and Greece are less well-off countries many of whose inhabitants are either too busy in their own tourist industry, or too poor, to take holidays outside their own country.

□ West Germany, Belgium and the UK are regarded as industrialised and so less attractive, as well as having less favourable climates.

The economic importance of tourism

Figure 14.9 shows that several EEC countries earn more from tourism than they spend on it (net gainers). Both Italy and Greece fall into this category, as will Spain and Portugal if they join the EEC. A major reason for Greece joining the EEC was to increase its tourism. In 1981 more people visited Greece than actually lived in it, and between 1970–80 the income earned from tourism increased by ten times. The net gainers tend to be in the poorer south of the continent, and without it, those countries would be even poorer. In 1982, Greece earned 20% of her income from tourism.

Using Figure 14.9 which country is the biggest net loser in tourism? What do you notice about the location of the three main net losers?

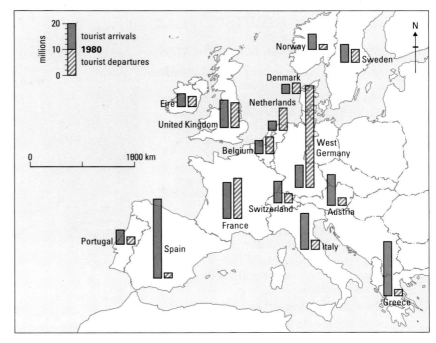

△ **Figure 14.8** Tourist arrivals and departures

▽ **Figure 14.9** Revenue from, and expenditure on, international tourism in the EEC

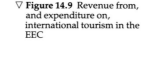

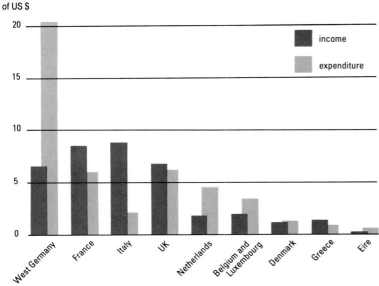

The EEC Policy on tourism

Article 2 of the Treaty of Rome gives the EEC the task of '*Promoting closer relations between states which belong to it*'. One way to achieve this is through tourism. Tourism, a labour-intensive industry, provides 4 million jobs in the EEC.

Aims

□ To stimulate trade and business.

□ To provide funds from the European Investment Bank and European Regional Development Fund.

□ Integrating transport routes. e.g. 'E' routes, Eurail.

□ To encourage 'Farm tourism' and local craft industries to try to reduce rural depopulation.

□ To improve services such as water supply, electricity and accommodation (hotels, holiday villages, camping and caravan sites).

□ To protect the environment – both the natural (beaches, seas, wildlife) and cultural.

□ To help the balance of payments for southern European countries.

Future plans include

□ The introduction of a common passport and driving licence.

□ To improve transport e.g. a new motorway from West Germany through Austria and Yugoslavia to Greece; to have a permanent link between the UK and the continent; and to increase travel on Eurail.

□ To create more jobs, e.g. redeveloping historic sites.

□ Since 1980 money has, and is, being spent on Community projects such as in Aquitaine, Languedoc-Roussillon (page 106) and the Mezzogiorno (page 114) as well as to a lesser degree in Ireland.

Winter resorts

Badgastein – a traditional resort (Austria)

Badgastein is an old Austrian spa town, situated in the glaciated Gastein valley (Figure 14.10). It is 105 km, and two hours by coach south of Salzburg. The town is well-known for its waterfall on the River Ache, which flows through Badgastein, and its thermal water and cures – in all there are 18 clear, hot springs. Much of the town is still medieval in origin, and its shops and boutiques occupy narrow, winding streets. Recent growth has resulted from its attractions as a tourist centre.

Natural advantages as a resort

☐ In winter the snow covered mountains offer ski-slopes of varying degrees of difficulty.

☐ In summer the same mountains offer spectacular scenery, ideal for sight-seeing, walking and climbing.

☐ Its healthy climate (clear air) and hot springs.

☐ Its accessibility to natural routeways through the Alps.

Purpose-built amenities

☐ Numerous hotels, many of which are not new in origin and contain luxurious suites and rooms (Figure 14.11). The Hotel Gasteinerhof, which is 5-star, overlooks the waterfall, has a 'Kellerbar', luxurious lounge and dining rooms, and most bedrooms have a bath and w.c. In its basement are the thermal baths and showers with the water obtained from the volcanic centre of the Graukogel mountain.

☐ The Felsenbad swimming complex (Figure 14.12) – a modern indoor pool built into the mountain side and with an outdoor heated pool and a sauna.

☐ Sporting facilities such as an indoor horse riding arena, indoor tennis and squash courts, a 9-hole golf course, and excursions by horse and trap.

☐ Cultural events are held in the local theatre and concert hall.

☐ Modern shopping complex.

Skiing The area offers 59 lifts and over 250 km of skiing (Figure 14.13). For beginners there are nursery slopes near the town, and its nearby neighbour of Bad Hofgastein. There is a good area for intermediate skiing as well as difficult runs down the Graukogel slopes. Badgastein itself has a cablecar, a triple chair lift, two double chair lifts, three single chair lifts and nine drag lifts, as well as a private skiers bus. Snowfalls in winter are heavy and reliable, yet the surrounding mountains protect the valley from very strong winds, and avalanches are less of a hazard here than in other Alpine areas.

What are the advantages of Badgastein to:
a) elderly summer tourists
b) younger age groups in summer, and
c) winter sports enthusiasts?

△ **Figure 14.10** Badgastein – a traditional ski resort

▽ **Figure 14.11** Badgastein, Austria

▷ **Figure 14.12** Felsenbad swimming complex at Badgastein

Key

hotel	
cable car	
chair lift	
drag lift	

beginners/easy runs
intermediate runs
advanced runs
difficult runs

△ **Figure 14.15** Les Arcs – a purpose-built ski resort

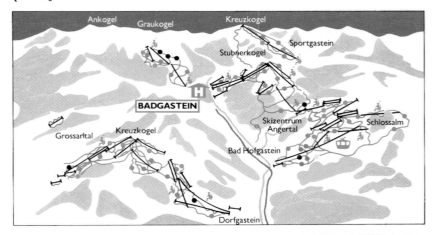

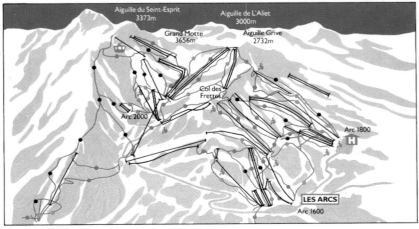

Les Arcs – a purpose-built resort (French Alps)

As the popularity of winter sports grew, and the traditional resorts became more congested and expensive, new purpose-built resorts have been created in Alpine regions. Les Arcs, in the French Alps and north-east of Grenoble, comprises three resorts (Figure 14.14). The original development was Arc 1600, so called because the centre was 1600 metres above sea level. As the number of visitors increased, newer complexes were built, firstly at 1800 metres, and more recently at 2000 metres. All three resorts are connected by newly constructed roads.

Accommodation consists of 14 blocks of self-catering apartments (Figure 14.15) with convenient access to a wide range of restaurants, bars and shops. Apartments have two bedrooms with a balcony. There are two single beds, or a double bed, and two or three bunk beds. The bathroom has a wash basin, bath, and a separate w.c. The kitchen has a sink, fridge, oven, dishwasher and two hot-plates.

Resort facilities include an open-air skating rink (floodlit in the evening), games arcade, snow-shoe excursions, bank, post office, food shops, bars and restaurants. The centre has its own doctor, nurse, surgery and X-ray facilities.

Advantages

43 lifts, and over 100 km of ski-runs
Ski facilities are in accessible places
Ski slopes begin and end at resort making the use of buses unnecessary
Graded runs at different levels of difficulty
Children on nursery slopes are looked after by instructors, allowing their parents time to use the more advanced slopes
No competition from other land-users, nor other forms of recreation
Functional accommodation
Provision of 'Night life' (après-ski)
Restaurants and food shops
Good access by road from Lyons airport
Numerous ski runs means little queuing for lifts
Costs are lower than in traditional ski resorts

Disadvantages

Unsightly buildings, not necessarily built to fit into the natural environment
No historic charms
No appreciation of, or contact with, any local community
Apartments the only form of accommodation
Over-organised for some tourists
Tends to close down in summer – really only a ski resort (i.e. not a mountain climbing area as well)

△ **Figure 14.13** Ski runs in the Gastein valley (middle)

△ **Figure 14.14** Ski runs at Les Arcs

▷ **Figure 14.16** Advantages and disadvantages of a purpose-built resort such as Les Arcs

	low season	mid season	high season	lift passes
Badgastein	£142	£152	£162	£38
Les Arcs	£117	£127	£137	£40

△ **Figure 14.17** Comparative costs per week

La Grande Motte

A purpose-built, government-aided resort

La Grande Motte is situated in Languedoc, and lies on the Mediterranean coast, immediately west of the Rhône delta. In 1963 the region was virtually uninhabited, mainly due to poor communications, deficient water supplies, and areas of marsh which were mosquito infested in summer. It was then that the French government decided to create six new tourist complexes. The decision was prompted because:

- The rapid expansion of tourism in the 1950s found France with insufficient accommodation and amenities, especially in comparison with Spain and Italy. This threatened France's position as a net gainer from tourism.

- The Côte D'Azur had become too expensive and too congested.

- The Côte D'Azur did not cater for the expansion in self-catering holidays, such as villas, and caravan and camping sites.

- Languedoc had a low standard of living, with an over-reliance upon wine production. The 200 km of sandy coastline west of the Rhône were virtually unutilised.

La Grand Motte was begun in 1965, and became noted for its modern architecture, and especially its 'pyramid' accommodation (Figures 14.18 and 14.19).

△ **Figure 14.19** La Grande Motte – the Aztec-like design of the buildings ensures that each window receives the same amount of sun

services
pine forests
open space
dual carriageway
road
holiday village
apartments
villas
camping
P   parking
*   entertainment
▲   hotel

0   100 m

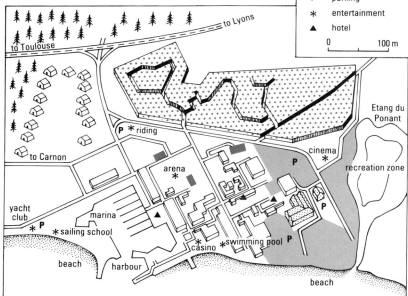

△ **Figure 14.18** Layout of La Grande Motte. What do you notice about the location of the apartments, the villas, the holiday village and camping areas? Why are there only three hotels? Describe the location of the parking areas, the open space and the woodland. What types of entertainment are shown?

▷ **Figure 14.20** Seasonal nature of tourism, 1980

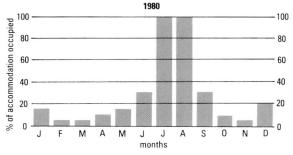

Advantages

- Long hours of sunshine with, in summer, very little rainfall.

- Over 5 km of sandy beaches with safe bathing.

- An enclosed lagoon, the Etang du Ponant, which can also be used for recreation (Figure 14.18).

- Pine woods behind the resort can be used for walking in.

- The central marina caters for all types of water sports, including windsurfing, sailing, fishing and water skiing.

- Many self-catering villas and campsites (Figure 14.18).

- Near to the main Toulouse–Lyons motorway, the airports at Nimes and Montpellier, and, since 1983, the TGV route between Paris and Montpellier (page 90).

- Amenities include nightclubs, a casino, cinema, tennis and horse riding. The shopping areas include supermarkets (for the self-catering) boutiques and souvenir shops. There are numerous bars, cafés and restaurants.

- Nearby is the Camargue National Park, famous for its white horses, black bulls and flamingoes, and the old Roman towns of Nimes and Arles.

Problems

- Much employment is seasonal. Figure 14.20 shows the resort is only full for the two months in the year coinciding with the highest temperatures and the school holidays.

- Little actual employment was created once construction work ended, as accommodation was self-catering (i.e. no holiday jobs).

- The cost of land and property has risen rapidly.

- An increasing amount of property is owned by people living elsewhere in France and indeed in NW Europe.

- Money spent on this region (since 1980 from the European Regional Fund) has meant less is spent on other tourist regions.

- Environmentally – the pyramid buildings do not blend in with the natural surroundings.

Impact of tourism

The growth of tourism can be both an advantage and a disadvantage to a local community and its natural environment. The advantages and disadvantages have been summarised in Figure 14.21.

Two areas which are becoming increasingly dependent upon tourism are the Swiss Alps, and the Spanish island of Ibiza. Study the table and Figure 14.22. Choose *either* the Swiss Alps *or* Ibiza, and then:

1 Describe the traditional way of life and the natural environment.

2 Describe the ways in which tourism has altered this traditional way of life, and the natural environment.

3 Complete the following table listing ways in which you think tourism has harmed or benefitted the local economy, local community and natural environment.

	harmed	benefitted
Local economy		
Local community		
Natural environment		

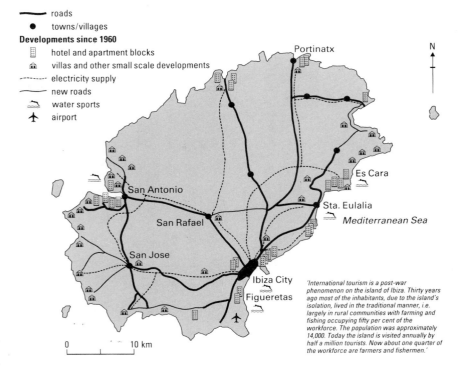

roads
● towns/villages
Developments since 1960
▦ hotel and apartment blocks
🏛 villas and other small scale developments
------- electricity supply
~~ new roads
🛥 water sports
✈ airport

N

Portinatx

Es Cara

San Antonio

Sta. Eulalia

Mediterranean Sea

San Rafael

San Jose

Ibiza City

Figueretas

0   10 km

'International tourism is a post-war phenomenon on the island of Ibiza. Thirty years ago most of the inhabitants, due to the island's isolation, lived in the traditional manner, i.e. largely in rural communities with farming and fishing occupying fifty per cent of the workforce. The population was approximately 14,000. Today the island is visited annually by half a million tourists. Now about one quarter of the workforce are farmers and fishermen.'

▽ **Figure 14.21** Tourism, and the local community and environment

△ **Figure 14.22** Ibiza – the influence of tourism

Gains to local community and environment

Increase in local employment – cafes, souvenir shops, and boutiques. Better paid jobs.

Decrease in rural depopulation

Increase in land values gave greater income to farmers since they sold land to developers

Farmers could sell produce to local hotels

Growth of local craft industries

Improved communications – new roads, modern airports, and ports to accommodate cruise liners

Improved services with better water supplies, sewerage and electricity

More entertainment

Preservation of the cultural, historic heritage

Improved links with other countries

Improves area's/country's balance of payment

Losses to local community and environment

Adverse visual impact (see Figures 14.3 and 14.15); hotels, car parks and airports spoil views

Congestion, especially on beaches, at airports, on main roads, at cafes and at places of historic interest

Increase in noise e.g. from planes and discos

Air pollution spoiling famous buildings (Acropolis) and paintings (Lascaux caves)

Damage to buildings, wildlife and vegetation

Destruction or exploitation of traditional way of life

Undermining social standards

Farmland lost to property developers

Increased cost of property means vacant properties become second homes beyond the reach of locals

Hotels run by outsiders. These often replace local boarding houses, and employ non-villagers.

Much employment is seasonal

Need to import food for hotels

A Swiss Alpine valley
– the Val d'Anniviers

The Val d'Anniviers was a prosperous valley in the nineteenth century, relying on agriculture (dairying and vines) and forest products. By 1900 a decline in prosperity had led to rural depopulation.

Tourism began in earnest in 1964, when an outside organisation bought two semi-abandoned hotels and turned them, together with an extension, into a 440-bed resort. In 1967 a ski-complex was added, with three ski-lifts and a cable railway. A mountain restaurant, hotel and swimming pool were built but created little employment for locals. A two-lane road was opened, a large car park, sewerage and water supply added, although these were partly paid for by the local inhabitants through increased taxes.

Meanwhile, the seasonal migration of farmers (page 40) had ended. Some vineyards had been sold to property developers, though new ones were established on higher land. Other farmers rented spare rooms and outhouses to visitors, whilst others found seasonal employment as ski-instructors, lift operators, and bed and breakfast proprietors.

The younger members of the community did find more job opportunities and entertainment, and rural depopulation was halted. The 2253 inhabitants of 1910 fell to 1512 in 1970, and rose to 1611 in 1974. By 1976, 50% of the workforce were employed in tourism in some form or other and the annual number of tourists had risen to 24 000 from 8000. Although greater consideration was given in this valley to traditional buildings and the environment, the new road was affected by landslides; the delicate ecology was harmed; footpaths were eroded; the risk of fires (as well as avalanches) increased. The traditional way of life had been altered.

Cultural – heritage holidays

GREECE

TURKEY

Delphi
(Oracle and Temple of Apollo)

Marathon

Corinth
(Temple of Apollo)

Athens
(Acropolis and amphitheatre)

Mycenae
(Citadel 1350 B.C.)

Sounion

Olympia
(first Olympic Games 776 B.C.)

CRETE

Knossos
(centre of
Minoan culture)

Classical Greece

Visitors to Italy in the nineteenth century went not for the sun, or the beaches, but to look at museums, works of art and famous buildings. Since the arrival of the aeroplane and cheap package holidays, Greece, and the remnants of its past, has increasingly attracted tourists (Figure 14.23). However in the twentieth century the demands of conservationists, archaeologists, historians, students and tourists are increasingly heard. They wish to see the preservation of:

☐ The character of older towns reflecting a now declining life-style.

☐ Individual buildings noted for their historical links, their architecture, or as homes of famous people.

☐ The contents of houses and important buildings such as paintings, sculptures, silverware, etc.

Such 'culture centres' tend to attract day visitors and people on touring holidays, rather than those on long-stay vacations, and the distribution of visitors tend to be less seasonal than at coastal or winter resorts.

Problems

☐ Buildings are decaying under extremes of wind, sun, rain and frost.

☐ Buildings, especially the Acropolis (Figure 14.23), are crumbling due to chemicals such as sulphur dioxide in the air.

☐ Wearing away of footpaths and steps by over-use.

☐ Many buildings are in large cities where they are surrounded by modern high-rise buildings and urban motorways.

☐ Effect of the vibration of heavy traffic.

☐ Visually spoilt by such 'commercial' enterprises as souvenir and ice-cream stalls.

Recently in Athens, buses and lorries have been re-routed away from the Acropolis, and the closure of a local power station and gasworks has cut atmospheric pollution which had been attacking the marble buildings. Figure 14.23 shows restoration work.

The EEC sees restoration of ancient sites, delapidated buildings and maintenance of those already restored as a source of future employment.

Rhodes

Rhodes has the double advantage of having hot, dry, sunny summers and sandy beaches as well as a diversified history which makes it an ideal resort for 'sunlovers' and those interested in 'culture'. The island's strategic position on important trade routes has led to a turbulent history.

☐ From the fourteenth to twelfth century B.C. the island was part of the Crete-based Mycenaean civilisation – until the destruction of the empire by the eruption on Santorini (page 10).

☐ The island then fell under the influence of various Greek states. In Greek mythology, Helios the sun god chose Rhodes as his bride and blessed it with light and warmth.

☐ In 226 B.C. an earthquake destroyed the town, and the famous Colossus (Figure 1.21) one of the seven wonders of the ancient world. The site is marked today by two deer (Figure 14.24).

☐ The Romans administered the island for several centuries.

☐ A.D. 653 the island was invaded by the Saracens, and in the eleventh century by the Crusaders.

☐ The thirteenth century saw power fall to the Byzantines.

☐ The dominant features today are the old walls of the town, and the palace of the Grand Master (Figure 14.24). These were built by the Knights of St John of Jerusalem who settled here after their expulsion from the Holy Land (and before they settled in Malta). Their living quarters remain in the Street of the Knights.

☐ On the way to the fifteenth century fortress (now a lighthouse) and the statues of the deer, are the medieval drum-shaped windmills (Figure 14.24).

☐ 1522 saw the island falling under Turkish rule. A mosque is named after Suleiman its conqueror, Figure 14.24. The old Turkish quarter is a maze of narrow cobbled streets and high arches.

☐ The island became Italian in 1912, and Mussolini restored the palace for his retirement. In 1947 Rhodes was returned to Greece.

Questions

1 What is a cultural centre?

2 How has the geographical location of Rhodes contributed to the remains of many cultures found on the island?

3 What might the tourist find that reflects Greek, Byzantine and Turkish influence on the island?

4 What modern cultural attractions have been added to Rhodes?

5 Why is it possible to combine a cultural holiday with a beach holiday?

6 Why are cultural resorts less hindered by seasonal unemployment than coastal resorts?

◁ **Figure 14.23** Classical Greece

▽ **Figure 14.24** Rhodes – a historic-cultural resort

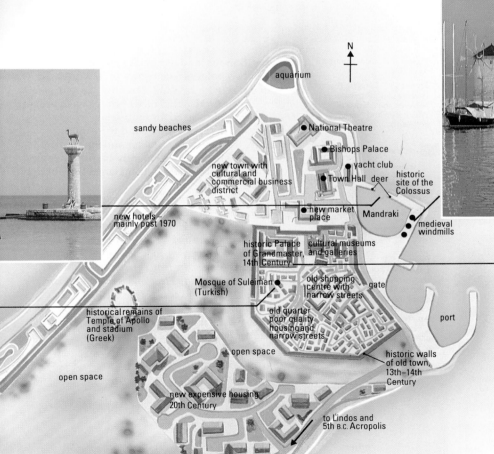

The Netherlands – environmental gain

The Zuider Zee scheme

Reclamation was necessary:

- To protect the land from the sea.
- To create hundreds of square kilometres of fertile farmland (Figure 15.1).
- To reduce salinisation in adjoining polders.
- To provide more land for a country with one of the highest population densities in the world.
- To cater for Amsterdam's overspill population.
- To shorten road connections (the Barrier dam reduced the length of the Dutch coastline by nearly 300 km).
- To provide drinking water.
- To provide leisure amenities.

How is land reclaimed?

- By building an enclosing dam (Figures 15.2 and 15.3), and then pumping out water since the land lies below sea level. Diesel pumps have now replaced the traditional windmills.
- By building a series of dykes and ditches to help to drain the land.
- Gypsum is added to help remove salt from the soil, and rape can be grown as it is insensitive to salt. Reeds are planted (by air) to add nitrogen to the soil, and later burnt to act as a fertiliser.
- The land is left as a fertile black silt, rich in humus and easy to cultivate. It is often ploughed for the first time by a machine capable of reaching 2 metres deep.
- The land is often used for state farming for five years before being leased for private farming, recreation and urbanisation.

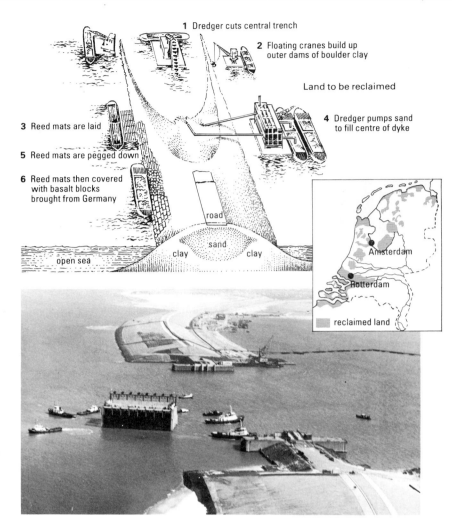

1 Dredger cuts central trench
2 Floating cranes build up outer dams of boulder clay
Land to be reclaimed
3 Reed mats are laid
4 Dredger pumps sand to fill centre of dyke
5 Reed mats are pegged down
6 Reed mats then covered with basalt blocks brought from Germany
road
clay   sand   clay
open sea

reclaimed land

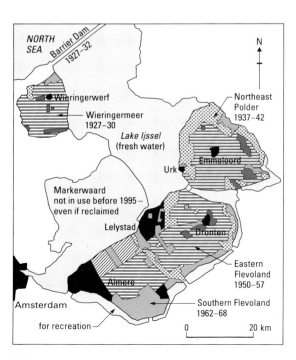

NORTH SEA
Barrier Dam 1927–32
Wieringerwerf
Wieringermeer 1927–30
Lake Ijssel (fresh water)
Northeast Polder 1937–42
Emmeloord
Urk
Markerwaard not in use before 1995 – even if reclaimed
Lelystad
Dronten
Almere
Amsterdam
for recreation
Eastern Flevoland 1950–57
Southern Flevoland 1962–68
N
0   20 km

△ **Figure 15.2** Constructing a dyke (top)

△ **Figure 15.3** Closing the 'Veerse Gat', the water between the islands of Walcheren and Noord Beveland

- residential
- industry
- horticulture
- woodland
- arable farming
- mixed farming and grazing

◁ **Figure 15.1** Land use in the Lake Ijssel polders. This shows the areas which have been reclaimed. Notice the changing land use with increased distance from Amsterdam. Describe and give reasons for these changes in land use.

Competition for land use on the polders

The first two polders (see Figure 15.1) were used almost entirely for farming, but now, despite a strong agricultural lobby, other groups wish to see the newer polders used for industrial development, urban growth and recreation, (compare the North-east Polder and Southern Flevoland). The biggest demands are from people living in Amsterdam, the second largest city in the Randstad conurbation.

'East Flevoland is basically farming country with small areas zoned for recreation and industry around three 'village' centres, and Lelystad, the polder's 'capital'. The plans for South Flevoland set aside far more land for non-agricultural purposes. Industry, arguably, provides better returns per hectare than agriculture. Moreover, the western end of South Flevoland is on Amsterdam's doorstep and could obviously help out with the city's overspill problem. These different points of emphasis will be just as relevant if the next planned polder – the Markerwaard – is to be eventually reclaimed.'

Land use %	Wieringermeer	NE Polder	E. Flevoland	S. Flevoland
farmland	87	87	75	50
woods and conservation	3	5	11	26
urbanisation	1	1	8	18
others	9	7	6	6

The Delta plan – why it was necessary

On the evening of 31 January 1953, a combination of storm force winds blowing from the north as a depression moved southwards down the North Sea, and spring high tides caused serious flooding in the Delta region. 1835 people were drowned, 10 000 houses were destroyed and many animals were lost. The island of Schouwen-Duiveland (Figure 15.4) was totally submerged apart from the sand dunes on the west coast. The disaster was mainly due to the tide racing up estuaries and breaching lower dykes on the inland side (page 15).

The Plan

Five primary dams were built to seal off estuaries, and several secondary dams to improve road communications. The dams were built one metre higher than the level of the 1953 flood – the highest tide so far experienced. Smaller dams were built first to increase the expertise of the builders, and later the longer, more difficult sections. The dates of completion are shown on Figure 15.4, and a photograph of the Haringvliet sluices is shown in Figure 15.5. This dam has to allow water from the Rhine and Maas to escape into the North Sea. Tidal scour made the final blocking of dams difficult and this has been achieved by using caissons (concrete blocks, with hollow centres) enabling them to be floated into position.

Two final schemes are the Philips Dam which is designed to separate salt and fresh water, and to keep the Scheldt–Rhine Canal non-tidal, and the Eastern Scheldt Dam. The plans for this 9 km long dam were changed at the last moment, so that the dam has 63 openings in it to allow the tide free entry, but which can be blocked off by steel gates (each 42 m wide) should there be a threat of flooding. This storm surge barrier was built mainly to protect the livelihoods of fishermen (and their oyster beds). It is hoped to have all schemes finished by 1985.

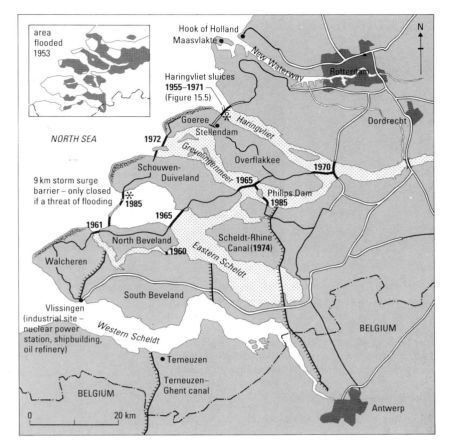

△ **Figure 15.4** The Delta scheme

◁ **Figure 15.5** The Haringvliet dam. The sluices are 60 m wide to allow ice flows out in severe winters.

Key:
- motorway
- road
- canal
- fresh water
- **1972** date of completion
- ≪ ship lock
- ✳ storm surge
- sand dunes

Aims of the Delta Plan

- ☐ Protection against future floods.
- ☐ Reduce salinisation of the islands.
- ☐ The dams would shorten distance by road (e.g. Rotterdam to Flushing reduced from 150 to 110 km), shorten the time taken by the journey (no waiting for ferries), and improve accessibility with the least prosperous parts of the country.
- ☐ Reduce the coastline by 700 km.
- ☐ To provide areas of sheltered water for recreation and fresh water for drinking and for the growing industries of the Maasvlakte area (page 93).
- ☐ To provide some new land for industry e.g. Vlissingen (Figure 15.4).
- ☐ To try to increase fishing areas.
- ☐ To allow access by shipping, and to make their journeys easier as the fast tidal waters became cut off from open sea.
- ☐ To provide a new fresh-water canal to link the Rhine and Scheldt (Figure 15.4).
- ☐ To use areas of deposition in front of dams as nature reserves.

Problems resulting from the Plan are few in comparison to the gains, but include an over-use of areas by an unprecedented increase in tourism, the growth of second homes (ruining traditional villages), an increase in ice as the moderating influence of the sea is reduced, and ecological problems due to the elimination of tides.

Environmental problems

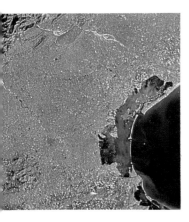

▽ **Figure 15.7** St Mark's square

Venice

Venice was one of 118 islands found in the shallow Venice lagoon. These islands were formed as rivers from the Alps deposited their silt in shallow water. The lagoon is protected from the open sea by the Lido, Figure 15.6. Early Venetians diverted rivers away from the lagoon to try to limit further silting.

Environmental problems

Flooding Venice is slowly sinking – latest figures suggest by 1 cm in the last decade, and over 2 metres since Roman times. St Marks Square may now be flooded over 100 times a year (Figure 15.7), and the inundations are becoming both deeper (the record in 1966 was 2 metres above usual) and more frequent. Flooding is worst in winter (November) when winds from the south-east cause a storm surge.

Flooding is the result of several factors:

☐ A slight world-wide rise in sea level.

☐ Buildings continuing to settle into the mud.

☐ Water extracted from underground sources for new industry on the mainland has caused the area to subside.

☐ A new deep water channel south of Venice takes oil tankers, but has increased the speed and height of tides.

☐ Over one third of the lagoon has been reclaimed for industry and fish farming giving tides less area to spread over.

Pollution The growth of the industrial town of Mestre and, since 1927, its new port of Porto Marghera, has led to a rapid increase in pollution of both the water in the lagoon and in the air above it. The 'acid rain' (page 116) attacks both buildings and their valuable contents. Also untreated sewage was put into the lagoon in the hope that tides would remove it (see Figure 15.6).

Seaweed Chemical fertilisers are added to farmland in the area and some reaches the lagoon causing an increase in seaweed which blocks the canals and gives off an unpleasant smell.

Decay of buildings (Figures 15.8 and 15.9)

△ **Figure 15.6** (Above left). False colour landsat photograph of the Venice region.
Key:
Light red – vegetation
Bright red – forest
Grey-blue – croplands
Blue-green – built up areas
Black – water
Light blue – pollution
Notice: (*a*) The long spit of the Venice Lido. (*b*) Light coloured streaks east of Lido showing sewage discharge. (*c*) Pale blue polluted areas of the Venice Lagoon. (*d*) The Causeway, in blue, linking Venice to the mainland of Mestre and Porto Marghera.

▽ **Figure 15.8** Results of changing sea levels, and building decay. As the land sinks, the protective stone is submerged, and damp rises upwards into the porous brick (Figure 15.9). Acid rain is causing marble buildings to crumble, and famous paintings to deteriorate. Salt in the seawater also corrodes buildings. Use of water buses and power boats instead of gondolas, causes bigger waves and increases erosion. 7000 large ships a year sail 'through' Venice on their way to Porto Marghera.

▷ **Figure 15.9** Water damage adjacent to Venetian canal (above right)

Overcrowding High housing density with little open space, though recently there has been rapid depopulation as people move away from the damp houses (50 000 migrated between 1960 and 1980).

Environmental solutions?

☐ A storm barrage across the three entrances to the Lido (as on the Thames and in the Netherlands – page 111). After nearly two decades of discussion, no plan has been approved.

☐ A sandbank barrier.

☐ Improved sewage and industrial waste treatment plants.

☐ Mestre and Porto Marghera now get water from a pipeline from mainland rivers. No new wells are to be sunk.

☐ In 1973 an international 'Save Venice Fund' was opened. Yet it was the 1980s before real attempts were made to improve buildings (by adding lead sheet to stop rising damp) and to restore chapels and their contents.

☐ No more land is to be reclaimed from the lagoon.

Can Mestre – Porto Marghera and Venice both survive?

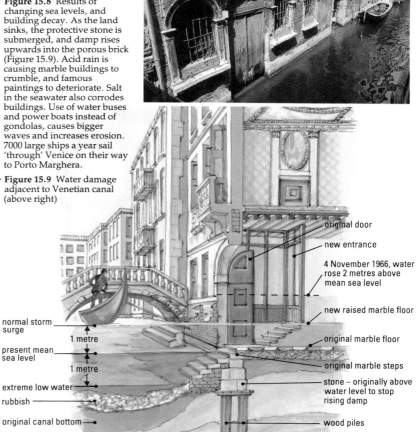

original door
new entrance
4 November 1966, water rose 2 metres above mean sea level
new raised marble floor
original marble floor
original marble steps
stone – originally above water level to stop rising damp
wood piles

normal storm surge
1 metre
present mean sea level
1 metre
extreme low water
rubbish
original canal bottom

The Ruhr – improving the environment

'Pit-heads and foundries, miners black with coal and panting steelworkers, slag-heaps and boggy industrial wastelands, smog and thunder, the sky full of smoke of chimneys in the daytime, and at night the glowing red reflections of 1000 soot-belching fires. Part pride, part revulsion, Germany's industrial heartland, the nation's environmental blackspot. The region made an early start in tackling its problems when, in 1920, the forerunner of the Ruhr planning region was set up.' (*Ruhr Planning Report*)

Parts of the Ruhr had 3000 people to every one kilometre of open space. The region had derelict mines and machines, disused transport routes, polluted rivers and air, slag and rubbish heaps, and lakes resulting from mining subsidence.

▽ **Figure 15.10** Leisure in the Ruhrgebiet

▽ **Figure 15.11** The Neinhausen Area Park – located between Essen and Gelsenkirchen (bottom)

The Ruhr plan

This began by creating, in the 1920s, a series of riverside walks in the Ruhr valley. This led to an integrated attempt to improve transport networks, create recreation areas and remove waste. By 1982 58.4% of the region was classified as 'Green areas'.

Green areas Five green belts (Figure 15.10) were created as 'Lungs' running north-south and separating the major urban areas. Over 27 million trees were planted in 30 years, and an attempt has been made to re-establish an ecological balance.

Area parks These five regional parks were built as near to large urban areas as possible. They are 25–100 hectares in size, and include swimming pools, fitness centres, solariums, and many team game facilities. Ideally 25–50 000 inhabitants should be within 15 minutes walking distance, and one million within 20 minutes drive of the area parks (Figure 15.11).

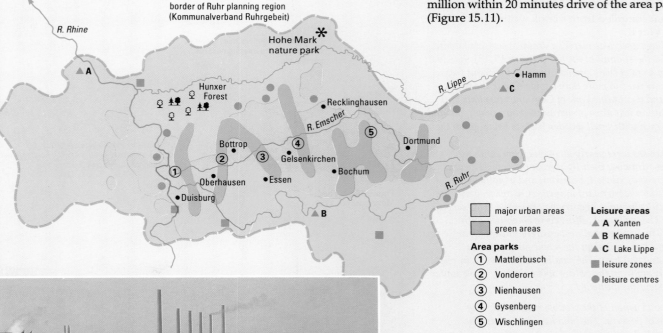

Area parks	**Leisure areas**
① Mattlerbusch	▲ A Xanten
② Vonderort	▲ B Kemnade
③ Nienhausen	▲ C Lake Lippe
④ Gysenberg	■ leisure zones
⑤ Wischlingen	● leisure centres

major urban areas

green areas

Leisure areas are up to 300 hectares in size with a minimum of 60 hectares of water (Figure 15.10). There is a strong emphasis on water sports in the three areas.

Leisure zones are smaller versions of leisure areas, being 150 hectares in size and including water sports.

Leisure centres usually are small, 10–25 hectares, and cater for small towns which are a longer way from larger leisure areas.

Conversion of industrial sites

'One example of a successful and almost completed development is the Emscherbruch area in Gelsenkirchen. In 1968 the Verband (planning authority) acquired a 2.6 million square metre colliery site on the former Graf Bismarck pit. One part is currently being used as a central rubbish dump and the other has been converted into a recreation area in which both forestry, in the form of recreational woodland, and agriculture, represented by a long-term pasture farming, are firmly established.' (*Ruhr Planning Report*)

113

Government intervention – The Mezzogiorno

This area lies south of Rome and includes the two islands of Sicily and Sardinia. Mezzogiorno means 'Land of the midday sun'. Along with Eire, it has been the poorest region in the EEC with, in 1950, still 53% of its workforce in farming. Figure 15.12 shows some of the causes of high unemployment, and why so many people have emigrated. To this list can be added the lack of mineral and energy resources, industry, commerce, services and skilled labour (24% illiterate in 1950). The resultant low standard of living meant that between 1950 and 1975 4.5 million people emigrated to 'The North', to the USA and as 'guestworkers' to West Germany and Switzerland (page 66).

The following account of Italy's extreme south has been compiled from a book written just before World War II.

'The village itself was merely a group of scattered white houses at the summit of the hill (Figure 15.13). It is like being on a sea of chalk, monotonous and without trees. The square was no more than a widening of the single street, and it contained one of Gaglianos two fountains. The fountain was always surrounded by women, old and young, each with small wooden baskets balanced on their heads.

The houses were nearly all of one room, with no windows, drawing their light from the door. The one room served as kitchen, bedroom, and usually as quarters for the barnyard animals. On one side was the stove; sticks brought in every day from the fields served as fuel. The walls and ceiling were blackened with smoke. The room was almost entirely filled with an enormous bed; in it slept the whole family, father, mother and children. The smaller children slept in reed cradles hung from the ceiling above the bed, while under the bed slept the animals.'

'The second aspect of the trouble is economic, the dilemma of poverty. The land has been gradually impoverished; the forests have been cut down, the rivers have been reduced to mountain streams that often run dry, and livestock has become scarce. Instead of cultivating trees and pasture lands there has been an unfortunate attempt to raise wheat in soil that does not favour it. There is no capital, no industry, no savings, no schools; emigration is no longer possible, taxes are unduly heavy, and malaria is everywhere. All this is in large part due to the ill-advised intentions and efforts of the State, a State in which the peasants cannot feel they have a share, and which has brought them only poverty and deserts.

Finally, there is the social side of the problem. It is generally held that the big landed estates and their owners are at fault, and it is true that these estates are not charitable institutions. But if the absentee owner, who lives in Naples, or Rome, or Palermo, is an enemy of the peasants, he is not the worst of the enemies they have to cope with. He, at least, is far away and does not interfere with their daily life. Their real enemies, those who cut them off from any hope of freedom and decent existence, are to be found among the village tyrants.'
(Carlo Levi, *Christ stopped at Eboli*)

Mezzogiorno – 1950

High summer temperatures (30–40°C). High evaporation rates giving a water shortage (page 48).

Low annual rainfall (under 500 mm) and a summer drought

Most farmers lived in isolated hillside towns of up to 20 000 people (defensive origins) – a long way from the fields.
Poor housing – 50% had no piped water, 40% no sanitation.

Scrub land or maquis (page 21), poor grass for sheep and goats

Latifundia – large estates of up to 1000 hectares belonging to absentee landlords, who had little interest in the land. 45% of farmers owned no land.

Rough track or poor road

Thin, dry limestone soils with little surface drainage (page 17)

Seasonal rivers caused problems of water supply for domestic and agricultural purposes

Rugged relief. 45% classified as hill country, 40% as mountainous and 15% as lowland.

River mouths silted up limiting port development and causing malarial marshlands

Small areas of fertile land giving low yields of olives, wheat, barley and vines

Soil erosion following centuries of deforestation, speeded up by convectional summer storms and landslides

△ **Figure 15.12** The Mezzogiorno, 1950

▽ **Figure 15.13** Hill village, Moureale, Sicily

Cassa per Il Mezzogiorno

This is an organisation created in 1950 by the Italian government to try to develop the south of the country. Since then, further aid has been given by the EEC and the World Bank. As the table below shows, from 1950–58 most of the money allocated to the Mezzogiorno was spent on improving farming, roads, and water supplies (for both towns and for irrigation), see the figures for 1955. More recently money has been spent on tourism and industry (e.g. in growth areas around Naples, between Bari–Brindisi–Taranto and in Sicily) as illustrated by the figures for 1980.

% of money spent by Cassa per Il Mezzogiorno

	1955	1980
improving farming	68%	21%
improving communications	14%	8%
improving water supply	10%	12%
developing industry	4%	43%
developing tourism	3%	6%
others	1%	10%

Figure 15.14 shows some of the improvements made by 1984. These included changes in housing, communications, farming and a diversification of jobs from an industrial viewpoint. Three main growth areas were encouraged:

(a) Around Naples with the Bagnoli iron and steel works, Alfa-Romeo, Olivetti, Pirelli and petro-chemicals.

(b) Between Bari, Brindisi and Taranto where one of Europe's largest steel works has been built at Taranto (page 69) based on imported raw materials, but using government grants and local abundant cheap labour. Other industries include oil-refining and petro-chemicals, cement and a brewery.

(c) SE Sicily, also with cement, petro-chemicals, and Fiat (Palermo).

Problems remaining in 1985

☐ Area is still very short of skilled labour.

☐ Car factories in the south still get all their components from the north.

☐ Such large, prestigious schemes as the Taranto steelworks cost vast sums of money, yet create relatively few jobs. How can smaller, more labour intensive industries be attracted?

☐ Although agricultural production has increased by 30% and the numbers involved have fallen from 53% (1950) to 21% (1983), there is still over-employment in farming.

☐ The newly created farms are often too small, and are too distant from EEC markets.

☐ Government grants have helped industry in three areas – but other rural areas have fallen further behind the north.

☐ Workers have a long way to travel to these 'growth areas'.

☐ A lack of investment.

☐ An increase in pollution – especially around Taranto.

☐ Aftermath of earthquakes (1980) and volcanic eruptions (1983) – page 12.

☐ Influence of the Mafia.

☐ Some of the funds have been misused, e.g. a dam was built in Sicily but without any means of getting the water to the farms.

▽ Figure 15.14 The Mezzogiorno. In August 1984 the application to renew the Cassa scheme was defeated. The Cassa employed 2550 – will they get alternative employment, or will they be retained in a possible new agency to help the Mezzogiorno? Even now rural depopulation is continuing and it is questionable if the Cassa scheme has repaid the investment made between 1950 and 1984.

Mezzogiorno – 1984

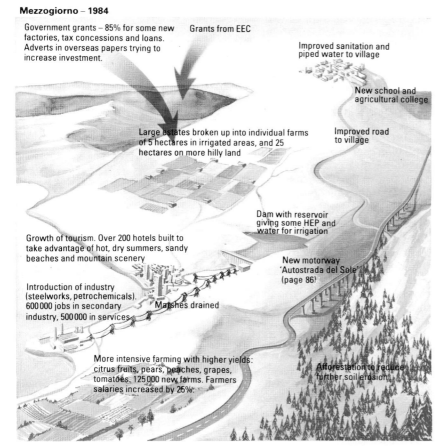

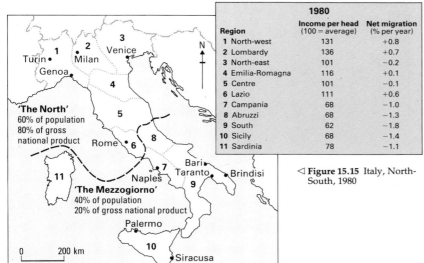

		1980	
Region		**Income per head** (100 = average)	**Net migration** (% per year)
1	North-west	131	+0.8
2	Lombardy	136	+0.7
3	North-east	101	−0.2
4	Emilia-Romagna	116	+0.1
5	Centre	101	−0.1
6	Lazio	111	+0.6
7	Campania	68	−1.0
8	Abruzzi	68	−1.3
9	South	62	−1.8
10	Sicily	68	−1.4
11	Sardinia	78	−1.1

◁ **Figure 15.15** Italy, North-South, 1980

Acid rain

'Perhaps the worst environmental threat ever to hit us.'

'Our biggest environmental problem now and for the future.'

These are quotations from Swedish and West German newspapers. Concern about acid rain was first expressed in the late 1960s by the Scandinavians. They claimed that the sulphur dioxides and nitrogen oxides produced by burning fossil fuels (Figure 15.16) were being carried into the lower atmosphere. These were then taken many kilometres (across seas and national frontiers) to be deposited directly onto the surface of the earth (dry deposition), or converted by chemical reactions into sulphuric and nitric acids and brought down with precipitation as ions of sulphate, nitrate, hydrogen and ammonium (wet deposition) Figure 15.17. The major source of the pollutants are said to be the coal and oil-fired power stations of the United Kingdom, France and West Germany, and that the problem worsened after the introduction of tall chimneys which were aimed at carrying the smoke away from local areas. The areas with the highest concentrations of sulphur dioxide are shown in Figure 15.18. Oxides of sulphur and nitrogen occur naturally in small quantities in the atmosphere, and European rainwater (if unaffected by man) would have a pH value of between 5 and 6 (pH7 is neutral). Today, over wide areas, the pH readings are between 4 and 4.5 with odd readings as low as 3 recorded. A falling pH is the sign of increasing acidity, and remember when pH falls by one unit it means that the concentration of acid (i.e. the number of hydrogen ions) has increased by ten times.

The effects of acid rain

Acidification of lakes Lakes with a slow-weathering, non-lime bedrock began to produce less fish in the 1950s. Tests carried out in west coast Swedish lakes (Figure 15.19) show a very marked increase in acidity – which kills fish and plant life. By 1984, 75% of lakes and rivers in south Norway had no fish in them.

Acidification of soils Soil has a greater resistance to acidification than does water, and lime-rich (alkaline) soils can often neutralise acid rain. However, regions with acid soils overlying granite rocks (e.g. Scandinavia) or heavily weathered sandy soils are more readily affected. So Scandinavia with thin sandy-glacial soils covered in coniferous trees (whose needles increase acidity) and slowly weathered parent material is much more likely to be affected by acidification than the more limestone soils on relatively rapid weathered parent rock of the Mediterranean lands.

Forests It is now believed that as acid rain penetrates the soil it leaches away important nutrients (e.g. calcium and potassium) and releases manganese and aluminium which poison the tree roots so restricting their ability to absorb moisture. The tops of the conifers turn yellow-green, growth stops, the lower branches shed needles, and the bark may split, letting the cold winds in in winter, and the bark beetle in summer. A report issued by the West German Government in 1983 claimed that *'Since 1980 one-third of the trees in the country had begun to die – and over half of those in the Black Forest were affected. 80% were fir trees, but 1983 showed signs that the beech was also affected. Between 1981–3 healthy firs decreased from 66% of their total to 1%, and the spruce could be dead by 1990.'*

Ground water As acid rain percolates downwards through the soil it is beginning to concentrate in underground supplies. Apart from possible future health dangers, it is even now corroding water pipes more rapidly.

Buildings are also crumbling under acid rain – it is claimed some are loosing 4% of their weight each year. The Acropolis in Athens is reported to have deteriorated more in the last three decades than in the previous 2000 years (page 108). Marble, limestone and granite are most easily eroded (Figure 15.20) and even new concrete buildings are only lasting half their expected life.

Health A link has been proved between the areas with high concentrations of sulphur dioxide (Figure 15.18) and people dying from lung cancer. Duisburg, in the German Ruhr, has four times more cases of bronchitis than the national average.

Agriculture In 1983, evidence was given, for the first time, of a decline in crop yields.

Climate An increase in sulphur dioxide produces a hazy atmosphere, and some experts believe that the constant haze in arctic areas in winter and spring is a consequence of this. There was twice as much sulphur dioxide in the air in West Germany in 1982 than there had been in 1952. Apart from short term reductions in visibility (and the effects on transport), in the longer term this could change the world's climate pattern.

sulphur dioxide + nitrogen oxides

Figure 15.16 Atmospheric pollution caused by the ICI plant at Wilton (main picture)

△ **Figure 15.17** Acid rain

▷ **Figure 15.19** (Top right) Acidification of fifteen lakes on west coast of Sweden (Source: *Acid Rain*, Ministry of Agriculture, Sweden)

▷ **Figure 15.20** Effect of acid rain on statues on the Acropolis (inset)

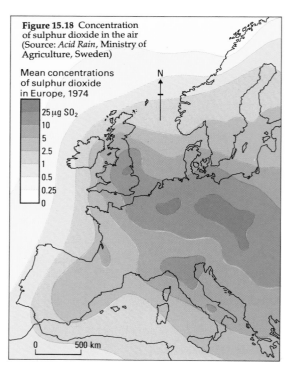

Figure 15.18 Concentration of sulphur dioxide in the air (Source: *Acid Rain*, Ministry of Agriculture, Sweden)

Mean concentrations of sulphur dioxide in Europe, 1974

25 µg SO₂
10
5
2.5
1
0.5
0.25
0

N

0   500 km

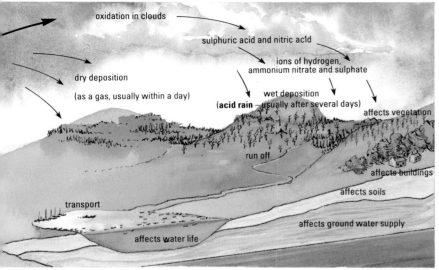

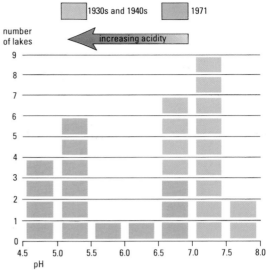

Possible solutions

- Trees are being sprayed in West Germany to try to wash off the acids – a losing battle. In 1984 an opinion poll showed Germans were much more anxious about their forests than about nuclear disarmament.

- Desulphurization technology can now prevent 90% of sulphur dioxide emissions, but companies are reluctant to use it due to the high costs. In Britain it would mean raising electricity charges by 15p in the pound to pay for conversions in power stations. In 1983 the UK and Scandinavia began a £5 m investigation into prevention methods.

- Reduce the number of coal and oil-fired power stations.

- In West Germany by January 1986 all new cars will have converters fitted, and all fuel will be lead-free.

- Add lime to lakes and the soil to try to neutralise the acid.

Polluted environments

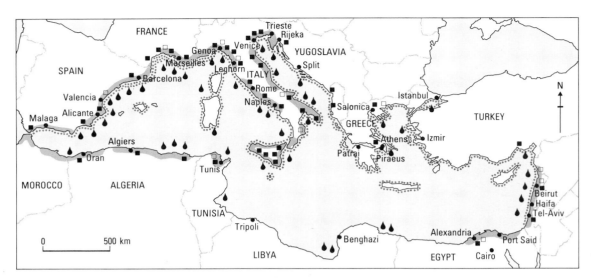

densely populated coastal regions
● pollution black spots – mainly untreated sewage
◆ oil
······· sewage and industrial waste
□ iron and steel industries
■ oil refining or chemical industries

◁ **Figure 15.21** Pollution in the Mediterranean Sea

The Mediterranean

The Mediterranean Sea is said to be 'The biggest open air swimming pool' and 'the biggest open sewer in the world' (Figure 15.21).

Causes of pollution

□ 90% of sewage from the 18 countries surrounding the Mediterranean flows into the sea untreated.

□ Chemical waste is either dumped directly into the sea, or, with pesticides and fertilisers, is brought down to the sea by big rivers.

□ Tourism. In 1980 over 100 million tourists visited the Mediterranean lands, and this could be 200 million a year by A.D. 2000. Tourism leads to visual and noise pollution, as well as an increase in litter.

□ Industrialisation, especially in the north-western areas, has seen the construction of oil refineries, coking plants, steel works, etc. all of which tend to dump their wastes back into the sea. The Rhône, Po and Ebro bring waste from inland industrial areas into the Mediterranean.

□ Oil. In 1980, 500 000 tonnes of oil found its way into the Mediterranean Sea. 470 000 tonnes of that was the result of accidents or direct spillage, 30 000 due to the illegal washing of decks and holds by empty tankers while at sea. The Mediterranean is on the major tanker route from the Middle East and North Africa to Europe.

□ Lack of international co-operation, especially between the richer 'Northern' countries and the poorer African states; and between political antagonists such as Lebanon and Israel.

□ Physical problems posed by: (*a*) Absence of tides (which would clean beaches twice daily). (*b*) The anticlockwise ocean current which carries pollutants along the coast. (*c*) The time taken (80 years) for the sea to clean itself. The only 'fresh' water is from rivers (if not polluted) or through the narrow, shallow Straits of Gibraltar.

Results include dirty beaches – under 75% of seawater off important resorts is safe for bathing; under 4% of mussels and oysters are fit for eating; fewer fish; the threat of extinction to such wild life as the Monk seal and marine turtle, (who can no longer find quiet stretches of beach on which to mate) and to human health (dysentery).

The Blue Plan

In 1972 the United Nations Environmental Organisation met to discuss the problems of the Mediterranean. Four years later the 18 countries which border the sea, produced the Blue Plan, and an agreement was signed in 1979. They agreed:

□ No more chemical dumping.

□ A united action plan to combat possible oil spillages.

□ To build new sewage treatment plants.

□ To create 83 marine laboratories which would then pool resources and information.

□ To work together to reduce pollution caused by agriculture, industry, transport, urban areas and tourism.

In 1983 a more detailed treaty was signed by six countries with the hope that more would join.

Will the Blue Plan work?

□ How long will it take to overcome the long-term build up of industrial waste?

□ Despite the ban on chemical dumping, a 'grey list' has been drawn up of chemicals which a country can dump providing it obtains a special permit.

□ High costs involved (and for little economic gain). Estimates suggest a minimum of £2500 million is needed just to solve the untreated sewage. The poorer countries cannot finance such schemes.

□ Who funds the projects?

□ Who will police the agreement?

▽ **Figure 15.24** An accidental release of chemicals into the Rhine in 1969 was the 'biggest catastrophe in the history of the Rhine' poisoning all the fish between Bingen and the North Sea

□ Conflict between countries to the North and those to the South. The North, which is now industrialised, and which has largely been responsible for the pollution, now wishes to clean up its beaches as tourism increases. The South, which needs to become more industrialised and to create more jobs, sees the protection of the environment as secondary to new industries.

□ Should new industrial developments be made inland rather than on the coast?

□ Can fish and animal life be guaranteed or will their mating and eating grounds be ruined? Decrease in sponges and coral which are used as souvenirs.

□ Less fresh water entering the sea as rivers become polluted, and rivers such as the Nile are dammed to store water for irrigation instead of, as previously, being allowed to flow into the sea.

□ Can the long standing view that the sea is a dumping ground be reversed?

▽ **Figure 15.22** Pollution points on the Rhine

▷ **Figure 15.23** Changing levels of oxygen and nitrates in the Rhine

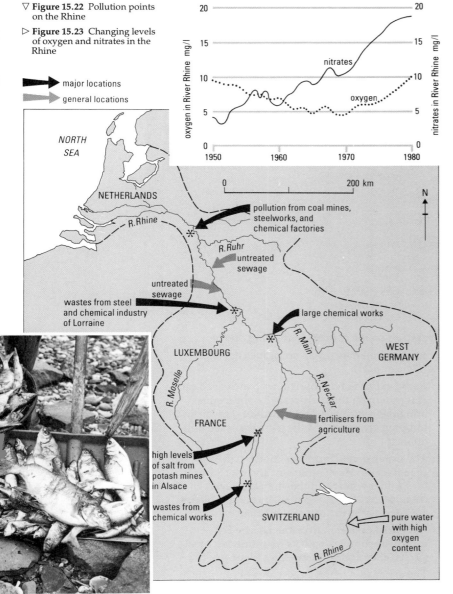

The Rhine

Forty million people live either along the 1200 km length of the River Rhine or in its drainage basin (Figure 15.22). For centuries the river has been used to cool machines in industry, as a dumping ground for waste, for irrigation, for drinking water (especially in the Netherlands), transport and recreation. The Rhine, which begins as melting Alpine snows, enters the North Sea heavily polluted.

Causes of pollution

□ A decrease in oxygen (Figure 15.23) has led to the death of fish. The last salmon was caught in 1950. In 1969 an accidental release of a chemical fertiliser killed the remaining 40 million fish north of Bingen (Figure 15.24). The pollution eventually flowed into the North Sea.

□ Industry, which was attracted to the river for transport, and its water for cooling purposes, now dumps its waste products into it. In 1976 the Rhine contained the following substances:

Total load in tonnes		lead	1200
arsenic	250	mercury	20
chromium	1500	salt	16
copper	950	zinc	8500

The Dutch claim that their market gardening loses output from salt in the water.

□ Chemical works and power stations send out hot water raising the temperature of the river.

□ Untreated sewage.

□ Oil leaks from factories and barges on the river.

Results The river can smell at low water, and affect the health of people living near to it. The pollution has killed fish and, when used in factories, corrodes machines. Water, taken from it for drinking purposes, needs greater treatment.

Problems Five countries lie within the drainage basin (Figure 15.22). Of these Switzerland uses the river least. France extracts little water from it, but allows waste into it. West Germany is the heaviest user, with 70% of its industry along it, whereas the Dutch extract most water and receive the waste of other countries. How can the countries agree to pollution control, who pays for it and who ensures that each country keeps its agreements?

Some solutions

□ To build more sewage treatment plants.

□ The Dutch have built larger purification plants and reservoirs. The latter, south-east of Rotterdam, are filled when the river is in flood and when impurity contents are at a minimum.

□ Fines for illegal dumping.

□ Potash waste from Alsace is to be stored underground and the cost to be shared by each country.

□ So far the Germans have put most money into trying to reduce pollution, but will they go on doing so?

Disappearing wetlands

Figure 15.26 Natural wild life of the Camargue

'The term wetlands is applied to such landscapes as fen, marsh and swamp, in which water plays a key role. Covering 6% of the world's land area, they form a transition zone between sea or lake and dry land. They may be inhospitable or unproductive, but they present an environment for special kinds of plant and animal life. Yet in the 1980's these areas are subject to increasing pressures which, according to many people, make them the most threatened of all landscape types.' (Geographical Magazine, 1983)

The Camargue

This area lies in the delta of the River Rhône (Figure 15.25). To the newcomer it is 'a flat bleak expanse of reed beds, salt-marsh and shallow etangs (lakes). The monotony is one of pale greens and greys of grass and scrub. Vegetation gives way to water and sky. The largest etang covers 150 km² yet is no deeper than one metre. There are few trees in this battlefield between fresh and salt water. The coastal etangs have been formed behind coastal spits.'

To someone familiar to the area, the water means the land is not dead. 'There are colours here, the ever changing blues and greys of the wind-rippled water, the faded yellows of the marsh beds lining the etangs, the near blackness of smooth crowned cypresses, the dark green of windbreak pines, the startling bright green of occasional lush grazing pastures, striking vivid against the brown and harsh aridity of the tough sparse vegetation and salt flats baked hard under the sun. And, above all, there is life here – birds in greater number, very occasional small groups of black cattle and, even more rarely, white horses.' (Alistair Maclean, Caravan to Vaccarès)

It is inhospitable due to

□ The rivers flooding in spring after snow melt in the Alps, or after a summer storm.

□ The sea flooding inland when the wind is in the south.

□ Mosquitoes between June and September.

□ The Mistral blows down the Rhône valley, especially in the autumn and winter (page 20).

It is a living environment for

□ Black bulls which are still used, but never killed, in local bullrings.

□ White horses (Figure 15.26) of which relatively few remain.

□ Pink flamingoes (Figure 15.26) which breed in their thousands along with egrets and purple herons.

□ A variety of marsh – both fresh and salt water – plants, fish and animals.

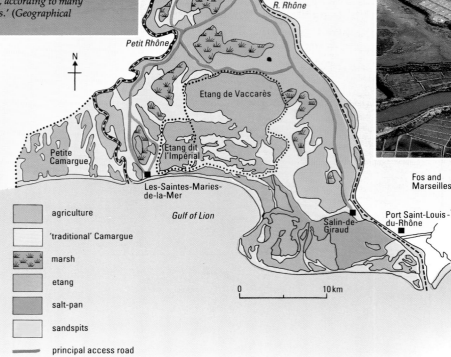

Map legend:
- agriculture
- 'traditional' Camargue
- marsh
- etang
- salt-pan
- sandspits
- principal access road
- ········· limit of reserves
- ----- boundary of Regional Park

Map labels: Arles 2 m above sea level, R. Rhône, Petit Rhône, Etang de Vaccarès, Petite Camargue, Etang dit l'Impérial, Les-Saintes-Maries-de-la-Mer, Gulf of Lion, Salin-de-Giraud, Port Saint-Louis-du-Rhône, Fos and Marseilles, N, 0 10 km

Pressures on the area are increasing due to

□ Encroachment of urban areas such as Arles (Figure 15.25).

□ Rapid expansion of tourism with increased car congestion on the narrow roads, the lorries bringing in supplies, the growth of caravan and camping grounds, and the increase in second homes.

□ The expansion of farming. Enough rice is grown to make France self-sufficient and more area is now under wheat and the vine. However, chemical fertilisers, weed killers and pesticides are altering the delicate water balance.

□ Industrial pollution from the nearby Fos industrial complex with its oil-refineries, steel works, chemical works and gas plant.

□ The expansion of the largest area of salt-flats in Europe (Figure 15.27).

△ **Figure 15.25** The Camargue Regional Park was created in 1972 and within it are two nature reserves. The object is to preserve the 'disappearing wetland' by conserving wildlife, and trying to prevent pollution. The Camargue remains, along with the Coto Donana (in south-west Spain) and the Danube delta, the only large expanse of marshland in Europe.

Lappland – Europe's last wilderness

The above claim, made by the Finnish tourist board, has much truth in it. Lappland is a region which spans across northern Norway, Sweden, and Finland. The climate is extremely cold and the vegetation is tundra (page 25). Such an area is both inhospitable to humans and possesses a delicate environmental balance (Figure 15.28). Wildlife in the area includes many rare species of birds who nest here in the Arctic summer, and large herds of reindeer who likewise migrate with the seasons. The 200 000 reindeer are now all privately owned, domestic animals, and are looked after by the Lapps (Figure 15.29).

The Lapps, who have their own language, and still dress in their colourful, traditional costumes (Figure 15.29) use the reindeer for food, milk, clothes, tents and draught purposes. Concentrated efforts are being made to preserve the vast tracts of tundra in their natural state for the Lapps to continue in their nomadic lifestyle. The reindeer are rounded up in autumn and brought down from their summer pastures beyond the Arctic Circle. The journey to their winter feeding grounds takes a month. This journey is now made easier as the Lapps use skis and snowmobiles, and can keep in contact with each other by wireless. The reindeer are now slaughtered every three or four years (previously every nine or ten years), and this improved management has helped to prevent overgrazing of the delicate tundra feeding grounds, and to improve the quality of the herds.

△ **Figure 15.27** The salt industry in the Camargue

Tourists are visiting Lappland in increasing numbers, especially between mid-May and the end of July, when the sun never sets. However, they are not allowed to fish for salmon, nor to shoot game. The Finnish Tourist Board recommend that visitors should *'stick to marked trails – it's easy to get lost in this sparsely populated region, and it will help conserve the natural beauty and wildlife of the region.'*

The EEC's Environment Policy

This policy was drawn up because *'industrial Europe can claim many achievements, including high material standards of living, high levels of literacy, high average life expectancy and adequate supplies of food. What it is in danger of losing are satisfying living and working conditions.'* (European Commission) The aim of a Community environment policy is to improve the quality of life and the surroundings and living conditions of the peoples of the Community – bearing in mind that most pollution problems do not stop at international frontiers. The six point plan aims to:

(a) Prevent, reduce and as far as possible eliminate pollution.

(b) Maintain a satisfactory ecological balance.

(c) Ensure sound management of, and avoid any exploitation of resources, or of nature, which might damage the ecological balance.

(d) Guide development by improving working conditions and the quality of life.

(e) Ensure that more account is taken of environmental aspects in town planning and land use.

(f) Seek common solutions to environmental problems with states outside the Community.

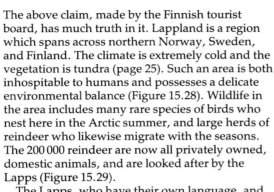

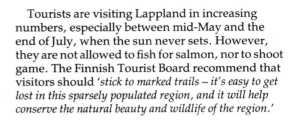

▽ **Figure 15.28** Swedish Lappland, Riksgrensen

◁ **Figure 15.29** Lapp with reindeer

Development

Key dates

29 November 1947
Formation of Benelux – a union for the free movement of money, people, services and goods across the three frontiers; and the working towards a common economic and trade policy.

18 April 1951
The six – France, West Germany, Italy, Netherlands, Belgium and Luxembourg agreed to form the 'European Coal and Steel Community' (ECSC) Figure 16.1. This was to *'abolish import and export duties, subsidies and restrictive practices, and to establish free and unrestricted movement of coal, iron ore, scrap and pig iron between the member countries.'*

25 March 1957
The six sign the treaty of Rome establishing the EEC. At the same time Euratom (European Atomic Energy Authority) was created for the co-ordination of nuclear research and the eventual production of nuclear energy.

November 1959
The European Free Trade Association (EFTA) was signed with the united object of abolishing all tariffs on industrial goods between the 7 member states of United Kingdom, Norway, Sweden, Denmark, Portugal, Switzerland and Austria.

8 November 1961
Negotiations begin on the United Kingdom's and Eire's application to join the EEC.

14 January 1963
France considers UK not to be ready for entry to the EEC.

29 July 1968
The six agree to the free movement of workers between member states.

1 January 1973
The UK, Denmark and Eire become full members of the European Community – 'the Nine'. Norway who had previously applied for membership, withdrew.

March, 1975
The Regional Development Fund was created.

May, 1975
The Lomé convention was signed by the nine EEC countries and 47 developing countries.

6 June 1979
First direct elections to the European Parliament.

1 January 1981
Greece becomes the tenth member of the Community.

14 June 1984
Elections to the European Parliament.

Mid 1980s??
Will Portugal and Spain be allowed to form 'the Twelve'?

What does the EEC do?

- It is a confederation of nation states, each with its own government. The heads of government meet at periodic 'Summit meetings', known as the '**European Council**'.

- The ten governments are each represented by a minister on the '**Council of Ministers**'. It receives policy proposals from the commission and takes back decisions to the commission for implementation. On major policy issues all member countries must agree.

- **The European Commission** is the executive with its headquarters in the Berlaymont Building in Brussels (Figure 16.2). It is directed by 14 members (see list on right).

The Commission administers the daily running of a customs union (countries with no barriers between them) totalling 260 million people.

2 members from
France
West Germany
Italy
The United Kingdom

1 member from
The Netherlands
Belgium
Luxembourg
Eire
Denmark
Greece

▽ **Figure 16.1** Development of the EEC

▽ **Figure 16.2** The Berlaymont Building in Brussels (bottom)

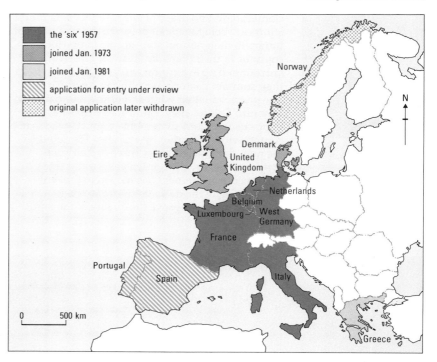

the 'six' 1957
joined Jan. 1973
joined Jan. 1981
application for entry under review
original application later withdrawn

□ 9000 people form the working secretariat for the Commission and Council of ministers.

□ The **Court of Justice**, which sits in Luxembourg, administers EEC law, and arbitrates in disputes between member states.

□ **The European Parliament**, at Luxembourg and Strasbourg, *'is unique in that it is the first ever Parliament to have been directly elected by peoples of different countries.*

Each of the four bigger countries in the Community has 81 members with varying numbers of members from the smaller countries depending on their population. (There are 434 members altogether).

In the Parliament, the members sit not by country, but by party affiliation. For example 117 Christian Democrats from nine of the countries sit as a single European group. Similarly, the British Conservatives are together in one group with Danish Conservatives and an Ulster Unionist.

The European Parliament is the democratic watchdog of the Community. Nothing can happen in the Community without the Parliament first being consulted. And the European Commission has to take note of what the Parliament wants. If it does not, the Parliament can exercise its right to dismiss the Commission from office.' (European Commission)

▽ **Figure 16.3** Aims of the EEC

▽ **Figure 16.4** EEC – winners and losers, 1983 (below right)

Freeing trade
Each of the countries of the European Community used to charge taxes – known as *tariffs* – on goods imported into that country. These have now been removed in order to create:
a larger home market,
cheaper goods,
a wider range of goods, and
a better standard of living for Community citizens.

Freedom to work
All citizens of the European Community are free to seek jobs in any Community country, on equal terms with the nationals of that country. Work permits are not required and there is no loss of social security rights. This applies to Greece after a period of transition.

Movement of capital
A series of international monetary crises has made it difficult for the Community countries to achieve the aim of allowing free movement of money for investment.
The European Monetary System has been set up in an attempt to recreate a stable system of currency exchange rates like that which existed up to the late 1960s. It is believed that linking Europe's currencies together, ultimately perhaps having a single European currency, will help in the fight against inflation and in the creation of more stable economic conditions.

Agriculture
It is vital that Europe can produce the food its people need. The Community's Common Agricultural Policy sets common prices for food in order to create a stable market and make sure that farmers are adequately paid.

The Community helps
The Community has funds to help regions and groups with economic difficulties. Special assistance is available to the coal and steel industries while the European Investment bank provides cheap finance for industrial development.

The Community and the World
The Community's Common Trade Policy enables it to negotiate as a united body. It also makes it possible to offer favourable trading terms and financial assistance to developing countries. Under the Lomé Convention most countries of Africa, the Caribbean and the Pacific have special relationships with the Community as a whole.

The future
The Community is developing other policies in areas where common action benefits all. An energy policy is a high priority and programmes for the environment and consumers are needed to protect all citizens.
Soon the Community must adapt to receive new members. Greece joined on January 1st, 1981, and Spain and Portugal are negotiating for membership.

Community Policies

These are summarised in Figure 16.3 which is taken from the EEC's own information booklet. Earlier in this book, reference has been made to:

□ Common Agricultural Policy (page 31)
□ Common Fisheries Policy (page 42)
□ Common Forestry Policy (page 47)
□ Common Policy on Shipbuilding and Steel (page 68)
□ Common Energy Policy (page 51)
□ Common Tourist Policy (page 103)
□ Common Policy on the Environment (page 121)

Future problems

□ Ambitious plans for full economic and political union have been set, but many member states do not want to give up too much independence.

□ Will there ever be a European currency, a common method of taxation or a common budget?

□ How can future policies regarding industry and technology be linked with environmental and social problems?

□ How long will it be before the slowdown in economic activity of the early 1980s is reversed?

□ The overproduction of certain farm products and the creation of 'mountains and lakes' (page 31).

□ The door to Spanish and Portuguese entry – with their reliance on agriculture and their low standards of living – appears to be opening very slowly.

□ Who pays for the budget?
The Community's annual budget of £15 000 million (1983) is raised from VAT, and from duties and levies on imports from non-EEC countries. Although this budget is small by national standards, some countries such as Britain and West Germany, contribute more than they receive (Figure 16.4). This produced the failure to agree on the EEC budget at the Athens Summit in 1984. As the Common Agricultural Policy accounts for two-thirds of the budget, solving this problem would make the finances of the EEC more stable.

	Trade balance of trade with other members (million £s)	**Budget** balance of payments to, and receipts from, EEC budget (million £s)
UK	−1140	−1122*
France	−7866	− 3.5
Germany	+5130	−1710
Netherlands	+7980[†]	+ 217
Italy	−1710	+ 830
Ireland	− 855	+ 447
Belgium/ Luxembourg	+1140	− 231
Denmark	+ 570	+ 192
Greece	−1539	+ 312

*without budget rebate
†figure highly inflated by oil imports through Rotterdam

Regional differences

After the enlargement of the EEC to nine members in 1973, pressure for regional aid increased due to the serious regional differences within countries (e.g. UK, Italy) and the peripheral nature of some member states (Eire). Some of these differences are given in Figures 16.5 and 16.6.

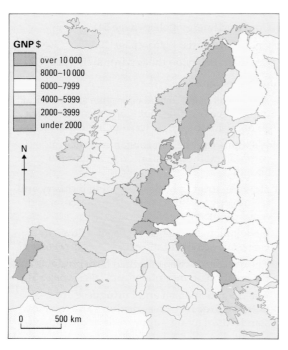

GNP $

	over 10 000
	8000–10 000
	6000–7999
	4000–5999
	2000–3999
	under 2000

N

0   500 km

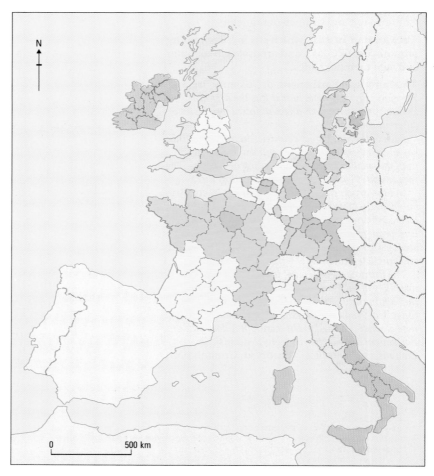

0   500 km

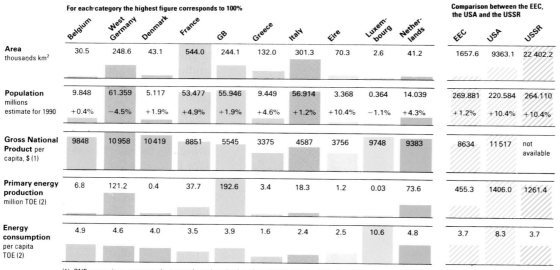

For each category the highest figure corresponds to 100%

Comparison between the EEC, the USA and the USSR

	Belgium	West Germany	Denmark	France	GB	Greece	Italy	Eire	Luxem-bourg	Nether-lands	EEC	USA	USSR
Area thousands km²	30.5	248.6	43.1	544.0	244.1	132.0	301.3	70.3	2.6	41.2	1657.6	9363.1	22 402.2
Population millions estimate for 1990	9.848 +0.4%	61.359 −4.5%	5.117 +1.9%	53.477 +4.9%	55.946 +1.9%	9.449 +4.6%	56.914 +1.2%	3.368 +10.4%	0.364 −1.1%	14.039 +4.3%	269.881 +1.2%	220.584 +10.4%	264.110 +10.4%
Gross National Product per capita, $ (1)	9848	10 958	10 419	8851	5545	3375	4587	3756	9748	9383	8634	11 517	not available
Primary energy production million TOE (2)	6.8	121.2	0.4	37.7	192.6	3.4	18.3	1.2	0.03	73.6	455.3	1406.0	1261.4
Energy consumption per capita TOE (2)	4.9	4.6	4.0	3.5	3.9	1.6	2.4	2.5	10.6	4.8	3.7	8.3	3.7

(1) GNP per capita = measure of a country's total production of goods and services divided by the number of people living in that country

(2) TOE = Tonnes of oil equivalent

	under 60%
	60–79%
	80–99%
	average = 100%
	100–120%
	over 120%

◁ **Figure 16.5** Basic statistics of the EEC and its ten member states, and comparison between the EEC, the USA and the USSR

△ **Figure 16.6** Gross National Product (above left)

△ **Figure 16.7** Regional differences in GNP within the EEC, 1980

The Regional Development Fund

This is money which can be allocated to poorer parts of the community. Criteria for aid:

1 A gross national product lower than the Community average (Figure 16.7).

2 A heavy dependence on employment in declining industries with at least 20% of local employment in such a category.

3 A persistently high rate of unemployment or, in the case of agriculture, underemployment.

4 A high and sustained rate of emigration (over 1% per year over a period of years).

5 All 'Development' areas designated by individual member states automatically qualify for supplementary grants from the Regional Development Fund.

Regional aid	% of total	
	1977	1979
Italy	31.5	39.4
UK	36.2	27.0
France	21.9	16.9
Ireland	5.9	6.3
W. Germany	2.1	6.4
others	2.4	4.0

Problem regions

These may be conveniently divided into four main categories:

(a) Backward agricultural regions especially those in upland areas and in more remote rural areas. Both the Mezzogiorno and Western Eire have over 30% in agriculture in comparison with the EEC's average of 9%. Such areas have little industry and much emigration.

(b) Long established industrial areas, especially coalfields, steel and shipbuilding districts, such as the Belgian Campine; the French Nord and Lorraine. Environmental problems here include poor housing, derelict industry and slag heaps.

(c) Mountains and hill-land such as the Apennines where a weak economic base leads to rapid depopulation.

(d) Old urban areas in Randstad-Holland, Belgium and north-east France with all the associated problems of pollution, traffic congestion and poor quality housing.

▽ **Figure 16.8** Eire – planning regions and regional development areas

▽ **Figure 16.9** Employment structures in Western Ireland (bottom left)

▽ **Figure 16.10** Co. Galway, Eire (bottom right)

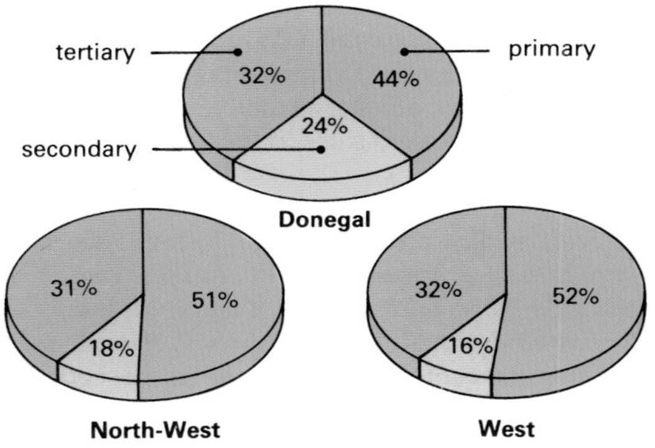

Western Eire

This is the extreme case in the Community of a peripheral, underdeveloped region suffering from endemic poverty and rural subsistence. Although the whole of Eire qualifies for aid from the Regional Development Fund, the western parts are markedly poorer than those in the east (Figure 16.8).

□ Less than 20% of the population live in towns, the remainder living in small, scattered villages or in isolated farmhouses.

□ Parts of the area have over 50% of their population engaged in agriculture (Figure 16.9) and at a level bordering on subsistence (Figure 16.10).

□ The absence of minerals and usuable forms of energy have prevented industrial growth. Less than 20% of the population in certain areas are engaged in the secondary sector (Figure 16.9).

□ The average income per head is only 60% of that of people in the Dublin area, and as was shown in Figure 16.7, the area is well below the average for the EEC as a whole.

□ Although emigration from Eire has declined in the last few decades, there remains a difference between the east (where migration in the 1970s was less than 1 person in every 1000) and the west (with 10 people out of every 1000). One claim is that *'The single most pressing problem is the maintenance of a viable population in Western Eire'*.

The Irish Development Authority (IDA) was created in 1949 to:

□ Encourage industrial investment by means of incentives.

□ End restrictions on foreign ownership of Irish companies. Following a report published in 1968, attempts to improve the standard of living in the west by 'means of the designation of Regional Development Centres and to assist the modernisation of local craft industries'. By the mid 1980s the only real growth area in the west is near the international Shannon Airport (Figure 16.8) with its 'Free Airport Scheme'. This allows companies to import and export without paying custom dues.

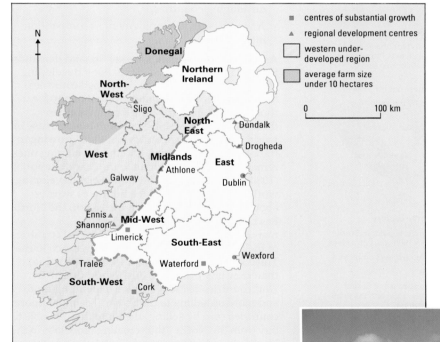

Legend (Figure 16.8):
- ■ centres of substantial growth
- ▲ regional development centres
- □ western under-developed region
- average farm size under 10 hectares

0 — 100 km

Figure 16.9 Employment structures:

Donegal: tertiary 32%, primary 44%, secondary 24%

North-West: 31%, 51%, 18%

West: 32%, 52%, 16%

Trade

Trade between the developed and developing world is essential (Figure 17.1). The developed countries produce 90 per cent of the world's manufactures and many of these are needed by developing countries. The developing countries account for 60 per cent of the world's exports of agricultural and mineral products, which are needed by the developed countries. However, although the prices of raw materials have increased, the prices of manufactured goods have increased much more. This means that a country exporting manufactured goods earns increasingly more than a country selling raw materials – and so the trade gap widens. The differences in the types of trade of developing and developed countries is given in Figure 17.2.

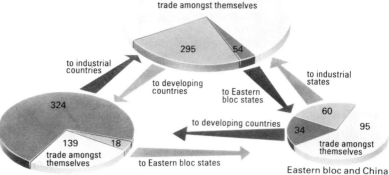

Exports 1982 in billion $

Western industrial states

823

trade amongst themselves

295 54

to industrial countries

to developing countries

to Eastern bloc states

to industrial states

60

95

324

139 18

trade amongst themselves

34

trade amongst themselves

Developing countries

to developing countries

to Eastern bloc states

Eastern bloc and China

△ **Figure 17.1** The triangle of world trade

▽ **Figure 17.2** Differences in trade between developed and developing countries

Trade of developing countries	Trade of developed countries
A legacy of former colonial economies, where a mineral once mined, or a crop once grown, is exported in its 'raw state'. Most exports are primary products	Mainly manufactured goods, as these countries have become industrialised, and cereals
	A wide range of items
Often only two or three items are exported	
Prices of, and demand for, these products fluctuate annually. Prices rise less quickly than for manufactured goods	Prices of, and demand for, these products tend to be steady. Prices have risen considerably in comparison to raw materials
The total trade of these countries is small	The total trade of these countries is large
Most exports come from multi-national companies who tend to send profits back to the parent company	Profits are retained by the exporting country
Trade is hindered by poor internal transport networks	Trade is helped by good internal transport networks

Advantages for the country	Disadvantages for the country
Employs local labour	Local labour often poorly paid; in Brazil the average wage in 1980 was £25 a week
Improves the levels of education and technical skill	Very few local skilled workers employed
Investment in, and aid given to, the country	Profits go overseas
Leads to development of mineral wealth and manufacturing	Minerals usually exported and cost of manufactured goods is beyond the price range of the local market
Companies provide expensive capital equipment such as machinery	Mechanisation reduces the size of the labour force
Leads to development of energy resources	Usually a need to import energy (e.g. oil) which increases the national debt

The importance of a multinational in a developing country

A developing country can be said to be making progress and increasing its level of industrialisation and volume of trade if it can attract such multinational companies as Shell, Unilever, Nestlé's etc. But does that country *really* benefit? Figure 17.3 shows some of the advantages and disadvantages of a multinational in a developing country.

△ **Figure 17.3** Advantages and disadvantages of a multi-national company in a developing country

Why are developed countries worried about industrialisation in developing countries?

They fear:

☐ Loss of markets as other countries produce their own goods.

☐ Cheaper imports from the lower-paid developing countries.

☐ An increase in unemployment as competition increases.

As a result, tariff barriers are set up, and demands for total import bans are made. *But* if developing countries cannot export to developed countries, they cannot earn the money needed to pay for those goods which the developed countries themselves wish to sell. The result is a decrease in world trade, with unemployment still growing in the developed countries, and the developing ones remaining poor. According to the Brandt Report (1980), referring to the developed and developing worlds as the North and the South, as worries about unemployment rise in the North, the North has been putting up more barriers to manufacturers from the South. But most countries of the North sell at least four times as much to the Third World by way of manufactures (in value) than they buy from the Third World Countries. And countries of the North are depending more and more on selling to the South. The more poorer countries earn by selling, the more they are able to buy from the North – thus creating more jobs in the North. As industries grow in developing countries, richer countries of the North may have to move some of their capital and workforce out of some industries and into others. While some jobs may be lost in countries like Britain because of imports from the South, at least as many new jobs are gained by increased sales to the South. As the Brandt Report says, *'a significant proportion of jobs in the North depend on trade with the South. There will be difficult conflicts within the North between those who have to change their employment and those who do not. But if the North fails to adjust, it will be more difficult for everybody.'* And *'Economic growth of one country depends increasingly upon the performance of others. The South cannot grow adequately without the North – the North cannot prosper unless there is greater progress in the South.'*

Aid – methods and problems

If a developing country wishes to develop and has a widening trade gap with the developed countries, then it has to borrow money from overseas. Aid can be given in three ways:

Bilateral aid This is government-to-government aid which goes direct from one developed country to a developing country. In 1960 60% of aid came from this source, but only 30% in 1980. The recipient country puts forward a development plan, which, if accepted, will be finalised, equipped and operated by the donor country. Although this method is quick to implement, and credit rates may be low, it has disadvantages in that the technology given is often unsuitable and linked to a particular project, and the recipient country has to buy goods from its donor country. Third World countries refer to this as 'economic colonialism'.

Multinational aid This type of aid comes from such international agencies as the World Bank, the International Monetary Fund, the Food and Agriculture Organisation (FAO) and UNESCO. By 1980 over 66 per cent of aid came from this source, with the advantage of having no political ties and not being linked to specific projects. However, the amount of aid available is too limited, much time is lost in organising projects, and the interest rates put the recipient deeper into debt, though the poorest borrowers do get interest-free loans which can be repaid over a 50-year period.

Charities Such voluntary organisations as Oxfam and Christian Aid raise money in the developed world to support projects in the poorer countries. Again no political ties are made, and projects are on a smaller and more realistic scale.

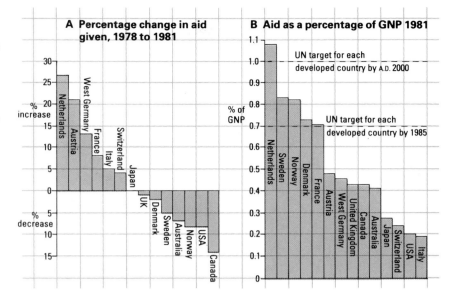

△ **Figure 17.4** European aid to the Third World

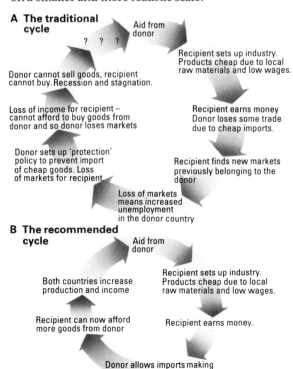

◁ **Figure 17.5** Aid or protection?

What are the basic problems?

☐ The countries that borrow money fall deeper into debt.

☐ World interest rates are tending to increase.

☐ In times of recession in the developed world, the amount of aid given is reduced (Figure 17.4A). The United Nations have set a target for developed countries to give 0.7 per cent of their GNP to developing countries by 1985, and 1 per cent by A.D. 2000. Figure 17.4B shows how far most countries are from fulfilling this aim.

☐ Also in times of recession, the developed countries try to protect their own industries from cheap imports from the developing countries (Figure 17.5A). Development agencies recommend free trade between the North and the South as a way to overcome recession and unemployment (Figure 17.5B).

☐ A new, single currency is needed for the whole world.

Questions

1 Why does the trade gap between developing and developed countries continue to widen?

2 Why should developing countries try to process their raw materials before export?

3 Make a list showing the main items in the two-way trade between developing countries and the EEC. Which side seems to benefit the most? Why?

4 Why is it important for the whole world that the gap between developing and developed countries narrows?

5 How can a multinational company benefit a developing country?

6 Why do some people regard multinationals as harmful to developing countries?

7 Why, during times of recession in the EEC, do many Europeans feel it necessary to impose tariffs on imports from developing countries?

8 Why does the Brandt Report believe that protectionism by the European countries increases unemployment in those countries, and decreases the volume of world trade?

9 In Figure 17.5, do you consider the traditional *or* the recommended cycle benefits (a) the donor country (b) the recipient country?

10 Do you think that the countries of the EEC should give more aid to the developing countries, or try to solve their own unemployment problems first?

11 Which form of aid do you consider to be the best for the recipient country?

12 What is meant by 'economic colonialism'?

13 Should the EEC try to increase trade *or* aid with the developing world?

Index